THE LAST CRUISE OF A GERMAN RAIDER

THE LAST CRUISE
OF A GERMAN RAIDER
The Destruction of SMS Emden

Wes Olson

NAVAL INSTITUTE PRESS
ANNAPOLIS, MARYLAND

First published in Great Britain in 2018 by
Seaforth Publishing,
An imprint of Pen & Sword Books Ltd,
47 Church Street,
Barnsley S70 2AS

Published and distributed in the
United States of America and Canada by the
Naval Institute Press,
291 Wood Road, Annapolis,
Maryland 21402-5034

www.nip.org

Library of Congress Control Number: 2018946934

ISBN 978 1 68247 373 3

Printed and bound in Great Britain

Contents

Glossary

Imperial German Navy ranks and positions relevant to *Emden*	Royal Navy equivalent or English translation
Offiziere	Officers
Vizeadmiral	Vice Admiral
Konteradmiral	Rear Admiral
Kommodore	Commodore
Kapitän zur See	Captain
Fregattenkapitän	Commander (Senior)
Korvettenkapitän	Commander (Junior)
Kapitänleutnant	Lieutenant Commander
Oberleutnant zur See	Lieutenant
Leutnant zur See	Sub Lieutenant
Fähnrich zur See	Midshipman
Marine-Oberstabsingenieur	Engineer Commander
Marine-Stabsingenieur	Engineer Lieutenant Commander
Marine-Oberingenieur	Engineer Lieutenant
Marine-Ingenieur	Engineer Sub Lieutenant
Marine-Oberzahlmeister	Senior Paymaster
Marine-Zahlmeister	Paymaster
Marine-Zahlmeisterapplikant	Deputy Paymaster
Marine-Stabsarzt	Surgeon Lieutenant Commander
Assistenzarzt	Assistant Medical Officer
Unteroffiziere mit Portepee	Senior Non-Commissioned Officers
Bootsmann	Boatswain
Feuerwerker	Gunner
Steuermann	Helmsman
Torpedoobermaschinist	Torpedo Chief Warrant Officer

Torpedomaschinist	Torpedo Warrant Officer
Obermaschinist	Engine Room Chief Warrant Officer
Maschinist	Engine Room Warrant Officer

Unteroffiziere ohne Portepee	**Junior Non-Commissioned Officers**
Oberbootsmannsmaat	Chief Boatswain's Mate
Obermaat	Chief Mate
Oberwachtmeistersmaat	Chief Master Sentinel's Mate (ship's police)
Obersteuermannsmaat	Chief Helmsman's Mate
Oberhoboistenmaat	Petty Officer Bandsman
Obermaschinistenmaat	Engine Room Petty Officer 1st Class
Obermaschinistenoberanwärter	Senior Engine Room PO Probationer
Maschinistenmaat	Engine Room Petty Officer 2nd Class
Diensttuender	Acting Engine Room PO
Maschinistenoberanwärter	Probationer
Oberfeurwerksmaat	Chief Ordnance Artificer's Mate
Obermaterialienverwaltersmaat	Chief Storeman
Oberbotteliersmaat	Chief Steward
Artillerieobermechanikersmaat	Chief Artillery Mechanic's Mate
Artilleriemechanikeroberanwärter	Chief Artillery Mechanic Probationer
Bootsmannsmaat	Boatswain's Mate (PO 2nd Class)
Feuerwerksmaat	Gunner's Mate/Ordnance Artificer's Mate
Funkentelegraphiemaat	Wireless Petty Officer 2nd Class
Funkentelegraphieoberanwärter	Wireless Petty Officer Probationer
Signalmaat	Yeoman of Signals' Mate
Steuermannsmaat	Helmsman's Mate
Torpedomaschinistenmaat	Torpedo Petty Officer
Zimmermannsmaat	Petty Officer Carpenter

Segelmachersmaat	Sailmaker's Mate
Sanitätsmaat	Sick Bay Mate
Schreibersmaat	Writer/Clerk's Mate
Wachtmeistersmaat	Master Sentinel's Mate (ship's police)

Mannschaften	**Men**
Obermatrose	Leading Seaman
Obersignalgast	Leading Signalman
Diensttuender Obersignalgast	Acting Leading Signalman
Oberheizer	Leading Stoker
Oberbottelier	Leading Steward
Oberzimmermannsgast	Leading Carpenter's crew/hand
Funkentelegraphieobergast	Leading Wireless Operator
Artillerieobermechanikersgast	Leading Artillery Mechanic's crew/hand
Torpedoobermatrose	Leading Torpedoman
Torpedooberheizer	Leading Torpedo Stoker
Matrose	Ordinary Seaman
Torpedomatrose	Torpedoman
Heizer	Stoker
Torpedoheizer	Torpedo Stoker
Signalgast	Signalman
Bäckersgast	Baker's crew/hand
Funkentelegraphiegast	Wireless Operator
Malersgast	Painter's crew/hand
Sanitätsgast	Sick Bay Attendant
Schneidersgast	Tailor's crew/hand
Schuhmachersgast	Shoemaker's crew/hand
Zimmermannsgast	Carpenter's crew/hand
Kriegsfreiwilliger Heizer	War Volunteer Stoker

Zivilpersonal	**Civilian personnel**
Offizierbarbier	Officer's Barber
Offizierskoch	Officer's Cook
Waschmänner	Washerman/Laundryman

Abbreviations and Conversion Table

Abbreviations

AWM	Australian War Memorial
BL	Breech-loading
EEACTC	Eastern Extension Australasia and China Telegraph Company
ERA	Engine Room Artificer
GMT	Greenwich Mean Time
GOC	General Officer Commanding
HAPAG	Hamburg-Amerikanische Packetfahrt Actien Gesellschaft
HIGMS	His Imperial German Majesty's Ship
HMAS	His Majesty's Australian Ship
HMS	His Majesty's Ship
NAA	National Archives of Australia
PO	Petty Officer
RAN	Royal Australian Navy
RN	Royal Navy
rpm	revolutions per minute
SBS	Sick Berth Steward
SMS	*Seiner Majestät Schiff*
SS	Steamship
(T)	Torpedo
W/T	Wireless Telegraphy

Conversion Table

1 centimetre (cm)	0.393 inches
1 metre (m)	3.280 feet (1.093 yards)
1 kilometre (km)	1,093 yards
1 tonne	0.984 (long) tons
1 (long) ton	1.016 tonnes
1 pound (lb)	0.453 kilograms

1 inch (in)	25.40 millimetres (mm)
1 foot (ft)	30.48 centimetres
1 yard (yd)	0.914 metres
1 fathom (6 feet)	1.828 metres
1 cable (202 yards)	185.2 metres
1 nautical mile (2,025 yards)	1.852 kilometres
1 knot	1.852 kilometres per hour

Acknowledgements

This book owes its existence to a request many years ago for a guest speaker. The Western Australian chapter of the Naval Historical Society of Australia was asked to provide a speaker for a Trafalgar Day dinner. The topic was the action between HMAS *Sydney* and SMS *Emden* on 9 November 1914. There were no takers, so I got the job. My research for that lecture led to a desire to gain a better understanding of why and how the two ships fought on that fateful day. This book is the product of that desire.

Many individuals contributed along the way, but the finished work would not have been possible without the generous help and advice of Rear Admiral (retired) Henning Bess, head of the *Emdenfamilie*. I also owe a huge debt of gratitude to the late Peter Günter Huff, whose study of SMS *Emden* continues to inspire me.

I also wish to acknowledge the invaluable assistance provided by John Perryman and Greg Swinden at the RAN's Sea Power Centre-Australia; Michael Gregg and Mack McCarthy at the Western Australian Museum; Geoff Vickridge, Murray Ewen and David Nicolson; Shane Casey, Ricky Phillips and the staff at the Australian War Memorial; Jenny Lee at the Telegraph Museum, Portcurno; the staff at the various offices of the National Archives of Australia; the State Libraries of New South Wales, Victoria and Western Australia; the Australian National Maritime Museum; and the Naval Historical Society of Australia.

I extend a special thanks to Desiree Lochau-Emden and her family for permission to quote from *On The Raging Seas*; John Glossop for permission to quote from his father's diary and papers; John Walter for permission to reproduce his line profile of *Emden*; Tim Cumming of the Western Australian Museum for the maps; and a very big thanks to Malcolm Wright and Julian Mannering for their confidence in me.

Last, but by no means least, I wish to thank my wife Dale, and children James, Caitlin and Claire for their ongoing love and support.

Wes Olson
February 2018

Introduction

For two months in 1914 a small German cruiser waged war on British and Allied trade in the Indian Ocean, carried out raids on the ports of Madras and Penang, then met her end trying to destroy the cable and wireless stations on the Cocos (Keeling) Islands. Handled with dash and daring, *Emden* operated like a twentieth-century pirate ship, stopping merchant vessels on the trade routes, taking what she needed to keep going, and sinking or releasing those she had no use for. But unlike the pirates of old, *Emden*'s commanding officer, Fregatten-kapitän Karl von Müller, upheld a strict code of chivalry. Enemy combatants were to be put to the sword while the battle raged, but merchant mariners and civilians were to be spared. Word of his 'knight-like' conduct quickly spread, and von Müller became widely known as the 'gentleman of war'.

During her brief career as a commerce raider in the Indian Ocean, *Emden* destroyed two enemy warships and intercepted twenty-nine merchant vessels. Of the latter, eleven were released, three were captured and kept for their cargoes of coal, and fifteen sunk. Two of the captured vessels were subsequently recaptured by British warships; the third was scuttled by her prize crew. This brought total British mercantile marine losses to sixteen ships totalling 70,360 tons which, together with their cargoes, represented an estimated monetary loss of £2,200,000. In 2018 values, this equates to over £200 million.

Emden also destroyed oil storage tanks at Madras (Chennai) containing over 1.9 million litres of kerosene, and her presence in the Bay of Bengal had an equally damaging effect on trade. The risk of ships and cargoes being lost resulted in heavy increases in insurance premiums, vessels being prevented from leaving port, and critical delays in the export of tea, jute and other commodities from southern India. The logistical cost to the British Admiralty was also considerable. A large number of British, Japanese, Australian, French and Russian warships were tied down guarding ports, providing escorts for convoys, and hunting *Emden*. With so many warships opposing the German cruiser it was only a matter of time before she was caught.

Emden met her nemesis, the Australian light cruiser *Sydney*, at the Cocos Islands on 9 November 1914. Out-gunned and unable to escape, her death was slow and brutal. Von Müller fought until *Emden* was a burning, shattered wreck, and then drove her ashore on North Keeling Island to save as many of his crew as possible. Of the 318 officers and men who were onboard at the start of the battle, 182 survived. Of these, twenty-one were seriously injured and forty-four were slightly wounded.

This is the story of *Emden*'s last cruise and final battle. It is told by the victors and the vanquished, and spares neither friend nor foe in the telling. It is a tale of war at sea at its worst, and of naval men and boys at their very best.

1

Swan of the East

Our Commander went aboard the flagship to report to
the Admiral of the squadron, and to submit to him the
proposal that the "Emden" be detached from the
squadron, and be sent to the Indian Ocean, to raid the
enemy's commerce.

Kapitänleutnant Helmuth von Mücke

Seiner Majestät Schiff (His Majesty's Ship) *Emden* was the second of
the *Dresden*-class light cruisers built for the Imperial German Navy.
Designed for service abroad or with the fleet, *Emden*'s construction
was authorised on 23 December 1905, and building commenced at the
Kaiserlichen Werft (Imperial Shipyard), Danzig, on 1 November 1906.
Officially named and launched on 26 May 1908, *Emden* was commissioned for trials on 10 July 1909. The latter revealed a propeller
defect which prevented the ship attaining the contract speed of 24
knots, but this was subsequently rectified and *Emden* passed her speed
trials on 20 August. Coal consumption, manoeuvring, gunnery,
torpedo and equipment tests were completed by 29 September 1909.[1]

Emden was built during a period of rapid expansion of the
Kaiserliche Marine (Imperial Navy), and warship construction out-
stripped the recruitment and training of essential personnel, especially
engineer officers.[2] The manpower shortage had an impact on the latest
addition to the fleet; despite costing 6,380,000 marks to construct,
Emden was decommissioned on 30 September and placed in reserve
until a crew became available.

Officially classed as a small protected cruiser, *Emden* had an overall
length of 118m (387ft), a beam of 13.5m (44ft), and displaced 3,664
tonnes (3,606 tons). Designed draught was 5.13m (17ft) forward and
4.53m (15ft) aft. Twelve transverse watertight bulkheads divided the hull
below the waterline into thirteen compartments, commencing with Compartment I at the stern and ending with Compartment XIII at the bow.

The tiller flat and rudder machinery were located in Compartment I. Compartment II housed the explosives and small arms cartridge room, and the shell fuze locker. Compartment III contained the after magazines and ammunition hoists. The auxiliary engine rooms were located in Compartment IV, and the main engines were in Compartment V; a longitudinal bulkhead ran down the centreline of these two compartments, providing watertight separation between the port and starboard engine rooms, and the port and starboard auxiliary engine rooms. Compartments VI, VII, VIII and IX housed the ship's boilers. Compartment X contained the main fresh water tanks and the torpedo flat. The forward magazines and ammunition hoists were located in Compartment XI. Compartment XII contained the ship's refrigerating equipment and the cool room. Compartment XIII was essentially a collision compartment, and the upper section of it, including the bow-ram, was packed with cork.[3]

All of these compartments and their important contents were protected by an armoured deck (*Panzerdeck*) varying in thickness from 10mm to 110mm. It also varied in height, and between Compartments II and XI it was well above the waterline; here the *Panzerdeck* took a high turtle-back form, having sloping sides crowned by a horizontal section of plating or armoured grating (above the engines and boiler uptakes) for greater protection against plunging shell fire. The steel decks above the *Panzerdeck* (upper, forecastle and poop decks) varied in thickness from 10mm (0.4in) to 25mm (1in). Teak planks covered the upper deck amidships and beneath the forecastle and poop deck guns. Linoleum covered the remaining upper and lower deck surfaces.[4]

Emden was the last German cruiser to be built with reciprocating steam engines, these being of the vertical triple-expansion type.[5] The two engines fitted to *Emden* developed 16,171 brake horsepower (bhp) at 141rpm, and delivered 15,683 shaft horsepower (shp) to the two 4.3m (14ft) diameter, four-blade propellers. There were twelve Schulz-Thornycroft type four-drum coal-fired boilers for steam production. These small-bore water-tube boilers were housed in four boiler rooms, for which three funnels were provided:

Kesselraum (boiler room) I housed two boilers – No. I port and starboard (their uptakes being trunked to the after funnel).

Kesselraum II housed four boilers – No. II port and starboard (their uptakes being trunked to the after funnel), and No. III port and starboard (their uptakes being trunked to the centre funnel).
Kesselraum III housed four boilers – No. IV port and starboard (their uptakes being trunked to the centre funnel), and No. V port and starboard (their uptakes being trunked to the forward funnel).
Kesselraum IV housed two boilers – No. VI port and starboard (their uptakes being trunked to the forward funnel).[6]

Coal for the boilers was stored in transverse and longitudinal bunkers located above (upper) and beside (lower) the boiler and engine room compartments. The coal stored in the upper and lower bunkers thus formed an additional layer of protection through which an enemy shell would have to pass before striking the *Panzerdeck* or the compartment bulkhead. Total bunker capacity was 790 tonnes (777 tons).

Emden was normally conned from an enclosed bridge on the forward superstructure, but an armoured conning tower was provided immediately below the bridge for the protection of the captain, gunnery officer, helmsman and other key personnel when the ship was in action. A steering stand (wheel) and a compass binnacle were provided in both positions; in the transmitting station three decks below the conning tower; and in the tiller flat in Compartment I. Directional compasses were also placed in the auxiliary steering position; on an elevated stand above the engine room skylight; and at the forward gunnery control station above the bridge.

The ship's rudder was turned by a steam-powered screw-spindle machine located in the tiller flat. This *Rudermaschine* could be controlled remotely from the bridge, the armoured conning tower and the transmitting station. In the event of a loss of steam to the *Rudermaschine*, or failure of the ship's electrical system, *Emden* could be steered from an auxiliary steering position on the poop deck. The auxiliary steering gear consisted of a pair of ship's wheels connected to the *Rudermaschine* via drive chain and rodding.

Emden's main armament consisted of ten 10.5cm (4.1in) C/88 (Model 1888) *Schnellfeuer-Kanonen* (quick-firing guns) on C/04 mountings. These central pivot mounts gave each gun an elevation of 30° and a maximum effective range of 12,200m (13,340yds). A well-trained gun crew was expected to be capable of loading and firing the 10.5cm C/88 L/40 gun sixteen times in a minute.[7] Six of *Emden*'s guns were fitted with splinter shields and roofs, these being No. 1 port and No. 1 starboard (forecastle deck), No. 3 port and No. 3 starboard (upper deck amidships), and No. 5 port and No. 5 starboard (poop deck). The four guns not fitted with shields were placed in sponsons below the forecastle deck (No. 2 port and No. 2 starboard) and below the poop deck (No. 4 port and No. 4 starboard); the crews of these guns were thus partially protected by the deck above, and by the ship's sides.

Ammunition for the 10.5cm guns was of the fixed type, in that the projectile (shell) was permanently fixed to a cartridge case which contained the primer and the propellant. *Emden* was authorised to carry 750 cartridges with a high-explosive internal-fuze shell, 720 with a high-explosive nose-fuze shell, and thirty with shrapnel shells – an allowance of 150 cartridges per gun.[8]

Emden was also equipped with eight 5.2cm (2in) *Schnellfeuer-Kanonen* L/55 guns. Two were placed in the bows below the forecastle deck, two were mounted on the forecastle deck above the No. 2 sponson guns, two were mounted on the poop deck above the No. 4 guns, and two were placed in the stern below the poop deck. In addition, *Emden* carried a wheeled, 6cm (2.4in) *Stahl-Bootskanonen* L/21 (steel boat's cannon) for use by the ship's landing party. A second 6cm gun was embarked when the ship was on foreign service; *Emden*'s allocation of two Maxim Model 1894 machine guns was likewise increased to four when on overseas duty.[9]

Two underwater torpedo tubes were provided, one to port and one to starboard; these were located in a flat directly below the No. 2 sponson guns. *Emden* carried five Model C/03 45cm (17.7in) torpedoes, which had a maximum range of 3,000m (3,300yds).[10] *Emden* was also equipped with four 150-ampere (A) searchlights; two were positioned on the foremast, and two were placed on the mainmast (aft). Eight ship's boats were carried, and pairs of radial davits were provided for each boat.[11]

Emden's sojourn with the Reserve Fleet came to an end on 26 March 1910 when the Kaiser, Wilhelm II, initialled her sailing orders. The cruiser was required for service with the East Asiatic Squadron, based at Tsingtau (Qingdao) in eastern China, and recommissioned on

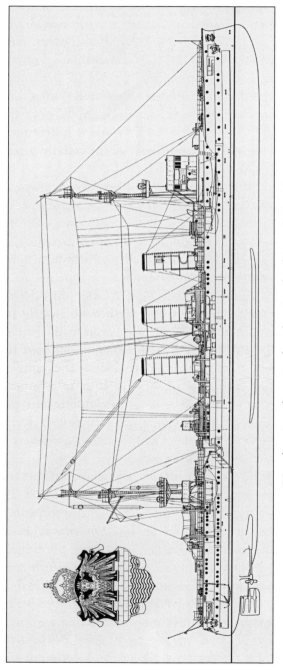

Line drawing of SMS *Emden*, showing the ship as designed. As constructed, *Emden* had longer propeller shafts and larger diameter propellers. (*John Walter*)

1 April under the command of Korvettenkapitän Waldemar Vollerthun. The majority of the 361 officers and men who formed the ship's company were experienced hands from the cruiser *Arcona*, which had recently completed a three-year deployment to the Far East and had returned to Germany for modernisation.

Emden, freshly painted for tropical service, sailed from Kiel on 12 April. Proceeding via the Cape Verde islands, she crossed the Atlantic, called at Montevideo and Buenos Aires, passed through the Strait of Magellan, and entered the Pacific Ocean in early June. After further stops at Valparaiso and Talcahuano for coal, *Emden* set off across the Pacific and reached Tsingtau on 17 September 1910.[12] Here, *Emden*'s elegant lines, gleaming white hull and stately appearance earned her the nickname '*Schwan des Ostens*' (Swan of the East).

Tsingtau, in Shantung (Shandong) Province, was seized by German naval forces in November 1897. Germany was then a rising power in Europe, but a newcomer to colonialism, having sought and acquired its first overseas territory in 1884. The acquisition of Togo, the Cameroons, German East Africa and German West Africa was quickly followed by concessions in the Pacific. These included the northeastern part of New Guinea (proclaimed Kaiser Wilhelm's Land in 1885), the adjacent Admiralty Islands, Duke of York Islands, Massau Islands, New Britain, New Hanover, New Ireland, and the Vitu Islands (collectively known as the Bismarck Archipelago) – thus forming the Protectorate of German New Guinea. In 1886 Germany acquired the Marshall Islands, and two years later the island of Nauru was annexed. Finally, in 1899 Germany purchased the Caroline, Pelew and Marianne islands (less Guam), laid claim to Bougainville and Buka islands, and assumed control of the western Samoan islands.[13]

The seizure of Tsingtau as a site for a naval base to protect Germany's Asia–Pacific empire had an immediate destabilising effect on the region. It prompted Russia to acquire Lushun (Port Arthur) 200 miles to the north, which in turn caused Britain to establish a naval base at Weihaiwai, midway between the two.[14] From 1894 to 1897 the *Kaiserliche Marine* maintained a cruiser division (four ships) in the Far East, but after the acquisition of Tsingtau the Kaiser approved the creation of a cruiser squadron (*Kreuzergeschwader*) of eight ships. When *Emden* arrived on station there were six cruisers in the East

Emden, in her tropical paint scheme of white hull and buff upper works. (*Author's collection*)

Asiatic Squadron, these being *Scharnhorst* (flagship), *Gneisenau*, *Nürnberg*, *Leipzig*, *Condor* and *Cormoran*. In line with German naval policy, each cruiser had a proportion of the crew trained in infantry weapons and tactics, to be sent ashore to resolve any colonial crisis that her guns or mere presence could not.[15]

Emden conducted her first police action at the end of December 1910 when she, *Nürnberg*, *Cormoran*, and the survey vessel *Planet*, were sent to the Carolines to quell a rebellion on the island of Ponape. *Emden* fired her guns in anger for the first time and her landing party took part in the ground-fighting which lasted for several weeks. The next incident was closer to home. A series of uprisings and revolts in China culminated in the 1911 Revolution, the creation of a national Chinese government, and the fall of the Qing dynasty. Unrest continued, however, and in July 1913 Nanking (Nanjing) was captured by anti-government forces. *Emden*, now commanded by Korvettenkapitän Karl von Müller, was ordered up the Yangtze River to help retake the city. The cruiser came under artillery fire on 27 August, but responded in kind and silenced the rebel guns. Von Müller, the 30-year-old son of a German army officer, had only been in command of *Emden* for four months – his first seagoing command – and was subsequently awarded the Royal Order of the Crown (*König-*

7

(*Western Australian Museum*)

8

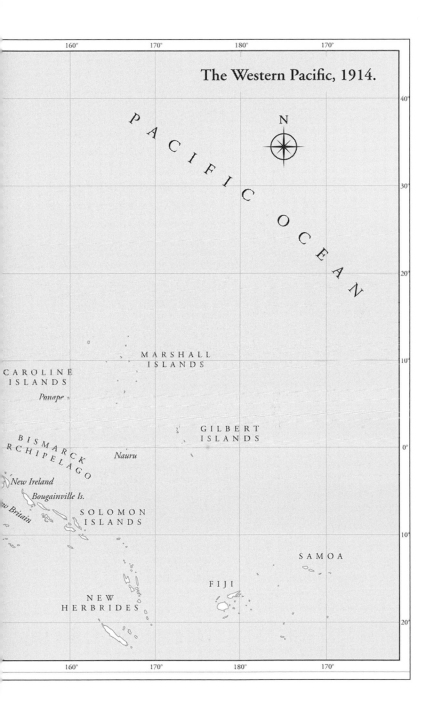

The Western Pacific, 1914.

PACIFIC OCEAN

N

40°

30°

20°

10°

MARSHALL
ISLANDS

CAROLINE
ISLANDS

Ponape

BISMARCK
ARCHIPELAGO

GILBERT
ISLANDS

0°

Nauru

New Ireland

Bougainville Is.

New Britain

SOLOMON
ISLANDS

10°

SAMOA

FIJI

NEW
HERBRIDES

20°

160°   170°   180°   170°

160°   170°   180°   170°

licher Kronenorden), 3rd Class with Swords, for his leadership and *Emden*'s performance at Nanking. He was also recommended for promotion.[16]

Von Müller was promoted to Fregattenkapitän on 12 March 1914. Three months later Kapitänleutnant Helmuth von Mücke was appointed as *Emden*'s first officer (second in command). A percentage of the ship's company was relieved every six months for return to Germany, and on 3 June the HAPAG liner *Patricia* reached Tsingtau with 1,500 replacements for the East Asiatic Squadron and the naval garrison.[17] One of them was 21-year-old Friederich Lochau, who had recently completed his training as an officers' cook at Cuxhaven. He

Emden's officers, August 1913. Standing, left to right: Oberleutnant zur See von Ruville, Marine-Ingenieur Francksen, Marine-Oberzahlmeister Oppermann, Oberleutnant zur See Gaede, Kapitänleutnant Peucer, Marine-Ingenieur Warnecke, Korvettenkapitän von Müller, Marine-Stabsarzt Luther, Kapitänleutnant Bess, Marine-Ingenieur Haaß, Marine-Oberingenieur Ellerbroek, Oberleutnant zur See Hillebrand, Oberleutnant zur See Witthoeft. Sitting, left to right: Fähnrich zur See von Guérard, Leutnant zur See Ladisch, Leutnant zur See Krauss, Leutnant zur See Haas, Fähnrich zur See Fikentscher. (*Western Australian Museum*)

noted the presence of *Scharnhorst*, *Gneisenau*, *Emden*, *Leipzig* and a few gunboats in harbour, and assumed that one of these vessels was to be his home for the next two years. On 4 June Lochau found himself in a draft of 150 assigned to *Emden*; a period of intensive training quickly followed: 'Once settled on board, gun drill as well as gun-firing practice, mine and explosive-charge exercises, debarkation man-oeuvres, and not to forget the daily deck-scrubbing with bare feet and pants rolled up to the knees, began.'[18]

Others did their training at sea. On 7 June *Leipzig*, with her quota of new men, sailed for Mexico to relieve *Nürnberg* on the West American Station. Thirteen days later the squadron commander, Vizeadmiral Maximilian Graf von Spee, took *Scharnhorst*, *Gneisenau*, and the squadron auxiliary *Titania* on a cruise to Samoa, leaving *Emden* as the sole modern cruiser at Tsingtau.

Storm clouds

Emden was scheduled to sail to Shanghai in July 1914, but an event in Bosnia changed everything. Fähnrich zur See Prinz Franz Joseph von Hohenzollern, a nephew of the Kaiser, and *Emden*'s second torpedo officer, recalled: 'On June 29th, 1914, there reached us, in Tsingtau, the fateful telegram saying that the Archduke Franz Ferdinand of Austria, the heir to the throne, and his consort the Duchess of Hohenberg, had been murdered in Sarajevo.'[19] The shots echoed throughout Europe, and the shock waves carried as far as Tsingtau. On 7 July von Müller received orders from Germany, cancelling *Emden*'s cruise and instructing him to remain in harbour. Then on 22 July the Austro-Hungarian cruiser *Kaiserin Elizabeth* unexpectedly entered port. Von Hohenzollern believed that their ally was worried about war with Russia, and was seeking shelter and protection.

Austria–Hungary blamed Serbia for the murder of Archduke Ferdinand and threatened war. In response, Russia began to mobilise her huge army in support of Serbia. There was a very real possibility that Russia would go to war with Austria–Hungary over Serbia, and if she did, a complicated arrangement of alliances and treaties would come into play; Germany would most likely declare war on Russia; in which case France would probably declare war on Germany. Europe was a powder-keg, and the fuse was lit on 28 July. A month to the day after the assassination of Archduke Ferdinand, Austria declared war on Serbia.[20]

Von Müller received the news on 29 July and, as senior officer of the squadron in the absence of von Spee, began preparing *Emden* and Tsingtau for war. On 31 July he received another telegram from Germany, warning of growing political tension between the Central European Powers (Germany and Austria–Hungary) and the Triple Entente (Russia, France and Britain). Von Müller ordered *Emden* to be readied for sea, as he wanted freedom of movement if it did come to war. Unnecessary items like carpets, curtains and furniture were landed, while coal, provisions, ammunition and torpedo warheads were embarked. Von Hohenzollern wrote that it was a severe task, especially since the gunnery officer, Kapitänleutnant Ernst Gaede, claimed a percentage of the ship's company to carry ammunition. He pitied von Mücke, who 'had work and worry to spare'.[21]

Marine-Zahlmeisterapplikant Franz Bordeaux went ashore with senior paymaster Woytschekowsky and four ratings to draw war contingency money from the Deutsch-Asiatische Bank. Bordeaux also had to order provisions, only some of which were delivered in time. When he returned to the ship most of the other work was complete; the bunkers were full, and bags of coal were standing on the deck. He noted that it was 6.30pm when *Emden* cast off from the coaling wharf: 'Our band is playing on deck "There resounds a call like thunder", which arouses great enthusiasm in everyone's heart. Then we escort the steamer *Elsbeth*, which is bound for the *Scharnhorst* and *Gneisenau* in the Pacific.'[22]

Emden had barely left harbour when 'Clear ship for action' was given by drum and bugle. It was a precautionary move in case hostile warships were waiting outside, but *Emden* and *Elsbeth* reached open water without incident and then steamed southward. At nightfall 'war watches' were set at the guns, searchlights, and in the torpedo flat. Extra lookouts were also posted on the masts, bridge and after gunnery control stand to give early warning of other vessels. Those men not on watch climbed into their hammocks and slept fully clothed so that they might reach their action stations more quickly in an emergency.[23] Later that night *Elsbeth* was detached for independent passage to Yap; von Müller chose to remain in the Yellow Sea, where he could monitor wireless news of the situation in Europe and return to Tsingtau if necessary.

Saturday, 1 August found everyone working hard, as stores and provisions had to be stowed, and fuzes needed to be fitted to the 10.5cm ammunition. On 2 August Bordeaux wrote:

One would never know that it is Sunday; we are still working at the priming [fuzing] of ammunition. At 11 o'clock in the morning all the ammunition (about 3,000 rounds) is primed. The crew has had to work very hard this last week.[24] At 11.40 sounds 'All hands aft'. In a few words the Commander [von Müller] thanks us for our excellent work. Then he reports that his Majesty the Kaiser on the 1st of August in the afternoon declared that the Army and Navy were to be mobilised. Our opponents so far are restricted to Russia. England's and France's conduct is still uncertain.[25]

Von Müller then told the ship's company that they were to act bravely and courageously if it came to war, so that at the end of the conflict each man could hold up a proud head before the Kaiser. According to von Hohenzollern, he ended his address with three cheers for His Majesty the Emperor, and every man joined in with enthusiasm.

Unknown to von Müller, Germany had declared war on Russia on Saturday evening (European time). The news did not reach *Emden* until early Monday. Bordeaux wrote in his diary, 'At 4.30 in the morning the boatswain's mate whistles to the watch, "War is declared". We are steering north.'[26] Von Müller had turned north in the hope of intercepting a Russian freighter on the Nagasaki–Vladivostok shipping route, but there was also a risk that *Emden* might encounter the cruiser *Askold* – a more heavily armed ship. Consequently, there was some apprehension when a vessel was sighted at 6.00am on 4 August. Bad weather and heavy seas hindered identification, and many feared the worst. Bordeaux heard the cry '*Askold* in sight – *Askold* is here', before rushing to his post – the first aid station in the tiller flat:

We are completely cut off from above down here and the heat is almost unbearable. We hear and see nothing. We are still of the opinion that the *Emden* must immediately engage action with the *Askold*. The engines increase their revolutions. The rudder is put hard to port with a terrible noise by the steering machine. Now they must certainly be about to begin. We can only hear shots when we listen most attentively. The engines run yet faster. It is becoming awful … Soon it becomes calmer, the engines slow down. The hatch is opened. In great excitement we asked what had actually happened. 'Oh, it's only a Russian steamer.'[27]

It was *Ryazan*, a fast cargo-liner of the Russian volunteer fleet. As such, her deck was stiffened for armaments, but she was yet to undergo conversion to an auxiliary cruiser. It took a dozen warning shots to bring her to a stop so that an armed boarding party could be sent across. *Emden*'s boarding officer, Oberleutnant zur See der Reserve Julius Lauterbach, was delighted with what he found. The naval reserve officer had, until recently, been captain of the HAPAG steamship *Staatssekretär Kraetke*. He had spent years in the Orient; he knew ships and he knew people; he also knew that *Ryazan* was a very good catch.[28]

Ryazan was declared a war prize, allowing Lauterbach and his men to take charge of the ship. Her master, crew and passengers were placed under German martial law and informed that they were now going to Tsingtau. Bordeaux watched as the Russian flags were hauled down, 'and soon we see the proud German war flag waving at the peak'. He thought *Ryazan* looked better for it. 'As she can work up to fourteen knots she comes along with us. Now we have to be careful if we wish to reach Tsingtau with her.'[29]

They were still in the Tsushima Strait when just after 5.00pm *Emden*'s crow's-nest lookout reported smoke from several ships off the starboard bow. Von Müller feared they were the French armoured cruisers *Montcalm* and *Dupleix* with accompanying destroyers, so turned away to avoid battle.[30] *Emden* and *Ryazan* escaped detection, but this was now the reality for von Müller and his men; *Emden* was but a single small cruiser in a hostile world. As yet, only Russian and French forces had to be faced, but Britain and perhaps Japan would soon be against them. Von Mücke was acutely aware of their predicament:

Yes, the English will surely join our enemies, but not until such a time as seems most favourable to them. Whether now, or later, whether by an immediate participation in the war, or not until towards the end, when Germany has been weakened, we cannot tell. But attack us, they surely will.[31]

In March 1911 *Emden* was repainted; the upper works became silver-grey, and the hull was painted a slightly darker 'squirrel-grey'. *Emden* retained this scheme until her loss. (*Western Australian Museum*)

War plans

The British Admiralty knew that if it came to war with Germany, trade in the Pacific and Indian Oceans would be seriously threatened by von Spee's Cruiser Squadron and the light cruiser *Königsberg*. This was reflected in the deployment of ships to counter the threat. *Scharnhorst* and *Gneisenau*, armed with 21cm (8.2in) guns and capable of 22 and 24 knots respectively, posed the greatest danger; the Admiralty therefore assigned the battleship *Triumph* (10in guns/19 knots), and the armoured cruisers *Minotaur* (9.2in guns/22 knots) and *Hampshire* (7.5in guns/22 knots) to Vice Admiral Martyn Jerram's China Squadron. Jerram also had the light cruisers *Yarmouth* and *Newcastle*, eight destroyers, and numerous gunboats at his disposal.

Upon Britain entering the war, the French Far East Squadron would also come under Jerram's command, giving him another two cruisers, *Montcalm* and *Dupleix*, plus ancillary vessels. The China Squadron would be further boosted by the fast passenger liners *Empress of Asia*, *Empress of Japan*, *Empress of Russia* and *Himalaya*, which were to be armed with 4.7in guns and commissioned as auxiliary cruisers.

Covering the southwest Pacific was Rear Admiral George Patey's Australian Squadron. This comprised the battlecruiser *Australia* (12in guns/25 knots), light cruisers *Melbourne*, *Sydney* and *Encounter*, small cruiser *Pioneer*, destroyers *Parramatta*, *Warrego* and *Yarra*, and the submarines *AE1* and *AE2*. Although the squadron was made up of ships of the Royal Australian Navy, it would come under Admiralty control upon the outbreak of war.[32] In addition there were three small Royal Navy cruisers, *Philomel*, *Psyche* and *Pyramus*, in New Zealand waters. They were operated by the New Zealand Naval Forces, and would also come under Admiralty control in the event of war.

Should von Spee cross the Pacific to operate in South American waters he would have to deal with Rear Admiral Sir Christopher Cradock's 4th Cruiser Squadron, which comprised the armoured cruisers *Suffolk*, *Lancaster*, *Essex* and *Berwick*, and the light cruiser *Bristol*. If the German admiral took all or part of his squadron into the Indian Ocean where *Königsberg* (based at Dar es Salaam in German East Africa) might join him, he would have to reckon with the battleship *Swiftsure* and the light cruisers *Dartmouth* and *Fox* of the East Indies Squadron. Covering South African waters were the light cruisers *Hyacinth*, *Astraea* and *Pegasus* of the Cape of Good Hope Squadron.[33]

Then there was Japan; she had a large and powerful navy, and had signed an alliance treaty with Britain in 1902. The treaty required neutrality should one signatory became involved in a war with another power, but support if one party went to war with more than one power. When the Anglo-Japanese Alliance treaty was renewed in 1905 it included a pledge of mutual assistance in the event of either signatory being attacked by a single power.[34] The Admiralty was hopeful that Japan would honour this pledge by siding with Britain in a war with Germany, but conceded that 'nothing beyond her benevolent neutrality could be counted upon'.[35]

Von Spee's squadron and *Königsberg* were not the only threat to trade in the Pacific and Indian oceans. The Austrian cruiser *Kaiserin Elizabeth* was known to be at Tsingtau, and the Italian armoured cruiser *Marco Polo* was at Kobe, Japan. Italy's intentions were not yet known, but it was feared that she would side with Germany. Worse, there were a large number of German merchant ships in foreign waters which might be fitted with guns and pressed into service as auxiliary cruisers.

Further complicating matters, Jerram and Patey were expected to mount offensive operations against German bases in the Asia–Pacific region, and seize or sink her merchant ships. The aim of these operations was to destroy von Spee's communications network and deprive him of coaling stations and supply ships.[36] Despite the fact that Jerram and Patey would be hard pressed by all these operational demands, the First Lord of the Admiralty, Winston Churchill, was confident that von Spee would be hunted down and his squadron destroyed. 'He was a cut flower in a vase; fair to see, yet bound to die, and to die very soon if the water was not constantly renewed.'[37]

Britain declared war on Germany at midnight on 4 August. *Emden* received the news by wireless the following afternoon. Bordeaux wrote, 'So that's another enemy. Out here the position for us is becoming fairly serious, for England has too many ships for us to be able to oppose them.'[38] Von Hohenzollern was equally concerned, and thought that British warships would already be lying in wait outside Tsingtau, ready to capture any ships entering or leaving harbour.[39] He need not have worried. Jerram's China Squadron was 1,300 miles away at Hong Kong.

When the Admiralty's telegram warning of possible war with Germany reached Jerram on 28 July he was at Weihaiwei with *Minotaur*, *Hampshire*, *Yarmouth* and six destroyers – ideally placed to blockade Tsingtau and to destroy *Emden*.[40] The precautionary telegram stated that all commanders-in-chief should be 'prepared to shadow possible hostile men-of-war and consider dispositions of HM ships under your command from this point of view'.[41] On receipt of this telegram Jerram sought information on the whereabouts of von Spee's squadron and other potential enemy warships. According to the available intelligence, *Scharnhorst* was at or near Yap, *Gneisenau* was reported (erroneously) to be at Singapore, *Leipzig* and *Nürnberg* were somewhere near Mexico, *Marco Polo* was at Kobe, and the gunboat *Jaguar* was at Shanghai. *Kaiserin Elizabeth* and *Emden* were at Tsingtau, as was *Cormoran*, the gunboats *Iltis*, *Luchs* and *Tiger*, and the torpedo boat *S.90*.[42]

Scharnhorst and *Gneisenau* were Jerram's main concern. He assumed that they would try to reach Tsingtau at the commencement of hostilities, so decided to take up a position 350 miles to the south

17

of the German base and establish a patrol line between Shanghai and southern Japan. Unfortunately, the Admiralty directed Jerram to concentrate at Hong Kong so that *Triumph* could form part of his squadron. This was achieved on 5 August, with *Dupleix* joining the squadron there the same day.[43] The Admiralty had instructed Jerram to concentrate at Hong Kong because it feared his squadron's margin of superiority over von Spee was too small without *Triumph*.[44] The end result was that none of Jerram's ships were in a position to deal with *Emden* when Britain entered the war.

Rear Admiral Patey had no such qualms about his powerful squadron, and he had his own ideas as to von Spee's likely movements. On 1 August Australian wireless stations heard *Scharnhorst* communicating with Yap and Nauru, and trying to contact *Nürnberg*. Working on the signal strength recorded at different receiving stations, von Spee's flagship was believed to be several hundred miles northeast of Port Moresby, British New Guinea.[45] Patey doubted that the German admiral would try to return to Tsingtau. He thought von Spee might concentrate his forces at Simpsonhafen (Simpson Harbour), New Britain, in preparation for an attack on Australian ports and shipping. Patey therefore took *Australia*, *Sydney*, *Parramatta*, *Warrego* and *Yarra* north to make a surprise raid on Simpsonhafen.[46]

Further wireless transmissions from *Scharnhorst* were picked up on 5 August, the day Australia learned that it was at war with Germany. Patey and Jerram were informed of these transmissions, which now placed *Scharnhorst* east of the Solomon Islands; it was thought that *Gneisenau* and *Nürnberg* were with her. As for *Emden*, Jerram received word that she and four colliers had departed Tsingtau on 3 August. Another, more accurate report, stated that the Norddeutscher Lloyd steamship *Yorck*, which was known to be stiffened for armaments, had left Yokohama on 4 August heavily laden with coal and supplies.[47]

Jerram, confident that Patey could deal with *Scharnhorst*, *Gneisenau* and *Nürnberg*, now thought it safe to split his squadron.[48] On 6 August he sailed with *Minotaur*, *Hampshire* and *Newcastle* in an attempt to cut off *Emden*, *Yorck* and the four colliers, which he believed were making for Yap. *Triumph*, *Yarmouth*, *Dupleix* and five destroyers were to head north and establish a watch on Tsingtau. Unfortunately for Jerram, the information he had received regarding *Emden* was incorrect.

18

Emden and and *Ryazan* reached Tsingtau just before dawn on 6 August. Von Müller expected British warships to be lying in wait, but was pleasantly surprised to find the approaches clear. After exchanging signals with the steamship *C Ferd Laeisz*, which was patrolling the harbour entrance, *Emden* was guided through the protective minefields and into port, followed by *Ryazan*. *Emden* secured alongside the coaling wharf and immediately started taking on coal; *Ryazan* went to another berth for conversion to an auxiliary cruiser.[49] Bordeaux was surprised to see that the Norddeutscher Lloyd liner *Prinz Eitel Friedrich* had already undergone this process, having been fitted with searchlights and guns taken from *Iltis*, *Luchs* and *Tiger*.

After arrival von Müller was handed orders from von Spee; *Emden* was to join the squadron at Pagan Island on 10 August. This meant sailing again the same day – and there was much to be done. The piano had to be landed, additional stores, provisions and hammocks embarked, and the ship's company brought up to war strength. Amongst those joining the ship was Bootsmannsmaat Joseph Ruscinski, who had been

The joys of coaling; dust-covered members of *Emden*'s ship's company pose with Fähnrich zur See Schall and Leutnant zur See Fikentscher (centre). (*Western Australian Museum*)

19

serving in the small gunboat *Vaterland* on the Yangtze. By the time *Emden* was ready to sail she had a complement of 398 officers and men, plus three Chinese laundrymen.[50] Bordeaux wrote of *Emden*'s departure:

> At 5.30 in the afternoon we put to sea again. There was a big crowd on the wharf. To the strains of our war song 'There resounds a call like thunder' we leave the harbour. Outside in the roadstead lies the HAPAG steamer *Markomannia* which we are to convoy. The *Prinz Eitel Friedrich* follows us.[51]

On 8 August *Markomannia* was sent ahead so that *Emden* and *Prinz Eitel Friedrich* could each hunt for enemy shipping. Despite taking on extra crew there was still a shortage of watch officers, so with little clerical work to do, Bordeaux volunteered to serve on the war watch of *Emden*'s forward searchlights. His new station was on the signal deck above the bridge, thus guaranteeing him a good view of any action. The only ships sighted, however, proved to be neutral Japanese, so *Emden* joined with *Prinz Eitel Friedrich* on 11 August and they resumed course for Pagan.

Admirals Jerram and Patey were meanwhile closing in on their objectives. On 11 August *Hampshire* intercepted and sank *Elsbeth*, and the following day *Minotaur* and *Newcastle* shelled and destroyed the German wireless station on Yap. Jerram failed to locate *Emden*, but Patey had even less luck. His destroyers, *Parramatta*, *Warrego* and *Yarra*, reached Simpsonhafen on the night of 11 August, but on entering the harbour found it empty. Subsequent searches of the neighouring bays, and around Bougainville by *Australia* and *Sydney*, also drew a blank. Capping off Patey's disappointment, he was unable to locate and silence the German wireless station on New Britain.[52]

There was good news – for some. On 10 August the Russian Pacific Squadron was placed under Jerram's command, giving him another two cruisers, *Askold* and *Zhemchug*, four torpedo boats, and four armed volunteer ships. The following day Japan announced its intention to declare war on Germany and capture Tsingtau. On 12 August the Admiralty sent a telegram to Jerram, informing him of this development, and advising, 'You may now leave whole protection of British trade north of Hong Kong to [the] Japanese, concentrating your attention in concert with Australian Squadron on destroying German cruisers.'[53] Bordeaux wrote: 'Last night the following news was picked up by wireless: "Japan intends to declare war on Germany". "The Japanese fleet is on the way to Tsingtau". Still more news but nothing good.'[54]

Emden and *Prinz Eitel Friedrich* reached Pagan late in the afternoon of 12 August. As they approached the bay where the squadron was anchored, *Emden* was challenged by *Titania*, conscientiously guarding the entrance; after exchanging recognition signals and pleasantries, *Emden* entered the anchorage. Bordeaux could scarcely believe his eyes. 'We steam round the Island and find lying in a bay the *Scharnhorst, Gneisenau, Nürnberg*, and from 10 to 15 colliers and provision ships.'[55]

Shortly after anchoring, von Müller, accompanied by his adjutant, Leutnant zur See Albert von Guérard, went across to *Scharnhorst* to report to von Spee. They returned with the news that von Hohenzollern and fellow midshipman Robin Schall had been promoted to Leutnant zur See, and that *Emden* would take on coal and provisions in the morning.

Early on 13 August *Staatssekretär Kraeke* was secured on *Emden's* port side, and *Gouverneur Jäschke* was brought alongside to starboard. Despite taking coal from the holds of both ships at once, the work, performed under a blazing sun, went slowly. The task of shovelling coal into sacks and baskets for conveyance to *Emden* was normally performed by Chinese labourers, so it was a new and unpleasant experience for the ship's company. At 9.00am von Hohenzollern paused from his work and noted the belated arrival of *Markomannia*; later in the day he was introduced to Leutnants Gyssling and Schmidt, who joined *Emden* from *Gneisenau*.[56]

While his men sweated and toiled, von Müller attended a conference onboard *Scharnhorst*. Von Spee announced to the assembled officers that he intended taking the whole squadron across the Pacific to the Americas, where they would have a better chance of obtaining coal. Although this would entail the suspension of attacks on enemy shipping for several weeks, he saw the value in maintaining his squadron as a 'fleet in being', thereby forcing the enemy to maintain large forces on the trade routes and focal areas. Von Müller respectfully disagreed, and suggested that at least one light cruiser be detached to operate independently in the Indian Ocean. Later, after he had returned to *Emden*, a secret order was hand-delivered to him:

> Accompanied by the steamship *Markomannia*, you are to be detached for deployment in the Indian Ocean, there to wage a vigorous cruiser war to the best of your ability.
>
> Enclosed is a copy of telegraphic communications with our southern supply network during the last few weeks. It lists the amount of coal ordered for the future, an amount that will be turned over to you.
>
> Tonight you will remain with the squadron. Tomorrow morning, this order will be set in motion by the signal 'Detached'.
>
> I intend to sail with the remaining formation to the west coast of America.
>
> Signed,
> Graf Spee[57]

Von Müller told no one of the order.[58] The squadron and attached merchantmen sailed that evening and set course eastwards. Bordeaux wrote in his diary, 'Destination unknown.'[59]

At seven the next morning *Scharnhorst* signalled to *Emden*, 'Detached. Wish you every success.'[60] To everyone except von Müller, the news was like a bolt from the blue. According to von Hohenzollern, the signal caused much rejoicing and excitement in *Emden*. 'At last we were to be on our own and could act independently, as we, or our Captain, pleased.'[61] Von Müller replied to the flagship, 'My dutiful thanks for the confidence placed in me. Success to the squadron and bon voyage.' With that, *Markomannia* was ordered to follow *Emden*. Both ships swung away to the southwest, closed, then stopped so that a signalman could be transferred from *Emden* to the collier for better communications. Von Mücke recalled: 'Ere long we had lost sight of the other ships of the squadron, which now were steering a course contrary to our own, and we all knew full well that we should never meet again.'[62] The ship's company still did not know where they were going, but when *Emden* and *Markomannia* settled onto a south-southwesterly course von Hohenzollern guessed they were heading for the Indian Ocean.

On 15 August *Emden* and *Markomannia* altered course westward, as von Müller wished to call at Angaur in the Pelew (Palau) Islands to take on more coal and provisions, and perhaps acquire another collier. A second support ship was vital, because if *Markomannia* broke down, was captured or sunk, *Emden* would be without a reliable supply of coal. While en route to Angaur further operational preparations were made and training conducted. The gun crews, ammunition handlers, and the range-takers received special training, for which *Markomannia* served as a practice target.[63]

Spare gun crews were also formed and underwent training. Bootsmannsmaat Ruscinski was assigned to the No. 2 port gun as a reserve gun-layer, whilst Matrose Lochau, who was now in charge of the warrant officers' galley, became part of the reserve ammunition crew for the No. 2 starboard gun. Von Mücke put others to work making woven rope (hawser) curtains, which were hung around the No. 2 and No. 4 guns to protect personnel against flying steel splinters when the ship was in action. Woven hawser matting was also placed around the wireless room and the after gunnery control stand.

Marine-Oberingenieur Friedrich Ellerbroek, *Emden*'s senior engineer, had the hardest job. He was responsible for the boilers, engines and auxiliary machinery, and would have to keep everything in working order for the duration of the cruise. The engines were sturdy and reliable, and gave no cause for anxiety, but the boilers needed constant attention. Leaking water tubes were the biggest problem. Fortunately, *Emden* carried an ample supply of spare tubes, and a strict maintence schedule enabled boilers to be shut down for cleaning, running repairs, and the replacement of water tubes and fire-bricks.

Great attention was also given to the selection of watch personnel and lookouts. It was imperative that *Emden* see enemy warships before she herself was seen, so that avoiding action could be taken. Thus far there were only British, Australian, French and Russian vessels to worry about. Japan's position was still uncertain, but became clearer over the next twenty-four hours. On 15 August Japan sent an ultimatum to Germany, demanding the immediate withdrawal of all warships and armed vessels from Japanese and Chinese territorial waters, and the unconditional surrender of Tsingtau by 15 September. Germany had until 23 August to respond.[64] *Emden* received the news by wireless from Tsingtau. Even Lochau grasped the significance of this. If Tsingtau fell, Germany would lose her only base in the Far East, and *Emden* would lose her last link with home. Unknown to Lochau and his shipmates, Japan was already in the war, having informed Britain that she would 'at once place cruisers on the trade routes to shepherd British and Japanese merchant ships and to round up enemy vessels'.[65]

Emden sighted the Pelews at first light on 19 August, and reached Angaur at 11.00am. There were no other ships about, so von Müller decided to take on coal from *Markomannia* while awaiting the arrival of *Prinzessin Alice*. He had heard the Norddeutscher Lloyd liner trying to contact von Spee by wireless the previous afternoon, so instructed her to proceed to Angaur. If her master was agreeable, *Prinzessin Alice* would accompany *Emden* and *Markomannia* into the Indian Ocean.

Prinzessin Alice arrived at 3.00pm, and brought confirmation of Japan's ultimatum to Germany. Von Müller hoped to obtain provisions from her, but was thwarted by a bureaucratic company accounts officer. He did, however, gain another six naval reservists, including Kapitänleutnant der Reserve Oskar Klöpper, and six of the liner's stokers, who volunteered for war service in *Emden*.

Emden sailed again that evening, followed by *Markomannia* and *Prinzessin Alice*. The latter was a reluctant companion, and after dark she slipped away. Von Müller could ill afford to lose the liner and her provisions, even if it did mean lodging forms for every item, so sent another wireless message to her. *Prinzessin Alice*'s captain replied that his boilers were in poor condition and he was short of coal, so would be unable to accompany *Emden* on her cruise. Von Müller then tried to contact von Spee to warn him of the situation with the Japanese, and was astonished to receive a call from *Geier*. The old cruiser was nearby, so a rendezvous was arranged and they met on the afternoon of 20 August. Although *Geier* had a collier (*Bochum*) with her, she was too slow for commerce raiding; von Müller exchanged information with her commanding officer and then they continued on their respective journeys.

Emden and *Markomannia* steered a southwesterly course. Von Müller wished to pass to the west of the Moluccas, cross the Banda Sea, and arrive off the eastern tip of Timor in time to meet the cargo

24

ship *Tannenfels*. On the morning of 23 August, eight hours after *Emden* crossed the equator, a smoke cloud was sighted ahead. Hopes of capturing an enemy freighter faded when the vessel came into view and was seen to be flying a Japanese flag. Von Müller did not know if Germany was as yet at war with Japan, so played it safe. According to Bordeaux, 'After showing the English flag we let her go.'[66]

Von Müller's use of a false flag was a perfectly legal ruse, and his decision not to attack the Japanese ship was also correct.[67] Japan's ultimatum did not expire until midday, and it was only then, when Germany failed to respond, that Japan formally declared war. This was a great relief to Vice Admiral Jerram, as it resulted in the Japanese assuming responsibility for the protection of trade north of Hong Kong, thus releasing British warships for operations to the south. The exceptions were the battleship *Triumph* and the destroyer *Usk*, which were to assist in the capture of Tsingtau; in exchange the Japanese sent the battlecruiser *Ibuki* and the light cruiser *Chikuma* to Singapore and placed them at Jerram's disposal.

Jerram was in need of such vessels because the military authorities were in the process of redeploying British and Indian troops to Europe, the Middle East and East Africa. The transports were given adequate protection against attack by *Königsberg*, but Jerram was worried that von Spee might take his cruiser squadron into the Indian Ocean and attack the convoys. His reasoning was based on the knowledge that a number of German merchant ships laden with coal and provisions were holed up in various ports throughout the Dutch East Indies (Indonesia), and these might be used to replenish von Spee's cruisers prior to an Indian Ocean raid. The entry of Japan into the war thus allowed Jerram to send *Minotaur*, *Hampshire* and *Yarmouth* to the Dutch East Indies to search for enemy shipping.[68] Patey was unable to help because his squadron was covering expeditions in the Pacific. *Australia* and *Melbourne*, together with *Montcalm*, were protecting a New Zealand expedition (escorted by *Philomel*, *Psyche* and *Pyramus*) to capture Samoa; the remainder of the Australian Squadron was assigned to an expedition to capture Rabaul.[69]

Emden reached the designated rendezvous with *Tannenfels* near the Leti Islands on the morning of 25 August, but the freighter failed to appear. *Emden* instead took coal from *Markomannia* before the pair steamed west, into the Flores Sea. According to the information supplied by von Spee, another collier, *Offenbach*, was to be found at Tanajampea. They reached the island on the morning of 27 August, and shortly afterwards were surprised by an approaching warship. *Emden* was preparing to open fire when the stranger was identified as the Dutch coastal defence ship *Tromp*; from her commanding officer von Müller learned that *Offenbach* had been ordered away. The Dutch were keen to preserve their neutrality, and would not allow the Germans to establish coaling points in their territorial waters. Furthermore, foreign warships were only permitted to remain in Dutch waters for twenty-four hours every three months. *Emden* and *Markomannia* therefore steamed north, shadowed by *Tromp* until they were beyond the three-mile territorial limit. Once *Tromp* was out of sight they turned and set course for the Lombok Strait.

Beyond Lombok Strait lay the Indian Ocean. Von Müller expected its southern exit to be patrolled by enemy warships, so decided to negotiate it under cover of darkness the following night. Von Mücke suggested that before doing so they alter *Emden*'s profile by erecting a false funnel. In poor light *Emden* might thus pass for a British cruiser. The idea had originally been conceived by Leutnant Erich Fikentscher, and was now acted upon. Just after sunset on 28 August, as they were preparing to enter the strait, a dummy funnel was erected between the foremast and the forward funnel. The disguise proved unnecessary. Several vessels were sighted in the strait, but none proved hostile, and there were no enemy warships patrolling the exit. *Emden* and *Markomannia* entered the Indian Ocean just after midnight. Von Müller had reached his hunting ground.

2

Cry Havoc

Our orders were quite definite ... destroy the enemy's
trade. To carry out this duty as completely as possible the
"Emden" had to remain as long as possible unassailed,
and this could only be achieved by avoiding a fight with
enemy warships as far as possible.

Leutnant zur See Prinz Joseph von Hohenzollern

Despite having reached the Indian Ocean, Fregattenkapitän von Müller
was not yet ready to commence operations in earnest. Because
Tannenfels and *Offenbach* had failed to rendezvous with *Emden*, he
had been forced to take coal from *Markomannia*, whose cargo he
wished to preserve for as long as possible. He had one last chance to
coal from a German supply ship; *Ulm* was reportedly waiting at
Simeulue, the northernmost island in the chain off Sumatra's west
coast. Von Müller therefore steamed south from Sunda Strait for sixty
miles before turning west to follow the coastline of Java to Sumatra.
Besides coal, he was also hoping to secure fresh provisions from *Ulm*;
Emden's stocks were almost exhausted, and nearly every meal now
consisted of tinned corned beef.[1]

While *Emden*'s navigating officer, Kapitänleutnant Hans Gropius,
plotted their new course, Kapitänleutnant von Mücke applied himself
to building a better dummy funnel. The one hurriedly produced the
day before consisted of 2m-wide sailcloth deck-runners hung from a
piece of timber. Viewed from the side, the screen gave the appearance
of a funnel, but from any other angle it failed to convince. It was also
in the wrong place, so von Mücke put his men to work on an improved
model. According to Steuermannsmaat Hugo Plötz:

This dummy funnel was made of canvas, being the same size as the other
three, namely 10 metres high and 3 metres in diameter, being of course
oval shape. It was hoisted by a rope through a pulley which was

attached to a piece of rope stretched from the aft funnel to the mainmast.[2]

This was a much better arrangement, allowing the fake funnel to be raised or lowered as required.

That night (30 August), *Emden*'s wireless operators heard several warships, believed to be British, transmitting cipher messages to each other. The one doing most of the transmitting used the call-sign 'QMD', and the strength of her calls indicated that she was uncomfortably close. It was *Hampshire*, and unknown to von Müller, she was searching the islands *Emden* was heading for.

Emden and *Markomannia* reached Simeulue on the evening of 3 September. They hoped to find *Ulm* waiting in a natural harbour halfway up the island's east coast, but upon entering the bay at first light, found it empty. Von Müller no doubt cursed his luck, but if he

HMS *Hampshire* was armed with four 7.5in guns, six 6in guns, and numerous smaller quick-firing weapons. She was also well protected with armour plate, and could make 22 knots. If *Emden* had been forced into action with her at Simeulue Island it would have ended disastrously for the German cruiser. (*Author's collection*)

had arrived a day earlier he would have encountered *Hampshire*, and *Emden*'s raiding career would have been over before it had even begun.

Marine-Zahlmeisterapplikant Bordeaux marvelled at the beauty of the bay. 'Langini harbour is a wonderful hiding place, surrounded by land and luxurious vegetation and having only a narrow passage leading to the open sea.'[3] Von Müller thought it perfect for coaling, so had *Emden* secured alongside *Markomannia*, and work commenced at 9.00am. The heat and humidity were oppressive, and only 450 tonnes were embarked during the day. Coaling resumed at 6.00am on 5 September, only to be interrupted by the arrival of a Dutch patrol boat two hours later. Von Müller was ordered to leave Dutch territorial waters, but managed to delay departure until 11.00am, by which time *Emden*'s bunkers were full and another 200 tonnes of bagged coal was stacked on the upper deck. *Emden* and *Markomannia* steered a false course until the patrol boat was out of sight, then swung in a wide arc to port before heading northwest. The following morning Bordeaux wrote in his diary, 'We are steering towards the Gulf of Bengal.'[4]

Leutnant Prinz von Hohenzollern was told that *Emden* was making for the steamship route between Colombo and Khota Raja (Banda Aceh), which she reached on 7 September. He wrote that a sharp lookout was kept, as everyone wished to be the first to report smoke in sight:

> Like the hunter, a sailor also needs a little luck, for which we in the *Emden* hoped in vain. Our many hours of cruising brought us nothing. We would have to search elsewhere, and so altered course and made for the steamer line from Negabatam to Khota Raja on our way to the line between Colombo and Rangoon [Yangon].[5]

Emden, followed by *Markomannia*, pushed deeper into the Bay of Bengal, and another day passed with no sightings. The ship's company was now genuinely hungry for a kill. Fresh food was but a memory, and everyone was sick of the sight and taste of corned beef. Worse, they were almost out of soap. To be able to wash away the coal dust and sweat with soap and fresh water (also in short supply) after a duty watch was one of the small luxuries of shipboard life – a luxury they were now forced to indulge in sparingly.

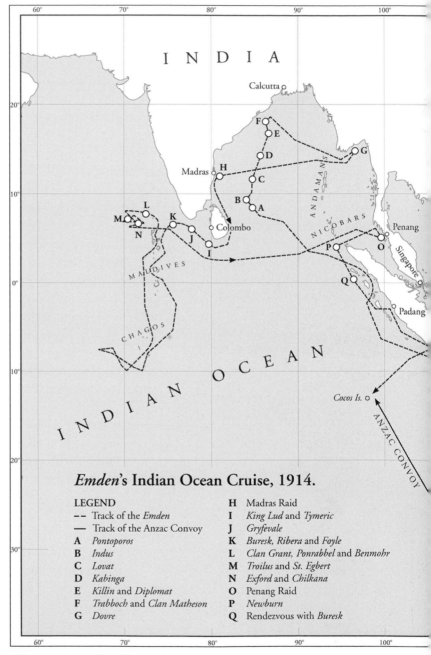

Emden's Indian Ocean Cruise, 1914.

LEGEND
- - Track of the *Emden*
— Track of the Anzac Convoy

A	*Pontoporos*
B	*Indus*
C	*Lovat*
D	*Kabinga*
E	*Killin* and *Diplomat*
F	*Trabboch* and *Clan Matheson*
G	*Dovre*
H	Madras Raid
I	*King Lud* and *Tymeric*
J	*Gryfevale*
K	*Buresk, Ribera* and *Foyle*
L	*Clan Grant, Ponrabbel* and *Benmohr*
M	*Troilus* and *St. Egbert*
N	*Exford* and *Chilkana*
O	Penang Raid
P	*Newburn*
Q	Rendezvous with *Buresk*

(*Western Australian Museum*)

Just before midnight on 9 September Bordeaux took over the middle watch (12.00–4.00am) on the signal deck. Permitted to doze while the lookouts swept the horizon with their night glasses, he was instantly awake when a light was reported off the starboard bow at 2.00am:

> Thereupon the call 'Alarm' immediately resounds from the bridge. It looked so funny when suddenly all the sailors and stokers appeared on the deck awakened out of their sweet sleep and rushed to their battle stations ... For the time being all that we can see is a dark spot which gradually comes closer and is soon distinguished as a steamer with one funnel.[6]

The rangefinder crew soon found the target and began calling out the range, which steadily decreased as *Emden* stalked her prey. Bordeaux continued:

> Our excitement continues to grow. We have now got to within a few hundred metres of the ship. Then the *Emden* fires the first shot and increases her speed. The steamer begins to signal in Morse but we can't make out what she wants and she continues on her way. Apparently she doesn't mean to stop. Our commander now gives the order to fire the second blank charge and at last she stops. Meantime a cutter is made clear and the prize crew has mustered on the deck. The prize officer of course is reserve Oberleutnant Lauterbach again. Now we are quite near to the ship which is to be seen quite plainly. It is a freighter. The cutter is launched and goes across to the steamer with the search party. A few exciting moments pass then the Morse light appears and gives us the following: 'The steamer is named *Pontoporos*, nationality Greek.'[7]

Hearts sank. Greece was neutral, so the vessel would have to be released. Lauterbach then signalled the good news – *Pontoporos* had been chartered by a British company to take 6,500 tons of coal from Calcutta (Kolkata) to Bombay (Mumbai). Bordeaux later heard that when Lauterbach, who spoke excellent English, reached the ship's bridge, the master asked: '"Why do you stop me, I am carrying coals for an English firm." "Yes" replied Lauterbach, "But we happen to be Germans." The man looked as if he had received a blow on the head. He had not expected that.'[8] Von Müller could not legally sink

Pontoporos, but he could confiscate the cargo, as it was owned by the enemy and therefore contraband. A compromise was worked out. The Greek master was asked if he was willing, on receipt of proper payment, to make his cargo available to *Emden*. He was. Lauterbach was instructed to remain onboard *Pontoporos*, and his boarding party was replaced by a prize crew. *Emden* then continued with the hunt, flanked by his new collier and *Markomannia*.

A few hours later, at 8.45am, a smoke cloud was sighted to the north. *Emden* went to battle stations, altered course to intercept, and began working up to full speed. Presently, the silhouette of a merchant ship appeared below the smoke. As the range reduced it was seen that the vessel flew the British Blue Ensign. Worryingly, she then turned towards *Emden*. Von Hohenzollern feared that the vessel might be armed: 'She was carefully studied from the *Emden* and we came to the conclusion that she was not armed. We therefore fired one warning round, hoisted the German ensign, and at the same time [hoisted] the international signal "Stop! Do not use wireless!"'[9] The British merchantman complied, and *Emden* closed with her so that a boarding and search party could be sent across. This party, under the command of Oberleutnant Ernst von Levetzow, signalled that the ship was the 3,413-ton *Indus*, and that she had been chartered by the Indian government to take horses and troops to Europe. These were yet to be embarked, but the ship had been fully provisioned. Von Müller couldn't believe it. *Indus* was carrying soap, foodstuffs, alcohol, cigarettes, chocolate, and all manner of luxury goods. He gave von Mücke six hours to collect whatever he could, and then *Indus* would be scuttled. In the meantime her crew was to be transferred to *Markomannia*.[10]

Indus died hard. After the scuttling party had opened the seacocks and returned to *Emden*, six shells were fired into the hull at the waterline to hasten her sinking. Despite this, an hour elapsed before *Indus* went down. Matrose Lochau was amongst the hundreds on *Emden*, *Markomannia* and *Pontoporos* who watched her die:

As the water entered through the portholes she sank even further to the level of the hatches which had been opened earlier. This sealed her fate. Gigantic fountains shot out from all the portholes, and then she dived bow-first, raising her propeller high up into the air, and disappeared, leaving behind black coal dust and some floating wreckage and lifeboats. As she dived to her grave she did so with a final diabolical mystic howling intermingled with a crescendo of crashing noises.[11]

Lochau was deeply moved by the sinking, and later heard that the captain of the *Indus* watched the death of his ship with tears in his eyes.

Von Müller had little time to reflect on such things. The British authorities were not yet aware of *Emden*'s presence in the shipping lanes, so it was vital that he strike again before they realised that *Indus* and *Pontoporos* were missing. He ordered a change in course and pushed deeper into the Bay of Bengal. The decision to head north proved sound, for at 2.00pm on 11 September smoke was sighted ahead. Bordeaux was in the ship's office, and heard the noise of the engines going faster: 'We could once again hear the cry "To the guns." When I came on deck a steamer was already in sight. Fortune had brought a second transport into our net. It was the steamer *Lovat*, and had the same destination as the *Indus* [Bombay].'[12] Like *Indus*, the 6,102-ton *Lovat* had been converted to carry troops – and suffered the same fate; her crew was transferred to *Markomannia* and then she was scuttled. *Lovat* did not sink quickly, so von Müller moved on, leaving the British ship to founder in her own good time.

The masters of *Indus* and *Lovat* divulged that three other vessels were due to depart Calcutta, and would be sailing on more or less the same route. Von Müller was keen to intercept them. *Emden*'s lookouts spotted the lights of one, the 4,657-ton *Kabinga*, at 10.00pm the following night. She was ordered to stop and not to use her wireless. *Kabinga*'s master, who had his wife and child onboard, willingly complied. Lauterbach led the boarding party, and discovered that the British-registered vessel was carrying American-owned goods. The ship could be legitimately sunk, but the destruction of a cargo belonging to a neutral country was another matter. Besides the adverse publicity such an act would generate, Germany would be obliged to pay compensation for the lost cargo. Von Müller decided to spare *Kabinga*; she would be detained, used as a dump ship for the prisoners, and released in due course. Until that time came Lauterbach and a prize crew under Leutnant Eugen Gyssling would ensure that she complied with instructions.[13]

Three hours later the 3,544-ton *Killin*, carrying 5,000 tons of coal from Calcutta to Colombo, was intercepted and silently captured. As her sinking was to be delayed until daylight, the boarding party took charge of the British collier and she joined von Müller's flotilla for a few brief hours. On the morning of 13 September *Killin*'s crew was transferred to *Kabinga*, and Lauterbach and Gyssling returned to *Emden*, leaving Oberleutant August Geerdes in charge of the prison ship. At 10.00am *Killin* was sunk by scuttling action and gunfire.

Sunday, 13 September was a busy day for *Emden*. When smoke was sighted at 3.00pm she steamed off to investigate, and found a ship flying the British Red Ensign. The vessel did not use her wireless, and stopped when ordered to, believing, like the others, that *Emden* was a British warship. Lauterbach and his boarding party then went across to inspect the ship's papers, and discovered that she was the 7,615-ton *Diplomat*, with a cargo of tea bound for London. They had hit the jackpot. *Diplomat* was only two years old, and insured for £81,000; her cargo, which included 30,000 chests of premium tea, was valued at over a quarter of a million pounds.[14] Von Müller decided to sink her at once, and ordered *Emden*'s torpedo officer, Oberleutnant Robert Witthoeft, to use explosive charges. *Diplomat*'s crew and their belongings were still being transferred to *Kabinga* when yet another ship came into view; *Emden* hastened off to intercept her.

The vessel was stopped and found to be neutral. The Italian *Loredano* was en route to Calcutta, so her master was asked if he would take and land the crews of ships *Emden* had sunk. Captain Giacopolo refused to accept them. Von Müller knew that once *Loredano* reached port *Emden*'s presence in the Bay of Bengal would no longer be a secret, so to gain a little more time he sought an assurance from Giacopolo that he would observe strict neutrality and not disclose the German cruiser's position. The Italian, despite witnessing the sinking of *Diplomat*, gave his word that he would not bring any hostile action against *Emden*.[15]

Loredano was released, and once she was out of sight von Müller steamed northeast, towards the Calcutta–Madras shipping lane. At 10.00pm the light of a vessel was sighted, whereupon *Emden* altered course to intercept. It was the fourth sighting for the day, and the fifth in twenty-four hours, but hopes of claiming another victim were dashed when the ship identified herself as the Italian *Dandalo*.

Late on the afternoon of 14 September preparations were made for *Kabinga*'s release. The crews from *Indus* and *Lovat* were transferred to her, and Geerdes, Klöpper, and their men returned to *Emden*. Before *Kabinga* was let go, however, another ship came into view. *Emden* steamed off to investigate, and returned with the 4,028-ton *Trabboch*. Her holds were empty, so von Müller decided to scuttle the British collier after her crew had been transferred to *Kabinga*. Seacocks were opened to flood the ship and explosive charges were used to blow holes in the hull. Von Müller did not want to use his guns to sink *Trabboch* because it was getting dark and the bright muzzle flash would give *Emden*'s position away.

Unfortunately, *Emden*'s explosives experts failed to take into account the coal dust in the empty holds. The first charge got the dust airborne; the second ignited it. There was an enormous flash which turned night into day, sheets of flame leapt from the holds, and then came the heavy boom of the explosion. Alarmed by the unexpected light and sound show, von Müller decided to leave the area as quickly as possible, and gave orders for *Kabinga* to be detached. Von Hohenzollern was surprised to hear the prisoners give three cheers for *Emden* as they steamed away. 'This unexpected ovation gave great pleasure in the *Emden* – recognition of the considerate treatment we had willingly conceded as far as the circumstances would allow.'[16]

Thirty minutes after *Emden*, *Markomannia* and *Pontoporos* had resumed their journey, a light was spotted off the starboard beam. *Emden* gave chase, and eventually forced the 4,775-ton *Clan Matheson* to stop by firing a shell across her bows. The British ship was found to be carrying a valuable cargo of steam locomotives, motor cars, machinery, bicycles and other goods, and quickly joined *Trabboch* at the bottom of the Indian Ocean. Her crew was embarked in *Markomannia*, and Klöpper was once again sent to the collier to supervise the prisoners.

Emden's wireless operators had meanwhile picked up a message warning all shipping of the German cruiser's activities, and naming the vessels she had sunk. Captain Giacopolo had gone back on his word.

It was clearly time to move on. Von Müller ordered a new course to the southeast, towards the Andaman Islands, where he hoped to find a secluded place to coal before resuming operations in the Andaman Sea.

The game begins

The British authorities learned of *Emden*'s presence in the Bay of Bengal through *City of Rangoon. Loredano* had met the British steamship, outward bound from Calcutta, on the afternoon of 14 September, and Giacopolo warned her master about *Emden. City of Rangoon* promptly turned back, and gave the alarm by wireless message: 'German *Emden* with four prizes sighted by Italian steamer, position 18° N, 86° 16' E.' Upon receipt of this message the port officer at Calcutta stopped all sailings, alerted other ports in the area, and informed the naval intelligence officer at Colombo of *Emden*'s arrival in local waters. The warning resulted in all vessels in the Bay of Bengal being detained in port, and the closure of the Colombo–Singapore shipping route.[17]

By coincidence, Monday, 14 September was the day von Spee chose to visit Samoa. He had received information that Apia, the capital of German Samoa, was occupied by enemy forces, and believed that a raid on the harbour might prove fruitful. There was the risk that the battlecruiser *Australia* would be defending the islands, but it was a risk von Spee was prepared to accept, as revealed by his orders:

> A surprise attack is to be made on 14 September, at dawn if *Australia* is to be reckoned with, otherwise later. The *Australia* is to be attacked by torpedo, the other ships by gunfire ... In the absence of *Australia*, *Scharnhorst* and *Gneisenau* will advance to the harbour from N and NE by E, in order to prevent ships leaving harbour.[18]

Disappointingly for von Spee, the harbour was empty, so he withdrew without firing a shot. The appearance of *Scharnhorst* and *Gneisenau* off Apia, however, and their departure in a northwesterly direction, had far-reaching consequences for von Müller.

In the days leading up to the declaration of war on Germany, Britain had received offers of troops from New Zealand and Australia. These offers were subsequently accepted, and both countries began raising and equipping expeditionary forces, and converting merchant ships to transport them. The Admiralty, mindful of von Spee's squadron and *Königsberg*, insisted that the transports sail in convoy via Fremantle, Colombo, Aden and the Suez Canal, and that the convoy be adequately protected against attack. After Japan's entry into the war, the Admiralty proposed that the New Zealand transports depart Wellington on 20 September, escorted by *Psyche* and *Philomel*, and join the Australian transports off Adelaide. *Melbourne* and *Sydney* would then escort the combined convoy to Europe. On 8 September it was decided that *Minotaur* and *Hampshire* should reinforce the escort between the Cocos Islands and Colombo. The Admiralty was worried that von Spee might take his squadron into the Indian Ocean and attack the transports. By 10 September they were concerned enough to add *Australia* to the escort.[19] Six days later the Admiralty received word of *Emden*'s activities in the Bay of Bengal, and the appearance of *Scharnhorst* and *Gneisenau* off Apia.

There was now a need to protect the New Zealand convoy against attack from *Scharnhorst* and *Gneisenau*. Sending *Australia* to Wellington to join the convoy escort was the logical solution, but the battlecruiser was required to help defend the Rabaul expedition against possible attack, and spearhead a hunting group once von Spee was located again. It was eventually decided that *Minotaur* and *Ibuki* should be sent to Wellington to pick up the New Zealand transports, and that *Melbourne* would join the escort at Albany, where the Australian transports would gather. A fourth warship, the Japanese armoured cruiser *Nisshin*, was to join the convoy escort off Fremantle.[20]

In the meantime, something had to be done about *Emden*. The Commander-in-Chief of the East Indies Squadron, Rear Admiral Richard Peirse, was unable to help because his ships were assigned to troop convoys soon to depart Bombay and Karachi.[21] It thus fell upon Vice Admiral Jerram to form a hunting squadron with *Hampshire*, *Yarmouth* and *Chikuma*. *Hampshire* and *Chikuma* sailed from Singapore on 16 September to patrol the shipping lanes between Colombo, Madras and Calcutta. *Yarmouth* sailed on 17 September to search the Nicobar and the Andaman Islands, but developed machinery problems the next day and was forced to put into Penang for repairs. *Hampshire* therefore took over the search of the Nicobars and the Andamans, leaving *Chikuma* to work the western side of the Bay of Bengal.[22]

Hampshire's commanding officer, Captain Henry Grant, believed that *Emden* would have to find a secluded anchorage, possibly in the Andamans, to take on coal. He underestimated his opponent. The sea was so calm on the morning of 16 September that von Müller decided to try coaling from *Pontoporos* mid-ocean. This involved placing fenders on *Emden*'s starboard side, going alongside the collier, and lashing the ships together with lines fore and aft. *Emden* then went slow ahead on one engine to maintain steerageway. Bags of coal were lifted from *Pontoporos*' after cargo holds by derrick, swung out over *Emden*'s upper deck, and dropped when the rolling of both vessels permitted them to fall safely. Damage to the cruiser's rails, deck surfaces, and the plating around the sponson guns was unavoidable, but the process allowed *Emden* to embark coal without the need to enter a harbour or anchorage.[23] 'This', wrote Bordeaux, 'saves us at least four days.'[24]

Emden took on 440 tonnes of coal from *Pontoporos* on 16 September, after which the collier was detached.[25] The time saved by coaling at sea permitted the German cruiser to proceed direct to her new hunting ground. Passing to the north of the Andaman Islands, *Emden* and *Markomannia* reached the intersection of the Calcutta–Singapore and the Madras–Rangoon shipping lanes on 17 September. Nothing was sighted until 4.00pm the following day when a smoke cloud was seen to starboard. Von Müller studied the smoke and thought the vessel might be heading for Rangoon, so set *Emden* on a converging course. Bordeaux hoped that it was a French or Japanese merchantman, but it proved to be the neutral Norwegian steamship *Dovre*. Lauterbach established that she was not carrying contraband, so would have to be released. The good news was that her captain was prepared to take the *Clan Matheson* crew and land them at Rangoon. According to Bordeaux:

He is ready to take them for 100 [Mexican] dollars. To my great pleasure I am allowed to go over and pay out the money. First of all we go to the *Markomannia* in order to transfer a few Englishmen over to the Norwegian. When the latter were on board and we were casting off the English captain called to his countrymen to give three cheers for the *Markomannia* for the good treatment which they had received on her.[26]

The Norwegian captain also agreed to delay his arrival in Rangoon, thereby giving *Emden* and *Markomannia* time to leave the area before word of their presence reached the British. That night *Emden*'s wireless operators picked up a transmission from a shore station, reporting that gunfire had been heard at Akyab (Sittwe), on the west coast of Burma (Myanmar), deep in the Bay of Bengal. They then heard other stations trying to contact the British warship 'QMD', and were delighted when one gave her real name – *Hampshire*. Von Müller thought that *Hampshire* was being sent to Akyab, so he decided to risk coaling from *Markomannia* again as the weather remained favourable.

The coaling on 19 September took eight hours, which delayed their passage through the northern Andamans until later that night. As they did so *Emden*'s wireless operators heard *Hampshire* sending messages; the loudness of the transmissions suggested that the British cruiser was not more than ten miles away. Bordeaux wrote that a special watch was posted when it was realised that the enemy was so close. He was relieved to add, 'We get through safely and steer for Madras.'[27]

Hampshire was searching the islands where *Emden* would have been coaling if von Müller had not done it at sea on 16 September. His decision to top up *Emden*'s bunkers on 19 September was also fortuitous. If *Emden* and *Markomannia* had steamed past *Hampshire* in daylight her lookouts could not have failed to see their smoke. Fortune favours the bold, and von Müller was now planning two especially bold raids. *Dovre*'s captain had mentioned that the French cruisers *Montcalm* and *Dupleix* were stationed at Penang, planting the seed in von Müller's mind for a surprise attack on them in harbour.[28] But first he wanted to damage British prestige in India by attacking the fortified city of Madras, the capital of the Madras Presidency and home to a large Tamil population.

Bordeaux was told that *Emden* was going to Madras to bombard the lighthouse, government buildings, gun batteries, and the oil storage tanks near the harbour.[29] The targets were specially chosen; by approaching on a particular bearing, *Emden*'s gun-layers could line them up, and simply had to increase or decrease gun elevation to engage each one. Equally important, any stray shells would land well away from the residential quarter of the city, thereby reducing the risk of civilian casualties. The attack was scheduled for the evening of 22 September, so the intervening days were spent training and preparing the ship for action.

Markomannia was detached at 5.00pm on 22 September after being given a rendezvous position for the following morning. *Emden* then began her approach. After dark the dummy funnel was hoisted, and just before 8.00pm Madras light became visible; this astonished everyone, as it was thought that the British had closed the lighthouse at the start of the war. Another surprise awaited them. The harbour lights were burning, and Madras was a sea of light. At 9.00pm the order 'Clear ship for action' was given, whereupon *Emden*'s searchlights and guns were manned. Von Hohenzollern wrote, 'We rushed towards the harbour at a speed of 17 knots, steering, thanks to their lights, so that at the order "Open fire" the oil tanks and the battery would be in line.'[30]

By 9.30pm *Emden* was 3,000m from shore, at which point von Müller ordered a turn to port and stopped engines. He then gave the order, 'Searchlights on. Open fire!' Bordeaux, manning the training gear for the No. 1 searchlight, had an excellent view:

Our first aim was the beacon [lighthouse], at which several broadsides were fired. It remained standing. Then we fired on the oil tanks. Soon one of them exploded, with tremendous flames shooting up to the sky. Then it was the next tank's turn. The first broadside was sufficient to reduce it to the same condition as the former. Meanwhile all four searchlights were showing ... the only thing that was lacking was an adequate reply to our bombardment ... the fort only fired three shots at us, of which none hit us, while we fired about 130 rounds. The whole bombardment lasted at the most 15 minutes.[31]

After ordering the searchlights to be extinguished and firing to cease, von Müller executed his escape plan, which involved steaming away in a northeasterly direction with *Emden*'s port lights showing. Once clear of the glare of the conflagration ashore, he had the lights switched off before steaming south under cover of darkness. Von Müller hoped that observers on shore would report his northerly course to the Royal Navy, thereby sending any would-be pursuers off in the wrong direction. Bordeaux wrote, 'Soon Madras was out of sight, and we could see nothing but the red glare of the fire in the sky.'[32]

The destroyed oil tanks had contained 1.9 million litres of kerosene, and five people were confimed killed by the shelling. Far worse was the disruption to trade. Shipping in the Bay of Bengal had to be stopped again – only eighteen hours after the trade routes were declared reasonably safe.[33] This had serious consequences; enormous stocks of jute and tea were accumulating in warehouses; hides and leather needed for the manufacture of army boots and saddles could not be sent to Britain; and gunny sacks urgently needed for the Australian wheat harvest could not be shipped. Still more serious was the effect the bombardment had on the local population. The alarm extended far beyond the port itself. Most of the local moneylenders in east-coast towns packed up and fled to the hills in panic, cutting off finance for commercial operations, and disrupting the whole course of trade in southern India.[34]

The oil storage tanks at Madras, still burning on the morning of 23 September. (*Mary Evans Picture Library*)

Equally concerning was the damage to British prestige. Despite assurances that the Royal Navy would hunt down and destroy *Emden*, the German cruiser seemed to be operating with impunity. It didn't help that von Müller had an uncanny knack of turning up where he was least expected. When he attacked Madras, *Hampshire* was 300 miles to the north, and *Chikuma* was a similar distance to the south.[35]

Emden met *Markomannia* at the agreed rendezvous at 5.00am on 23 September. After a quick foray along the coast south of Madras, von Müller decided to quit the area for a new hunting ground. He set course to the southeast, towards British Ceylon (Sri Lanka), to prey on the vessels entering or leaving its principal port, Colombo. The plan was to skirt around the island and work along the Colombo–Penang–Singapore shipping lane. Marine-Stabsingenieur Ellerbroek prayed that they might capture an Admiralty collier laden with Cardiff coal. *Markomannia*'s cargo of Shantung coal was nearly exhausted, and the Indian product taken from *Pontoporos* was a stoker's nightmare; it burnt poorly and produced a lot of smoke, soot, clinker and ash.[36] Lochau wrote of their normal steaming routine:

> We usually used only six boilers and could run 18 knots on them. Four boilers were always on standby to be ready to be steamed up in 30 minutes if needed, and two were always in repair. It was our routine to thoroughly clean one boiler every fifth day, while water [in each boiler] had to be changed every ten days, and a thorough overhauling was done every third or fourth week, as circumstances permitted.[37]

When Indian coal was used in a boiler, it had to be cleaned after twenty-four hours.

Early on the afternoon of 25 September *Emden* caught the 3,650-ton *King Lud*, which was en route from Alexandria to Calcutta. The British steamship was in ballast, but had a good stock of provisions; she was relieved of a considerable quantity of flour, potatoes, fresh meat and canned goods, and then scuttled. Once again Klöpper and an armed guard were sent over to *Markomannia* to receive and take charge of *King Lud*'s crew. At 9.00pm the Norwegian *Oceanus* was intercepted and, being neutral, allowed to proceed. Just before midnight the 3,314-ton *Tymeric* was captured; she was outward bound from Colombo with a cargo of sugar, and was being prepared for sinking when *Emden*'s lookouts spotted yet another vessel. This was believed to be the Dutch mail ship *Konigin Emma*, which had announced her impending arrival in Colombo by wireless, so was not challenged; once she was out of sight *Tymeric* was scuttled. Von Müller now steered northwest, in order to follow the Colombo–Aden shipping lane as far as Minicoy Island, 400 miles west-northwest of Colombo.

A bundle of newspapers had been taken from *Tymeric*, and *Emden*'s officers spent the morning of 26 September devouring the latest news. Von Hohenzollern was pleased to see that their recent activities were well covered, and that the Royal Navy was being roundly criticised for its inability to catch *Emden*:

> For the *Emden* herself, and for Kapitän [*sic*] von Müller, there was nothing but praise. The papers talked enthusiastically of 'fair play', and said that the Captain of the *Emden* must be a real sportsman – great praise from English mouths, for in England sport is of national interest.[38]

Shortly after midday *Emden*'s lookouts caught sight of another victim. Bordeaux wrote: 'About 1 o'clock in the afternoon the steamer *Gryfevale* runs into our net. Home port London. *Gryfevale* had been held up by the *Königsberg*, but for some reason or another had been let go again.'[39] The 4,437-ton *Gryfevale* was spared because her holds were empty and von Müller needed a dump for the crews of *King Lud* and *Tymeric*. That night a fast, brilliantly lit vessel was seen heading towards Colombo. She was thought to be the neutral Danish motorship *Fionia*, so was not challenged, but Lauterbach, watching from *Gryfevale*'s bridge, was convinced she was a British mail ship. Any qualms about letting her go vanished a few hours later. Bordeaux was halfway through his 12.00–4.00am watch when a white light was spotted:

> From afar we could make out that she was a fully laden collier. She brought us 6,000 tons of Cardiff coal – the best coal there is on God's earth. This prize was a Godsend for us … We took her along with us after a crew from the *Emden* had been put onboard the Englishman. The prize crew consisted of Kapitänleutnant der Reserve Klöpper, Leutnant Schmidt, Leutnant Gyssling, and some sailors plus one engineer.[40]

Ellerbroek's prayers had been answered.

Von Müller decided to keep the 4,337-ton *Buresk* as his collier and detach *Markomannia*, so after dawn the prisoners were transferred to *Gryfevale*. *Buresk*'s master and several of his crew requested permission to stay with their ship, and von Müller was happy to oblige them in the short term. Less pleased was Bordeaux, who was informed that he was to join *Markomannia* before she was detached. As 27 September was a Sunday, breakfast was followed by Divisions and Church. What should have been a day of rest soon turned into a day of action alarms. Just after midday the 3,500-ton *Ribera* was stopped and boarded. The British steamship was travelling in ballast, so her crew was taken off and she was sunk by gunfire. Then at sunset the 4,147-ton *Foyle* was captured; the London-registered vessel was also empty, but before she could be scuttled, another ship appeared. Bordeaux was ordered to get ready to join the boarding party: 'I arm myself with prize papers and writing material ... bayonet and revolver. I also put a few dollars in my pocket so as to be able to buy some cigarettes for the mess in case it happens to be a neutral ship.'[41] The ship, *Djoca*, was Dutch, and not carrying contraband, so was released.

It was once again time for *Emden* to disappear. *Foyle*'s crew was transferred to *Gryfevale*, and then she was sunk. At 10.00pm, after all the prisoners were safely onboard, and Lauterbach and the guards had been taken off, *Gryfevale* was released with instructions to proceed to Colombo.[42] As she pulled away von Hohenzollern heard the former prisoners give three cheers for von Müller, three cheers for *Emden*'s officers, and three cheers for the crew.[43]

Emden was in need of coal again so she, *Markomannia* and *Buresk* headed south, towards the Maldives. Monday, 28 September passed quietly, and the following morning the islands came into sight. Coaling from *Markomannia* commenced at midday and continued until 9.00pm. Upon completion on 30 September the coaling equipment, spare oil and water were transferred to *Buresk*. When Bordeaux was told that he was to leave with *Markomannia* that evening, he turned to his diary and confessed, 'I haven't been in particularly good spirits these last few days. I have a sort of feeling that I shall not meet the *Emden* again.' At 9.00pm he bid adieu to his friends then boarded the now empty collier; as he did so he heard music coming from *Emden*:

The ship's band is on the bridge playing. Then suddenly comes the order to cast off and everybody joins in the cry, 'A German cheer for *Markomannia* and her crew', which is returned by the *Markomannia*. To the strains of the beautiful marching song 'He to whom God wants to show his favour' ... my *Emden*, of which I had grown so fond ... gradually disappeared astern.[44]

Emden and *Buresk* continued on their southerly course as von Müller wished to rest his crew and repair his ship before resuming operations in the waters beyond the Chagos Archipelago. The Australia–Suez shipping lane lay just south of the Chagos, and he believed (erroneously) that Australian troop transports proceeding to Europe would use this route. Von Hohenzollern liked the plan. 'To surprise such a transport by night would be good sport for us.' Even more mouth-watering was the thought of capturing an Australian meat ship on her way to Britain.[45]

It took five days of slow steaming to reach the new hunting area. During this time all of *Emden*'s boilers were thoroughly cleaned and overhauled. The condensers and auxiliary machinery also received attention, and the main engines were stopped in turn to allow work on the bearings and glands to be carried out. Gunnery and ammunition supply training for the regular and reserve crews was also conducted, followed by practice firings at a target towed by *Buresk*. *Emden* then cruised along the Australia–Suez and the Mauritius–Calcutta shipping lanes for three days without sighting a single ship.

On 9 October *Emden* and *Buresk* entered the harbour of Diego Garcia, the chief island of the Chagos group. They spent a day and a half at the remote British outpost, coaling and entertaining the local managers, who were blissfully unaware that Britain was at war with Germany. Concurrent with the coaling, *Emden*'s fore, aft, port and starboard lower compartments were alternately flooded to raise the opposite sections of keel, allowing some of the speed-reducing weed and barnacle growth to be scraped away. Upon completion of this work, von Müller thanked his unsuspecting hosts then headed northeast to patrol the Australia–Aden shipping lane. He had intended to push east and carry out his planned attack on Penang, but an intercepted wireless message, reporting that the Aden–

Colombo route was now 'fairly safe' for shipping, tempted him to prove otherwise.[46]

The reopening of the Aden–Colombo route came after *Hampshire*, now supported by the auxiliary cruiser *Empress of Asia*, completed a fruitless hunt for *Emden* to the west of Ceylon. The pair then coaled at Colombo before proceeding south to search the Chagos Archipelago. The plan was sound, but five days too late. As the British warships patrolled south, on a track well to the east of the Maldives, *Emden* and *Buresk* steamed north, on the western side of the island chain. Von Müller was lucky on another count. If he had pressed ahead with his raid on Penang he would almost certainly have encountered *Chikuma*, *Zhemchug* or *Yarmouth* in adjacent waters.[47]

On 15 October *Emden* topped up with coal from *Buresk* then set course for Minicoy Island. Von Müller was convinced that he would again find enemy shipping on the Colombo–Aden route. Later that evening, eight hours after clearing the northern Maldives, Minicoy lighthouse came into view. Thirty minutes later the lights of a ship were sighted. The chase ended just after midnight when *Emden* drew within hailing distance and ordered the vessel to stop. She proved to be the 3,948-ton *Clan Grant*, laden with piece goods, fire-bricks, soap, cigarettes, bottled soda water, foodstuffs and livestock. This was much-needed booty, especially the cigarettes, so von Müller ordered Lauterbach and the prize crew to take charge of the British ship and fall in astern of *Emden*.

They steamed west, and at 7.00am on 16 October the transfer of prisoners, provisions, and 500 fire-bricks for *Emden*'s boilers commenced. This work was still in progress when smoke was sighted on the horizon. *Emden* sped off to investigate, and returned with the 473-ton *Ponrabbel*, an ocean-going dredger being delivered to Tasmania. Her crew was embarked in *Buresk* and then she was sunk with gunfire. *Clan Grant* met with a similar fate a short time later. Von Müller then recovered his boats laden with provisions, and resumed his journey westward. That evening he claimed his third victim for the day. At 8.50pm the boarding party signalled: 'Nationality British. Name BENMOHR, Leith. Crew 19 Britishers, 1 Russian, 1 Japanese, 25 Chinese. Cargo 6,700 tons, general cargo from London to Penang, China and Japan. Coal 300 tons in addition to bunkers. No newspapers on board.'[48] Von Müller ordered *Benmohr* to be sunk at once, and her crew transferred to *Buresk*.

Emden and *Buresk* continued westward until 2.40am on 17 October. Having failed to sight anything else, von Müller then turned back and commenced a zigzag sweep of the area southwest of Minicoy. Just after midnight they encountered the neutral Spanish ship *Fernando Po*. The dearth of enemy shipping was puzzling, so von Müller turned east-northeast. He assumed that vessels sailing from Colombo were perhaps taking a more northerly route, and was rewarded when he intercepted the British steamship *Troilus* on the afternoon of 18 October. The 7,562-ton vessel had only recently been completed, and was on the return leg of her maiden voyage.[49]

Troilus was laden with 10,000 tons of general cargo, which Lauterbach valued at 20 million marks (the cargo was insured for £130,000). She was also carrying eighteen passengers (including a woman), and a crew of sixty-six – too many to be accommodated in the now very crowded *Buresk*. Von Müller had little choice but to keep everyone onboard until another dump ship could be found. At 7.15pm he received a very informative message from Lauterbach, who had been in conversation with *Troilus*' master. It read, 'The Authorities at Colombo have instructed British Masters to pass Minikoi [Minicoy] 40 miles to the northward.'[50] Von Müller now knew that he was on the right track. The proof came at 9.00pm when *Emden* caught the British steamship *St Egbert*. By chance, she was carrying an American-owned cargo, so couldn't be sunk; however, von Müller had found his prisoner dump.

Shortly before midnight *Emden* captured another vessel, the 4,542-ton *Exford*. The British collier was carrying 5,500 tons of prized Cardiff coal. Such success was not without its problems. Each capture required two officers and a detachment of men, either in the form of a boarding and search party, or a prize crew. With four vessels under guard, von Müller now had more officers off *Emden* than on. Klöpper, Gyssling and Schmidt had charge of *Buresk*; Lauterbach and von Guérard were onboard *Troilus*, Geerdes and Fikentscher were with *St Egbert*, and von Levetzow and von Hohenzollern were on *Exford*. Von Mücke joined the list of exiles on the morning of 19 October when he was sent to *Troilus* to oversee the ransacking of her cargo. This left

Emden and the Ocean Steam Ship Company Limited vessel
Troilus, photographed from *Buresk* on 18 October. (*Peter Günter
Huff collection*)

von Müller, Gropius, Gaede, Witthoeft, Zimmerman and Schall as the
only naval officers onboard the cruiser. Von Hohenzollern thought that
if *Emden* was surprised now by an enemy warship, von Müller would
be 'fairly well caught'.[51]

Any doubts that von Müller would not give battle in such
circumstances were dispelled when a smoke cloud was sighted just after
8.00am. He quickly recovered a cutter then steamed off to investigate,
not knowing if the smoke was coming from a merchantman or a
warship. It proved to be the former. Only one officer, Leutnant Fritz
Zimmermann, could be spared for the boarding party, and he signalled
that she was the British *Chilkana*, with 5,000 tons of general cargo for
Colombo, Madras and Calcutta.[52]

The 5,146-ton *Chilkana* was also on her maiden voyage, and was
taken back to the group so that her crew could be transferred to *St
Egbert*. *Chilkana* was sunk that afternoon, and *Troilus* shared her fate
at 6.00pm. *St Egbert*, crammed with 343 passengers, officers and crew
from *Buresk*, *Clan Grant*, *Ponrabbel*, *Benmohr*, *Troilus*, *Exford* and
Chilkana, was released a short time later. *Emden*, with most of her
officers back onboard, then led *Buresk* and *Exford* (now commanded
by Kapitänleutnant Gropius) away on a false course before heading in
a southeasterly direction.[53]

St Egbert put in to Cochin (Kochi) on the southwest coast of India on 20 October to disembark the former captives and to raise the alarm. News of the raider's activities quickly reached Captain Grant in *Hampshire*, now patrolling off the south coast of Ceylon with *Empress of Asia* in company. Grant reasoned that *Emden* would need to coal, and thought she would head for the Maldives to do this, so he now steered for the islands. Von Müller, having no need to coal just yet, maintained a course well to the east of the Maldives. Grant's and von Müller's paths crossed on the morning of 21 October, but they failed to sight each other. The Admiralty later found out why: 'Rain squalls obscured the view, and the little German squadron passed unobserved only 5 miles astern of the *Empress of Asia*. It was the narrowest escape of the *Emden*'s adventurous career.'[54] Von Müller, unaware just how close he came to being caught, maintained course and speed until 2.00pm, when he stopped to effect a change of personnel in *Exford*. She was detached two hours later, with instructions to meet *Emden* on or about 7 November, forty miles north of the Cocos Islands.

Emden and *Buresk* continued south until 23 October, when they turned east, towards Penang. That afternoon *Emden* conducted action drills, followed by gunnery practice at a target towed by *Buresk*. Von Hohenzollern considered this vital, because they expected to find enemy warships at Penang. Their initial destination, however, was Nancowry Island in the central Nicobars, where von Müller intended to coal before making his attack. They reached Nancowry on 26 October, anchored in the natural harbour, and immediately commenced coaling. Once again luck was on von Müller's side. *Zhemchug* had just completed a sweep of the Nicobars and the Andamans and had returned to Penang; *Chikuma* was off Sumatra, 350 miles to the south; and *Yarmouth* was at Colombo. He was therefore able to coal without interference, detach *Buresk*, then set course for Penang that evening.[55]

Penang was a difficult target. It was little more than a sheltered anchorage, formed by a channel running north and south between the island of Penang and the Malay Peninsula. The southern entrance was only three fathoms (5.4m) deep, so *Emden* would have to enter and leave via the deeper northern entrance. The anchorage, a mile wide at its narrowest, was expected to be occupied by one or two enemy cruisers, several merchantmen, and defended by an unknown number of torpedo boat destroyers. Von Müller therefore timed his approach so that *Emden*, with her dummy funnel hoisted, reached the northern entrance just before dawn on 28 October. He was relying on disguise and surprise to gain entry to the anchorage, guns and torpedoes to deal with the enemy warships found inside, and luck to get out. The destroyers were the greatest danger; there would be little room for evasive manoeuvring once inside the anchorage, and if one got close enough to *Emden* to fire a torpedo, they might not be able to avoid it. *Emden* could survive shell damage, but a torpedo hit would be fatal.[56]

Lochau was one of those tasked with keeping a sharp lookout for destroyers. He was stationed on the aft searchlight platform, and at 4.45am noticed the hazy outline of palm trees about a mile off their starboard bow. Five minutes later *Emden*, steaming at 11 knots, reached the light-buoy marking the entrance to the anchorage. *Emden* then swung to starboard, and the 'town presented itself before us, brilliantly illuminated'. Several small fishing boats appeared in their path, forcing *Emden* to swerve to avoid a collision; the cruiser was barely on course again when a pilot boat was passed, and left rolling in the wake.[57]

Von Mücke, who had worked hard training and preparing *Emden* for the attack, was also on watch, keen to see the fruits of his labours. He noted that they reached the inner roadstead just as dawn was breaking, and in the half-light he was able to make out a large number of merchantmen, but nothing that resembled a warship.[58] Suddenly a darkened vessel was spotted off the starboard bow; the ship was anchored in the north-flowing current, which meant that her stern was pointing towards *Emden*. All eyes were glued on the vessel, which began to take on the shape and form of a large cruiser. The engines were quickly stopped, followed by the announcement 'Clear for action'. Simultaneously, the ensigns were hoisted, identifying *Emden* as a German warship. The sleeping enemy cruiser, now less than 500m away, was *Zhemchug*.

Oberleutnant Witthoeft was in charge of battle tactics, and stood in the armoured conning tower with von Müller; having reduced *Emden*'s speed for his torpedo shot, Witthoeft had the engines started again and waited for his director sight to align with *Zhemchug*. Von Hohenzollern was standing by in the torpedo flat below the waterline, ready to launch the starboard torpedo should the remote firing gear in the conning tower fail. At 5.18am he saw the 'Fire' indicator light illuminate, and the torpedo hissed from the tube a second later. From his vantage point Lochau was able to follow the trail of foam on the surface of the water as the torpedo sped towards its target:

> After a few seconds of fatal silence a hollow detonation like thunder vibrated through the air. Our missile had found its mark. At the moment of the explosion our artillery started roaring and shrieking and kept up a continuous bombardment of the front part of the *Zhemchug* in order to prevent the crew from reaching their battle stations.[59]

The torpedo blew a large hole in the Russian cruiser's port quarter, flooding the engine room. Kapitänleutnant Gaede was meanwhile directing the fire of his starboard battery against *Zhemchug's* forecastle, where the crew was quartered. Von Mücke saw many of the 10.5cm shells hit. In each instance there was a bright, sharp flash, which gave way to a fiery ring, and then black smoke poured from the shell hole. He did not see a single man emerge from this part of the ship.[60]

Despite the destruction and carnage on the Russian ship, at least one gun was brought into action against *Emden*. Twelve shells were fired, but all passed harmlessly overhead. Von Müller decided to end the argument with another torpedo. *Emden* continued on for a short distance, turned sharply to port, and then commenced a second run. During the turn the French gunboat *D'Iberville* was seen at anchor behind several merchantmen. There was no time to engage her, but Witthoeft ordered the starboard torpedo tube to be reloaded just in case; he then readied himself to fire the port tube at *Zhemchug*. Von Hohenzollern heard the torpedo leave the tube, and shortly afterwards there was a heavy explosion which was felt by everyone in *Emden*. The torpedo had detonated *Zhemchug's* forward magazine, blowing the ship apart. Pieces of the Russian cruiser splashed noisily in the water close to *Emden*, and then it was strangely quiet. A huge cloud of yellow smoke obscured the target for several minutes; when it cleared *Zhemchug* was gone, only the top of her mast being visible above the water.[61]

Von Müller now turned his attention to *D'Iberville*. He was in the process of turning back to attack her when another vessel was seen approaching from the north. It was feared that the newcomer was a warship, so the turn was immediately checked and *Emden* steamed for the exit at full speed. Gaede opened fire on the vessel a short time later, but ceased when it was identified as a government launch. By this time *Emden* was outside the inner roadstead, and von Müller thought it too risky going back for *D'Iberville* and the merchantmen.

As *Emden* was leaving the anchorage, a freighter was observed preparing to enter. Von Müller decided to stop and board the ship, which was flying a red danger flag at her masthead. Lauterbach discovered that she was the 4,696-ton *Glenturret*. The master, Captain Jones, claimed that he was carrying highly inflammable paraffin, but before Lauterbach could confirm this (*Glenturret* was actually carrying ammunition), he and his men were recalled to *Emden*.[62] The reason for the urgent recall was the sighting of another vessel to the north.

The intruder was soon identified as a small French destroyer, and was promptly fired upon. Gaede scored a hit with his third salvo. The shell exploded in *Mousquet*'s boiler room, releasing a cloud of black smoke mingled with white steam. The 298-ton *Mousquet* was soon dead in the water, though still full of fight. According to von Mücke, she opened fire with her forward 65mm gun and launched two torpedoes, but failed to hit *Emden* before being overwhelmed. 'Mast, funnel, forward tower, superstructure, ventilators – everything on the Frenchman was shot away.'[63]

Von Hohenzollern, knowing that Witthoeft would not waste a torpedo on such a small vessel, watched the uneven fight from *Emden*'s after gunnery control stand. 'Our gunnery was excellent. Once the range had been found, every shell thumped home.' After the twelfth salvo *Mousquet* disappeared under a pall of yellow smoke. Von Müller ordered Gaede to cease fire as he wanted to see if his opponent would raise the white flag, but when the smoke cleared away the destroyer showed no sign of surrendering. It took another ten salvoes to sink *Mousquet*, after which *Emden* closed to rescue survivors.[64] The destroyer had entered the fight with a complement of seventy-eight; *Emden*'s boat crews plucked one officer and thirty-five men from the sea.[65]

53

It was nearly 7.30am when *Emden* recovered her boats and got underway again. The air was now alive with W/T transmissions reporting *Emden*'s presence at Penang, and another destroyer could be seen leaving harbour, so von Müller ordered full speed (22 knots) on a northwesterly course. The destroyer was *Pistolet*. She gave chase, but gave up a few hours later when mechanical problems reduced her speed and *Emden* disappeared in a rain squall. At 4.00pm, having shaken off *Pistolet*, von Müller ordered a reduction in speed to 17 knots and a new course to the southwest.

Emden safely negotiated the Nicobars that night, but stopped at 8.00am the next morning for the burial at sea of two French sailors who had died of their wounds. Others needed to be hospitalised if they were to avoid a similar fate, so von Müller decided to follow the Singapore–Suez shipping lane in the hope of stopping a vessel which could take the prisoners to the nearest port. He knew that enemy warships would be searching for *Emden*, but was prepared to risk all for the sake of *Mousquet*'s wounded – men he had been trying to kill the day before.

No ships of any kind were sighted on 29 October, and another Frenchman died that evening. However, just before 6.30am on 30 October smoke was sighted, and *Emden* sped off to investigate. A short time later she stopped the British steamship *Newburn*. Von Müller could have added the 3,000-tonner to his list of victims, but spared her because the master agreed to take *Mousquet*'s survivors and land them at Khota Raja. *Emden* then steamed west, stopped briefly at 9.00am for the burial of the deceased French sailor, and as soon as *Newburn* was out of sight, turned southeast for her rendezvous with *Buresk*.[66]

Emden found *Buresk* just before dawn on 31 October. The pair then headed southeast, as von Müller wished to coal at North Pagai, one of the southern islands off Sumatra's west coast. It was during this operation, conducted on 2 November, that *Emden* sustained her first casualty; a sack of coal fell on Torpedomatrose Friedrich Possehl, breaking his left thigh. The raider and her collier resumed their southerly journey that evening. Von Müller wanted to try his luck in the Sunda Strait, but after running through it and back without sighting anything, gave up the hunt.

On 5 November he set course for the Cocos Islands to meet *Exford* and swap Lauterbach for Gropius. Von Müller planned to raid the cable and wireless stations on Direction Island on 8 November, and wanted Gropius to do the navigating. His logic was simple. Apart from the material damage the enemy would suffer by the destruction of the wireless station and the telegraph cable linking Australia with Britain, he wanted to give the impression that *Emden* was about to commence operations in the waters south and west of Australia. Von Müller hoped that this would draw enemy cruisers away from the Arabian Sea and the northern Indian Ocean. As he later explained: 'My intention was, after carrying out the raid on the Cocos group, to make for Socotra and cruise in the Gulf of Aden, and then on the steamer-route between Aden and Bombay.'[67] Fate, however, was about to intervene. Unknown to von Müller, the Australian and New Zealand troop convoy, and its powerful escort, was scheduled to pass the Cocos Islands on the night of 8/9 November.

3

The Cocos Raid

Frequent rumours were current regarding the possibility
of encountering the enemy, the greatest concern being
attached to the possibility of meeting the famous German
cruiser "Emden".
  Captain Arthur Croly, 11th Australian Infantry Battalion

The ten transports which formed the New Zealand component of the
convoy departed Wellington on 16 October 1914, escorted by
Minotaur, Ibuki, Philomel and *Psyche*.[1] Upon learning that they had
sailed, the Australian Naval Board authorised the departure of the
twenty-eight Australian transports from Sydney, Melbourne, Adelaide
and Hobart.[2] The Australian ships were to sail independently and reach
Albany, the port of concentration, by 28 October. They would be
followed across the Great Australian Bight by HMAS *Melbourne*.[3] By
this time *Scharnhorst* and *Gneisenau* were known to be in the eastern
Pacific, so the only real threat to the transports was in the Indian Ocean
– in the form of *Emden* and *Königsberg*.[4]

Nisshin was to have reinforced the convoy escort for the passage
across the Indian Ocean, but the Japanese cruiser struck a rock off
Sandakan on 12 October and was forced to put in to Singapore for
repairs. Consequently, the Admiralty proposed that *Pioneer*, stationed
at Fremantle, help escort the convoy as far as the Cocos Islands where
another Japanese cruiser, *Yahagi*, would relieve her.[5] HMAS *Pioneer*,
armed with eight 4in guns and capable of 20 knots at best, was more
of a liability than an asset, so it was decided to detach *Sydney* from Rear
Admiral Patey's squadron at Suva and add her to the convoy escort.[6]

Like *Melbourne*, HMAS *Sydney* was a relatively new ship of the British
Chatham class.[7] She was laid down at the works of the London &
Glasgow Engineering & Iron Shipbuilding Company Limited, Govan,
on 11 February 1911, and completed on 26 June 1913. The 5,400-ton

HMAS *Sydney*, as she appeared in 1913. (*Sea Power Centre-Australia*)

cruiser had an overall length of 457ft (139m) and a beam of 49ft 10in (15.2m), and was commissioned on 26 June by her commanding officer, Captain John Glossop, RN.[8] The *Chatham*s were well-armed and better protected than previous classes of British light cruisers. They carried eight 6in BL Mark XI* guns with an effective range of 14,300yds (13,075m), two 21in underwater torpedo tubes, and four 3pdr Hotchkiss guns.[9] A belt of armour plate 3in thick protected the twelve coal-fired boilers and the four Parsons turbines which drove the ship's four propellers. The class also had a good turn of speed, and during a full-power trial on 16 April 1913 *Sydney* achieved 25.7 knots.

Ship for ship, *Sydney* and *Melbourne* were thus vastly superior to *Emden* and *Königsberg*. They were bigger, faster, better protected, and carried heavier guns and torpedoes. Gun calibre and weight of shell counted more than anything else. The 10.5cm guns carried by *Emden* and *Königsberg* fired a shell weighing 38lb (17.2kg); the 6in (15.2cm) guns carried by *Sydney* and *Melbourne* fired a 100lb (45.4kg) shell.

On 14 October 1914 *Sydney* was ordered to return to Australia for immediate docking. She reached Port Jackson (Sydney) on 21 October and secured alongside Garden Island to exchange a damaged torpedo and to offload unnecessary furniture. The next day she was towed to Cockatoo Island Dock for an examination of her underwater fittings, a bottom scrape and a hurried refit. On 23 October *Sydney* was moved back to Garden Island to embark stores and 800 tons of coal. Petty Officer Frank Etheridge noted that coaling resumed the following morning, but it was very slow work as many ratings had returned from overnight leave with hangovers. On 25 October he wrote: 'All men returned off leave this morning, except for ten, who have missed the ship, and we got under way again at 10am, proceeding to sea at 11 knots, with many sore hearts and many more sore heads.'[10] Two officers, several ratings and one boy joined *Sydney* before she sailed. Amongst them was Surgeon Arthur Todd, who was new to the navy, but had a good grasp of the situation in the Pacific:

> By mid-October ... all the German Pacific Stations were in the hands of those of our allies, her colonies had fallen and her Naval Squadron dispersed and on its way to South America with the *Australia* and other ships in pursuit. Australian waters were free from the menace of hostile warships, for with their bases gone the Germans were like rabbits without a burrow.[11]

Todd discovered that he was to share *Sydney*'s wardroom with fifteen other officers, seven of whom were Australian by birth. The others were Royal Navy, but 'thanks to an acquaintance born of several commissions served on the station, had become Australian by inclination'. As for the men, 'about half were Australian, the more skilled ratings such as gun-layers being of course Englishmen'.[12]

The run to Albany was expected to take six days, and Todd wrote that each day the ship's company was exercised at general quarters (action stations):

> The guns are swung out and connected up by telephones and voice-pipes with the fire control from which the Captain and Gunnery Officer direct

58

the fire of the ship; the rails are lowered; the boats are turned in; and the ship is generally cleared for action.[13]

He noted that they exercised all manner of battle scenarios, including the loss of fore and aft gunnery control, in which case the guns go into independent firing. In another exercise *Sydney* was first steered from the bridge, then from the upper conning tower, and finally from the lower conning tower; when this too was declared out of action, a party of men in the tiller flat above the rudder steered the ship by hand.

The gathering

Melbourne, under the command of Captain Mortimer Silver, RN, reached Albany on the afternoon of 25 October, having passed several of the transports along the way. Albany, on the southern coast of Western Australia, was chosen as the port of concentration because it was blessed with a large natural harbour (King George Sound), and a smaller inner harbour (Princess Royal Harbour) – the entrance to which was protected by three 6in and two 6pdr guns.[14] *Melbourne* now provided an outer layer of defence by anchoring in the entrance to King George Sound and challenging all inbound shipping.

The last of the Australian transports reached Albany on 27 October, although two, *Ascanius* and *Medic*, bypassed the port and sailed direct to Fremantle to embark the Western Australian contingent. The New Zealand transports entered King George Sound on 28 October, and that afternoon *Ibuki*, *Philomel* and *Pyramus* (which had replaced *Psyche* at Hobart) sailed for Fremantle.[15]

At 3.45am on 29 October the first shot in defence of the convoy was fired. *Melbourne* had earlier received a signal from the Breaksea Island Signal Station, advising that the steamship *Essex* was approaching. *Essex* was required to remain outside King George Sound until daylight, so *Melbourne* signalled her to stop.[16] According to Ordinary Signalman Stan Gedling, the cruiser's guns and searchlights were manned when she failed to comply:

We then informed her that there were ships at anchor inside without any lights, and we then ordered her to stop engines and anchor, but she kept coming in and not obeying our orders. We then switched our

59

Sydney's officers and commissioned personnel, December 1914.
Back row, left to right: Assistant Paymaster Kingsford-Smith,
Engineer Lieutenant Dennis, Sub Lieutenant Johnstone, Artificer
Engineer Hutchison, Lieutenant Bell-Salter, Lieutenant Cavaye,
Lieutenant Garsia, Surgeon Todd, Lieutenant Rahilly. Middle row,
left to right: Surgeon Darby, Engineer Lieutenant Fowler,
Lieutenant Commander Finlayson, Captain Glossop, Staff
Paymaster Norton, Chaplain Little, Lieutenant Pope. Front row,
left to right: Boatswain Martin, Carpenter Behenna, Gunner
Salter, Gunner (T) McFarlane. (*AWM EN0163*)

searchlights on her but she still kept closing us, so we fired a blank 3-
pounder [charge] and then fired a six inch shell which landed about 10
feet astern of her and exploded and she at once dropped her anchors
and put out her steaming lights.[17]

Gedling acknowledged that it would have been a frightening
experience for *Essex*'s passengers, but a potentially disastrous collision
between the steamship and a darkened transport was averted. 'This
was', he added, 'the first angry live shell we had fired since the
beginning of the war.'

Sydney reached Albany just before dawn on 31 October, and spent the day taking on 700 tons of coal. The coaling and watering of the transports was completed that evening, and on the morning of 1 November the great convoy put to sea. *Minotaur* led *Sydney* out of harbour at 6.25am, and the first of the transports, *Orvieto*, followed twenty minutes later. *Orvieto* was the flagship of the convoy's Principal Transport Officer, Captain Arthur Gordon-Smith, RN, and also carried the commander of the Australian Imperial Force, Major General William Throsby Bridges. The eight other transports of the first division followed *Orvieto*, and at 7.15am the second division (seven ships) began leaving harbour. The third division (ten ships) sailed at 7.55am, followed by the New Zealand transports at 8.20am in two divisions of five. At 8.55am *Melbourne* weighed anchor and followed the last ship out.

By 10.30am the whole convoy had formed up and was steaming for Cape Leeuwin at 9 knots. The three divisions of Australian transports were arranged in three columns a mile apart. The New Zealand transports followed in two columns, also a mile apart. Each ship was required to steam 800yds astern of the one ahead, so when every transport was in its correct position the convoy stretched for seven and a half miles. *Minotaur* was stationed five miles ahead of the convoy, *Melbourne* was four miles off the starboard beam, and *Sydney* was a similar distance off the port beam.[18]

Glossop wrote of convoy escort work, 'We had to do sheepdog on the line, worry in & bark out'. Just after midnight the convoy rounded Cape Leeuwin and entered the Indian Ocean. Dawn on 2 November found the columns strung out due to poor station-keeping, and *Sydney* and *Melbourne* were kept busy getting the transports back into formation. Glossop noted in his diary, 'War now declared with Turkey, should think it would alter destination of our convoy'.[19] *Ascanius* and *Medic*, escorted by *Ibuki* and *Pioneer*, having departed Fremantle on the morning of 2 November, joined the convoy the following afternoon. *Ibuki* then took station on the starboard beam, allowing *Melbourne* to drop astern to police stragglers and protect the rear of the convoy. *Pioneer* reinforced the port flank, but engine problems soon forced her to return to Fremantle.

The remaining four escorts and the thirty-eight transports, carrying 30,000 soldiers and nurses, now settled down for the long trip to

Colombo. Speed was increased to 10 knots but *Southern*, the slowest ship in the convoy, struggled to keep up. Todd was told that her maximum speed was 'nine and a quarter knots – downhill'.[20] Darkening of all ships at night was also strictly enforced as the convoy moved further north. Captain Croly, travelling in *Ascanius*, wrote on 7 November: 'Today rumours regarding the possibility of touch with the enemy have become more pronounced, and the additional precautions taken indicate that there is some substance to the rumour.'[21]

The need for light discipline and vigilance was rammed home that night. Using her low-power W/T buzzer, *Minotaur* informed all ships: 'Press News November 6th: A small British squadron composed of *Good Hope*, *Glasgow* and *Monmouth* engaged the whole German cruiser squadron consisting of *Scharnhorst*, *Gneisenau*, *Dresden*, *Leipzig* and *Nürnberg* off Valparaiso. An unconfirmed report states that *Monmouth* was sunk.'[22] The news cast a great gloom over *Sydney*'s officers. According to Todd, 'Navy lists were got out, and very many had to mourn the loss of old messmates.'[23]

It was actually much worse. Late on the afternoon of 1 November Vizeadmiral von Spee's reinforced *Kreuzergeschwader* encountered four ships of Rear Admiral Cradock's recently formed South American Squadron off the coast of Chile. The light cruiser *Glasgow* and the auxiliary cruiser *Otranto* managed to escape, but the obsolete armoured cruisers *Good Hope* and *Monmouth* were overwhelmed and sunk. Their combined complements totalled over 1,600 officers and men; all perished, including Cradock.[24]

The disaster forced the Admiralty to redeploy a number of ships to deal with von Spee and counter his likely move into the South Atlantic. *Minotaur* was one of them. On the night of 7 November Captain Edward Kiddle received orders (via the Direction Island cable and wireless stations at Cocos) to proceed to South Africa to reinforce the Cape of Good Hope Squadron. Kiddle did not respond to the messages sent to him, and delayed his departure until 7.00am the next morning as he needed to hand over responsibility for the convoy to Captain Silver. Upon *Minotaur*'s departure, *Melbourne* took station at the head of the convoy.

Minotaur was clearly needed elsewhere, but the timing of her withdrawal couldn't have been worse as far as the convoy was concerned. The transports were now less than a day's steaming from Cocos, and entering waters where *Emden* and *Königsberg* might possibly be encountered. For this reason the convoy was steaming well to the east of the regular Cape Leeuwin–Colombo steamship route.

Emden and *Buresk* had in fact crossed ahead of the convoy on the night of 6/7 November in order to meet *Exford*. They were now thirty miles north of North Keeling Island in the Cocos group, and wondering why *Exford* was not at the rendezvous. *Emden*'s wireless operators had also picked up the messages sent to *Minotaur*, but were unable to read them because they were in cypher. The transmissions, made hourly, worried Fregattenkapitän von Müller; he did not know what they signified, so decided to postpone his planned raid. Provided *Exford* turned up, he would attack the cable and wireless stations on 9 November.

Exford appeared early on the morning of 8 November, and von Müller's decision to delay the raid seemed vindicated when *Minotaur* finally responded to the Direction Island wireless operator as she was steaming away from the convoy. Von Müller was greatly alarmed when his wireless operators reported that a British warship was nearby and using the signal letters 'NC', which, they assumed, were those of the light cruiser *Newcastle*. He confessed, 'When on the morning of the 8th I picked up the warship's conversation with the shore station, I debated whether I should not delay for another day.'[25]

Exford had meanwhile joined with *Emden* and *Buresk* for the exchange of personnel. Gropius returned to *Emden*, Lauterbach took charge of *Exford*, and Fikentscher and Schall went to *Buresk* in exchange for Gyssling and Schmidt. By midday von Müller's other problem had resolved itself:

> The (decreasing) strength of the warship's signals showed us that her distance from the Cocos was increasing; and about noon on the 8th, when this wireless conversation, after being resumed again, finally ceased, we estimated that she was about 200 miles from the *Emden*.[26]

Kapitänleutnant von Mücke was told to continue with preparations for the raid.

Emden's first officer was to be in charge of the raiding party, and he had already selected the men he wished to take ashore. Some were chosen for their specialist skills, whilst others were going for training and promotion purposes. As Leutnant Prinz von Hohenzollern explained, many were 'nine-year men': seamen who had signed on for nine years and aspired to become petty officers. Two officers, Gyssling and Schmidt, were to accompany them.[27]

Exford was detached at 4.35pm with orders to wait for *Emden* at a new rendezvous some 900 miles away in the direction of Socotra. *Buresk* was detached a few hours later. Kapitänleutnant Klöpper was ordered to remain to the north of Cocos until summoned; if the situation in the morning proved favourable, von Müller intended to coal from *Buresk* at Direction Island.

Von Müller began his approach at sunrise on 9 November. A pre-dawn raid would have been preferable, but he needed to be able to see if it was safe to enter Port Refuge at Direction Island. According to Matrose Nicolaus Mayer:

> The whole night was spent searching the vicinity for enemy ships; the result being favourable, we steered towards morning for Cocos Island. At 6am we sighted the Island and the lookouts keeping sharp watch reported the harbour free of enemy warships, and a sailing schooner as the sole occupant.[28]

Emden steamed straight in, swung into the outer anchorage just after 6.00am, and immediately lowered the steam pinnace and two cutters with the raiding party.

Von Müller still had to guard against the possibility that British troops were defending the island, so the pinnace was armed with two machine guns, and each cutter carried one in the bow. The pinnace crew and landing party comprised three officers, seven non-commissioned officers and forty men (see Appendix 1). Between them they carried twenty-nine rifles and twenty-four pistols. Each rifleman was supplied with sixty rounds of ammunition, and there were 12,000 rounds for the four machine guns.

Von Mücke had orders to destroy the telegraph and wireless stations, seize all code books and records of messages, and cut the underwater telegraph cables to Australia, South Africa and the Dutch East Indies. He had three hours to complete his work, but a recall signal was agreed upon in case of emergency. If the island was found to be garrisoned and in a state of defence, the raiding party was to withdraw; *Emden* would then bombard the wireless and telegraph installations. It was hoped that the wireless station could be taken by surprise, but if the operator began to send messages, *Emden*'s wireless operators were to drown them out by transmitting at the same time.[29]

As soon as von Mücke stepped onto the pinnace, which already had steam up, it commenced towing the cutters towards the objective, 3,000m away:

> Direction Island is very flat, and is covered with a luxuriant growth of tall palms. Among their towering tops we could discern the roofs of the European houses and the high tower of the wireless station. This was our objective point, and I gave orders to steer directly for it.[30]

Several men on Direction Island were watching the approach of the boats. Amongst them was the Eastern Extension Australasia and China Telegraph Company medical officer, Dr Harold Ollerhead. He studied the parent warship through a telescope, and was convinced that the fourth funnel was a dummy, so drew Dover Farrant's attention to it. Farrant was the superintendent of the EEACTC's cable and wireless stations on Direction Island:

> Quickly investigating, and finding that the fourth funnel was palpably canvas, I found Mr La Nauze and instructed him to proceed immediately to the wireless hut, and to put out a general call that there was a strange warship in our vicinity, asking for assistance and signing our naval code. At the same time I proceeded to the office and sent services, as previously instructed, to London, Adelaide, Perth and Singapore.[31]

At 6.24am, just as wireless operator George La Nauze was about to make his call, 'Kativ Battav' blasted through his earphones. The strange Morse message was very loud, very clear, and had the distinctive high-pitched note of German Telefunken wireless equipment. When it was repeated a short time later La Nauze responded with 'What is that code? What is that code?'[32]

'Kativ Battav' was the previously arranged signal for *Buresk* to join *Emden* at Direction Island. Von Müller had decided that it was safe to coal: 'As conditions in Port Refuge were favourable for coaling, and no enemy warship seemed to be in the immediate vicinity, I had the wireless message sent to the *Buresk* as soon as the boats neared the landing-stage, ordering her to join *Emden* forthwith.'[33] Orders followed for the dummy funnel to be lowered, and the wire stays supporting *Emden*'s genuine funnels to be removed in preparation for coaling.

It was a fateful decision. *Emden*'s wireless transmission, and La Nauze's response, was picked up by every ship in the convoy, now some fifty miles to the northeast. All maintained wireless silence and continued to listen for further calls. Presently, the Direction Island station was heard transmitting the message 'Strange warship approaching', followed by 'SOS Strange warship at entrance'.[34] Lance Corporal Ted Gwyther, of the Australian Divisional Signal Company, onboard the transport *Karroo*, wrote: 'On Cocos calling for help, the foreign warship, which proved to be the *Emden*, sent a mass of figures to blur the S.O.S. calls of Cocos, but did not fully succeed.'[35]

Farrant entered the wireless hut while La Nauze was making his calls, and was told that the warship was trying to interrupt them. He instructed La Nauze to continue calling, because the 'strong Telefunken notes could only be regarded as a matter for suspicion' if picked up by *Minotaur*. Moments later a German naval officer burst into the hut and ordered them to cease transmitting and leave the building. Farrant recalled, 'Armed guards ran to all buildings, and the office was taken possession of in force and the staff ordered out.'[36]

Robert Saunders had watched the Germans come ashore, and saw them rush the office, wireless hut, and staff quarters. They quickly had everyone mustered outside under armed guard, where 'with a Maxim gun trained on us – just to show there was no ill feeling – we were perforce interested, if not unwilling spectators of what followed':

One party tackled the wireless mast & hut whilst others attended to the smashing up of the office & engine room, an operation greatly facilitated by the use of huge great American axes.[37]

Two of von Mücke's men (second from left and second from right) keep watch over the wrecked instruments in the telegraph office. (*AWM P11611.009.002*)

Maschinistenmaat Adam Härttrich and his two men were responsible for much of the damage to the wireless hut:

As soon as we landed on the island we got to work in double quick time. I and the two W/T operators [Georg Hilbers and Rudolf Wichert] were the first at the W/T station, where calls for help were still being sent out. We at once destroyed accumulators, electric engines, motor engine, switch-board, etc, etc.[38]

Another party, under Maschinistenmaat Paul Rossbach, was ordered to smash up the telegraph office. After completing his work Härttrich joined Rossbach. 'Together we forced open a safe to look for secret papers, but only found 40 American dollars, which we gave up [returned].'

When Farrant was brought before von Mücke he was informed that the cable and wireless equipment would be destroyed. 'Further than this, he said, they would not go, and all private property would be respected.'[39] Farrant was then instructed to collect his staff and take them to a place of safety, as the wireless mast was about to be demolished. According to Saunders, three charges of dynamite had to be used before it was toppled. 'Very obligingly the officer in command saw to it that it fell well clear of any buildings & our tennis court which was close alongside.'[40]

Farrant was now able to study *Emden*, and noted that she circled over the underwater telegraph cables before anchoring outside the entrance to Port Refuge, obviously to 'watch for anything coming up'. Closer inshore, the pinnace was in the process of raising a section of cable. Farrant recognised it as the half-mile length of spare cable he had placed in the lagoon as a decoy, and was pleased to see the Germans spending a lot of time and effort hauling it up. He later reported that 'it did not appear to strike them that there was a considerable slack for a laid cable'.[41]

Unknown to Farrant, *Minotaur* had received La Nauze's calls, and at 6.30am Kiddle sent a message to Silver, suggesting he send a ship to Cocos to investigate.[42] *Emden*'s wireless operators picked up the distant transmission, and estimated that the sender was between 200 and 250 miles away. Von Müller assumed that it was a British cruiser, and if it came on at full speed, it could reach Cocos in ten hours. This made an extended stay too risky, so he abandoned his intention to coal and cancelled the arrangements made for it.[43]

Marine-Stabsingenieur Ellerbroek was informed of this, and warned that they would now sail as soon as the work ashore was completed. He ordered that steam be maintained in eight boilers, and that both engines be readied for starting at short notice. Little steam was required while the ship was at anchor, however, so Ellerbroek permitted the fires in the boilers to be kept low to save coal.[44]

Von Müller would have been even more concerned had he known that Farrant's telegraph operator managed to inform Singapore and Perth of *Emden*'s whereabouts before his equipment was smashed. When the warning telegram reached Vice Admiral Jerram he ordered *Hampshire*, *Empress of Asia* and *Empress of Russia* to sail from Colombo to reinforce the convoy escort. The telegraph station at Cottesloe (Perth) reacted by forwarding the message from Cocos to Navy Office in Melbourne; Navy Office in turn sent a telegram to the

Admiralty, informing them, 'Cable just received from Cocos Island states warship three funnels at Cocos Island landing men 7am. I am informing *Melbourne* by Perth Radio.'[45]

Navy Office believed that the three-funnelled warship was *Emden*, so instructed Perth Radio to transmit the following wireless message 'three times at hourly intervals on highest power' to *Melbourne*: 'Very urgent do not reply. KJ. [*Melbourne*] Information just received from Cocos Island by cable. Warship probably *Emden* at Cocos Island 7am 9th November sending boats ashore. Admiralty and Commander-in-Chief China have been informed.'[46] Silver was already fully aware of the situation, having received La Nauze's calls and *Minotaur*'s message. Upon hearing the Direction Island transmissions, and a German station attempting to drown them out, Silver immediately altered course to investigate. He then remembered his duty to the convoy, turned back, and signalled to *Sydney*, 'Raise steam for full speed and report when ready.'[47]

Glossop received *Melbourne*'s flag signal at 7.00am, and promptly ordered Engineer Lieutenant Commander Arthur Coleman to raise steam for full speed. This was achieved in fifteen minutes, whereupon Glossop altered course to port and commenced working *Sydney* up to her maximum speed.[48] Leading Seaman Ernest Newman was at the helm, and recalled: 'Captain's Orders – "Full Speed Ahead", "Helm Hard to Starboard", to which I put helm hard over [to port]. On "Steady" being given we were steering S.40.W, direct for Cocos Island.'[49] The urgent need for *Sydney* to investigate the strange ship at Cocos caught many by surprise. Lieutenant Rupert Garsia was having a bath when Lieutenant Bell-Salter informed him that they were within forty miles of the enemy:

> I, of course, took it for a 'leg-haul', but he soon convinced me, and the noise made by the propellers going at rapidly increasing speed soon left us in a state of great elation ... though I had a half-formed thought at the back of my mind, wondering whether I might be knocked out.[50]

It would take about two hours for *Sydney* to reach Cocos, so hands were piped to breakfast at the regular time of 8.00am. Newman was relieved by the quartermaster, then went below for his breakfast before the order came to prepare the ship for action. This involved all tables

69

and stools being placed flat on deck, tubs and buckets filled with water, and fire hoses rigged. Newman added that hammocks were also taken up to the fore bridge and placed around the searchlights.[51] Additional splinter protection was provided by a canvas deck awning which had been rolled up and wound around the upper bridge railing. Despite having an armoured conning tower at his disposal, Glossop preferred to command and fight his ship from the exposed compass platform on the upper bridge.

When Surgeon Leonard Darby was informed that an unknown warship was at the Cocos Islands he instructed Sick Berth Steward Tom Mullins to get everything below and prepare for action. Darby subsequently reported:

> The stations for the surgical party are the fore and after ammunition lobbies for the stretcher bearers with their stretchers, and two theatres, one for each Surgeon and his assistants, are prepared in well separated stokers bathrooms, which are situated in the tube running up the centre of the ship. The bathrooms are 10ft by 8ft by 7ft in size and are supplied with hot and cold water; also they contain lockers in which dressings can be stowed. Though not quite below the water line they are well protected – above by two decks, and on the sides by armour and by coal bunkers.[52]

Todd was assigned to the aft theatre, but took little comfort in its so-called protection:

> The surgeons are supposed to have the safest billet obtainable in action; but in a ship of the *Sydney* class with her thinly armoured sides, such cover as exists is probably only sufficient to make a well-aimed shell, if fired at reasonable range, burst the better. The coal bunkers which are supposed to form a further [layer of] protection were always the first emptied when the ship went to sea.[53]

At 8.30am Garsia took up his position on the compass platform as officer of the watch. Thirty minutes later he was relieved by the navigator, Lieutenant Cuthbert Pope. *Sydney* was now cleaving through the water at 22 knots and throwing up an enormous plume of thick black smoke.

The calm before the storm

It took von Mücke's men about twenty minutes to smash up the wireless hut and telegraph office. They then began searching the other buildings for reserve equipment, spare parts, and anything else that looked useful in a wireless station. This work was relatively simple, and was completed in a timely manner. By 7.30am all that remained to be done was the cutting of the underwater cables, and the scuttling of the schooner. Von Mücke admitted that cutting the cables was 'the most difficult part of our task'.[54] After grappling and pulling up a cable, the pinnace crew had to hack through the outer sheathing of tarred jute yarn and galvanised iron wire with axes and chisels to get at the brass tape and gutta-percha (tree gum) insulation which encased the copper conductor.[55] No one had foreseen how arduous this work was, or how long it would take to complete.

A great deal of time was spent on the first cable, and more was lost dragging one of the severed ends into deeper water to make the repair task more difficult. Having unwittingly wasted the best part of an hour on a decoy cable, the pinnace crew then began looking for the next one. Amongst those watching the pinnace going about its work was Matrose Lochau. He had spent the past hour in *Emden*'s cookhouse, helping prepare the midday meal:

> As I had just completed all the preparations for the coming lunch and had a few moments to spare, I went on deck and towards the railing, and saw our men still searching for the cable in the ocean that connected to the cable station on land.[56]

They soon found the main cables, which could be plainly seen in the clear, shallow water. Lifting one of these larger, 4½in diameter cables proved much harder, as did cutting through the extra layer of tarred jute and heavy-gauge galvanised iron wire. The men wielding the axes sweated and cursed as they struck blow after blow on the heavy cable. The sound did not carry to *Emden*, and this bothered Lochau. 'An uneasy feeling grew stronger inside me. The entire atmosphere was too quiet and thus laden with foreboding.'[57]

Lochau had been told of the SOS sent out by the island's wireless operator and the distant response from a vessel, which all assumed was

One of *Emden*'s Maxim Model 1894 machine guns, set up on
Direction Island on the morning of 9 November. (*AWM 305139*)

an enemy warship. Another sailor then remarked that loud noises were
again coming from the wireless room. 'As more men joined our group,
I could not help but notice that a general feeling of oppression prevailed
amongst all of us': 'Suddenly there was movement on the communication bridge above. A runner was seen hurrying on some errand
and in passing he informed us that a smoke cloud had been reported
on the horizon to the north.'[58] *Emden*'s lookouts had sighted the smoke
at 9.00am. Von Müller initially thought it was *Buresk*, but then began
to have doubts, as the collier did not usually produce smoke in this
quantity. Leutnant von Guérard offered a logical explanation; *Buresk*
had had a fire in one of her bunkers, and the smoke might be attributed
to the stokers using up partially burnt coal.[59] The subsequent report
from the crow's nest – that the smoke was coming from a ship with
one funnel and two masts – reinforced the belief that it was their collier.
The matter was seemingly settled when von Guérard joined the lookout
in the crow's nest and confirmed that only one funnel and two masts
were visible. It had to be *Buresk*.[60]

When Matrose Mayer heard about the smoke he went onto the
upper deck to see it, and was satisfied with the explanation offered:

It was said to be our collier *Buresk*. As I had plenty of work on hand I went to the 'tween decks and told off my men as there was some repairs to be done to the aiming gear [on one of the guns], and I intended to have completed same by evening.[61]

Von Müller was meanwhile growing impatient with the landing party, which should have returned to the ship by now. At 9.15am he sent a signal to Gyssling, ordering von Mücke to speed up the work.[62] Von Mücke, however, would not be rushed. His men had just finished cutting the second cable, and by his calculations they had one more to go. They would return to *Emden* when the work was completed. Lochau couldn't believe the lack of urgency ashore: 'What were they doing over there? In spite of the order to "speed up", men were still running and searching. Certainly no sign of any preparations for return to the *Emden* could be detected'.[63] A few minutes later the crow's-nest lookout reported that the vessel under the smoke cloud had tall masts like a British warship.

The real *Buresk* was over the horizon, about twenty miles north of *Emden*; Klöpper had also seen the smoke, and was trying to identify the vessel making it:

This was at first taken for a merchant ship, but was later recognised by her masts as a warship. The number of her funnels could not at first be clearly made out. No wireless message was sent, for fear of betraying *Emden*, as the smoke seemed to be trailing away to the S [south], past the islands.[64]

Von Müller also noticed that the enemy warship was not making directly for Port Refuge, but seemed to be trying to pass to the east of the island:

What followed now happened extraordinarily quickly, as the enemy warship was coming on at high speed – 20 to 25 knots. I ordered steam up in all the boilers and repeated several times the recall for the landing party: then I gave the orders 'Up anchor', 'Clear ship for action' [and] 'Get up steam immediately to put on all possible speed'. By this time it was seen that the enemy ship had four funnels, and we guessed it was the English cruiser *Newcastle*.[65]

Upon hearing the warning bell for 'Clear ship for action', Mayer sent his work party to their battle stations then hurried to his. Mayer's was on the forecastle deck, where he was to assist Oberleutnant August Geerdes with the forward guns. As he raced up the ladder in front of the armoured conning tower he heard orders being shouted:

> I then heard the chief signaller's mate call 'The smoke comes from at least four funnels'. It soon became clear to all of us, with the naked eye, that she was a warship. As I came on the upper deck the anchor was being got up as quickly as possible and the siren hooted to bring the landing party back.[66]

Härttrich was in the telegraph office when he heard the recall signal. 'While we were working, the *Emden* suddenly blew her siren; we collected everything quickly, got into the boats and left the island.'[67] Robert Saunders witnessed the departure of the landing party, and believed there was little or no haste on the part of von Mücke and his men: 'After saying a few words of thanks to the Superintendent & saluting, the officers marched their men off to their boats & we gave them a good cheer as they left the jetty.'[68] Von Mücke could not see the smoke off to the northeast, so saw no reason to rush. 'As I was boarding the steam launch, I saw that the anchor flag on the *Emden* was flying at half-mast, which told us that she was weighing anchor.' He and his men were not even halfway back to *Emden* when she put to sea. 'The reason for this great haste was a mystery to me, and, for the present, was no concern of mine.'[69]

Von Mücke couldn't have been more wrong. By failing to return to the ship in good time he deprived *Emden* of essential personnel, including gun-layers, signalmen, and himself. This alone should have been of great concern.

The order to clear the ship for action was given at 9.30am, at which point von Hohenzollern proceeded to the torpedo flat and the senior command team entered the conning tower. The latter comprised von Müller, Kapitänleutnant Gaede, Oberleutnant Witthoeft and Leutnant Zimmermann (assistant gunnery officer). They were accompanied by Steuermann Mönkediek (battle helmsman), Feuerwerksmaat van Rysse, Artillerieobermechanikersgast Hartmann and Matrose Tietz. Due to a

Emden, as she would have appeared after getting under way on the morning of 9 November. Upon receiving the order 'Clear ship for action', the Imperial German Ensign would have been hoisted to the top of both masts. The steel plates around the sponson guns would have been lowered before the commencement of the raid. (*Western Australian Museum*)

lack of space inside the conning tower other key personnel, including Gropius, Matrose Werner (von Müller's runner), and a few signalmen, stood outside in the 'fire lee' — the side of the ship away from the enemy.[70]

Emden's gunfire was to be controlled by Gaede. The orders to the guns were to go through Fritz Zimmermann, who was in charge of the fire control instruments and transmitters. Geerdes had command of the fore battery of 10.5cm guns, whilst Oberleutnant von Levetzow commanded the aft battery. Von Guérard's action station was in the crow's nest on the foremast. Von Hohenzollern wrote: 'Guérard's duty was the observation of the effect of our shooting, and the giving of information to the conning tower about it, so that the direction, range and deflection might be passed correctly to the guns.'[71] This data was passed to each gun by electric transmitter, but speaking tubes were provided in case of power failure or damage to the instruments.

As soon as the anchor was weighed von Müller ordered full steam ahead on a northwesterly course 'so as to improve still further our favourable position with regard to the wind' before the shooting started: 'My object was to attempt to inflict on the enemy such damage by gun-fire that her speed would be seriously lessened, and I might be able to bring on a torpedo action with some chance of success.'[72] Von

Müller believed that the enemy cruiser was *Newcastle*, which he knew to be armed with two 6in and ten 4in guns, and capable of 25 knots. Failing a speed-reducing hit, if he could disable one or both 6in guns quickly, *Emden* would be able to fight on more or less equal terms.

When Ellerbroek received the order 'Full speed ahead', he had the manoeuvring valves on both engines opened, allowing a full head of steam to be admitted to the cylinders, but knew that it would take time for *Emden* to reach full speed because steam pressure was low. Some of the available steam was used to draw air through the boilers already lit, as well as those being fired up. Despite the use of forced draught, steam pressure could not be maintained, and Ellerbroek noted that it fell to about 170–199lb/sq in. He added:

> When all the boilers had been started, measures were taken to ensure the protection during the action of the supply and exhaust steam pipes. The supply pipes to the spaces above the armoured deck (No. III Turbine, steam whistle, sirens, steam heating, capstan and stern windlass) and to the fresh water pump in the fore part of the ship were turned off.[73]

This meant that all steam produced was fed into the engines, and in consequence engine (and propeller) revolutions slowly rose to about 130 per minute. According to Obermaschinenmaat Michael Jaguttis, this equated to a speed of about 20 knots.[74]

Marine-Ingenieur Haaß was responsible for the boiler rooms. His counterpart, Marine-Ingenieur Stoffers, should have been in charge of the engine rooms, but he was suffering from pneumonia and instructed to shelter in one of the boiler rooms. *Emden*'s fourth engineering officer, Marine-Ingenieur Andresen, commanded the damage repair party in the central command station below the *Panzerdeck*.[75] Von Mücke should have been manning this important post, three decks below the conning tower, because it formed the reserve command position, but he was stranded ashore.

Emden's medical arrangements, like *Sydney*'s, were split to avoid the loss of all surgical personnel through a single hit. The principal dressing station was the ship's hospital in the forecastle, but as it was exposed to shellfire, Marine-Stabsarzt Luther set up his medical station in a boiler room. Assistenzarzt Schwabe, assisted by Marine-Oberzahlmeister Woytschekowsky, manned the reserve dressing station in the steering flat at the stern of the ship.

Action imminent

Despite having had two hours to prepare for battle, *Sydney* was not ready. Glossop was a man of routine, and even though his ship might soon be in action, adhered to his daily ritual of Divisions and Prayers when at sea. At 9.00am the ship's company was mustered on the quarterdeck, and when all divisions were reported as present and correct, Glossop addressed the assembled officers and men. He warned them of the possibility of action, stressed the 'necessity for steadiness in battle', and 'requested the older men to set an example for the younger'.[76]

After Divisions, Chaplain Vivian Little asked Glossop, 'Shall I read the Prayer before Action, Sir?' Glossop replied, 'Yes, I suppose so.'[77] *Sydney*'s captain then returned to the compass platform and ordered a reduction in speed to 'Slow Ahead' (about 13 knots). Little meanwhile led the ship's company in 'The Prayer to be said before a Fight at Sea against any Enemy' from *The Book of Common Prayer*:

> O most powerful and glorious Lord God,
> the Lord of hosts, that rulest and commandest all things;
> Thou sittest in the throne judging right,
> and therefore we make our address to thy Divine Majesty
> in this our necessity, that thou wouldest take the cause
> into thine own hand, and judge between us and our enemies.
> Stir up thy strength, O Lord, and come and help us;
> for thou givest not always the battle to the strong,
> but canst save by many or by few.
> O let not our sins now cry against us for vengeance;
> but hear us thy poor servants begging mercy,
> and imploring thy help, and that thou wouldest be
> a defence unto us against the face of the enemy.
> Make it appear that thou art our Saviour and mighty
> Deliverer, through Jesus Christ our Lord. *Amen.*[78]

While Little tended to his congregation, Petty Officer Lynch, the gun-layer of the No. 1 starboard gun (S-1), led the Roman Catholics in prayer.

After prayers the first officer, Lieutenant Commander John Finlayson, read out the requirements of 'Clear ship for action' for the benefit of those who had recently joined *Sydney*. According to Shipwright William White, Finlayson was interrupted by the order from the bridge to clear for battle.[79] The torpedo gunner, John McFarlane, was amongst those still on the quarterdeck when the bugle sounded 'Action'. He quickly made his way forward to the conning tower, and from its upper level focused his binoculars on a distant smoke cloud. He could barely believe his eyes. 'I saw a three-funnelled cruiser on the starboard bow, standing off an Island & about one mile distant from shore.'[80]

Direction Island had come into view at 9.15am, and smoke was sighted by the lookouts in the fore control top four minutes later. Almost immediately afterwards Glossop spotted a warship, 'coming out towards me at a great rate'.[81] At 9.23am the vessel was challenged, using signal projector and flag hoist. The enemy cruiser, believed to be either *Königsberg* or *Emden*, failed to reply.[82]

Von Müller was carefully watching the British cruiser, which now turned and came straight at him. She was closing fast, and when about 13,000m (14,220yds) distant, 'and bearing about four points on the bow, swung round to a converging course'.[83] Mayer recalled: 'The guns were loaded and pointed. Everyone thought we had to deal with the *Newcastle* or the *Yarmouth* and I was pleased about it. Both of them were about our own age (class) and cruised in these waters.'[84]

Von Müller now asked for regular reports from his rangefinder operator. The maximum effective range of *Emden*'s 10.5cm guns was 12,200m (13,340yds), but he needed his opponent to get much closer before he opened fire. Surprise and early hits were vital. Von Müller waited until the range had reduced to 12,000m (13,120yds); then he waited until it was eleven kilometres (just under seven miles). Presently, the rangefinder operator reported that the enemy was 10,000m (10,940yds) away.

The watching and waiting was hard on the nerves, and no one could understand why the British cruiser had not opened fire. *Newcastle* was known to carry two 6in guns, whilst *Yarmouth* was armed with eight such weapons; surely *Emden* was well within their range. Still von Müller waited. The critical moment came at 9.38am when the rangefinder operator reported that the distance between ships was

9,000m (9,840yds). Von Müller, having ordered Gaede to fire his ranging shots at a gun range of 9,400m (10,280yds), now gave him permission to open fire.[85]

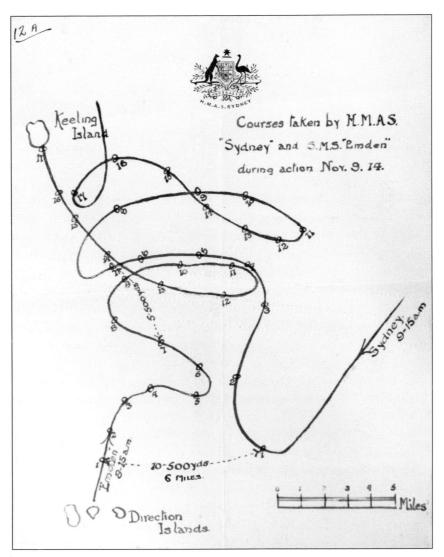

A copy of the track chart of the action produced by Captain Glossop onboard *Sydney* on 14 November 1914. (*AWM 3DRL/2190*)

4

Action

We closed very fast, and at 9.40, much to our surprise,
the "Emden" opened fire at 10,500 yards, having made
no real attempt to run away. Her opening fire was a
surprise because it had previously been thought that her
extreme range was only about 9,500 yards. We at once
opened on her and the firing became general.

Captain John Glossop

Lieutenant Garsia was in charge of *Sydney*'s foremost group of guns,
which comprised the forecastle gun, No. 1 starboard and No. 1 port.
He had gone to his action station immediately after Divisions, and was
still in the process of checking that everything was in order when he
heard the report 'Enemy in Sight' at 9.20 am.[1] Captain Glossop
responded to the sighting by ordering 'Half Speed'. He delayed going
to full speed because he wanted the ship's company to complete their
preparations for battle.[2] His gunnery officer, Lieutenant Denis Rahilly,
wrote:

> My station is Primary Control Officer on the Fore Upper Bridge, and I
> repaired there as soon as the enemy was reported in sight. The ship was
> closing very fast and there was barely time to Clear and prepare for
> Action before it was necessary to go to Action Stations.
>   Quarters were reported cleared away when the range was about
> 20,000 yards, still with a very fast closing rate. The ship was rolling
> about 3 degrees and pitching about 2 degrees, and the vibration was
> considerable, but ranges were taken very well and quickly, and a good
> Rate [of closing] was found.[3]

When the range was reported as 17,000yds (15,545m) Glossop ordered
a turn to starboard to reduce the rate of closing and to allow his port
battery to bear on the enemy cruiser. At the same time he ordered that

the report 'Enemy in sight' be sent to *Melbourne*.[4] Garsia, upon receiving the order 'Port Side', went to each of his guns, checked that the crews were properly closed up then stood behind the No. 1 port gun. As the enemy ship came within range the gun-layer, Petty Officer Bertie Atkins, asked if he should load the gun. Garsia, 'deadly keen there should be no flap', responded, 'No, don't load till you get the order.'[5] Atkins calmly replied that the enemy had just fired.[6]

Lieutenant Commander Finlayson was still making his way to his action station when *Emden* opened fire. He was on the boat deck on the port side when he saw the flash from what he thought was the enemy's No. 2 starboard gun. 'While the projectile was in flight I proceeded to my station in the Lower Conning Tower.'[7] Finlayson had thirteen seconds to get below deck before the shell arrived.[8]

Lieutenant Basil Bell-Salter was already in the upper level of the conning tower with Gunner (T) McFarlane. As third control officer, he was closely watching the enemy cruiser, and saw her open fire with the starboard forecastle gun (No. 1 starboard). Bell-Salter, like everyone else, was amazed when the shell fell '200–400 yards short of the ship, in line with the forecastle'.[9] Rahilly was stunned, as the range was well in excess of what a German light cruiser was believed to be capable of.[10]

The accuracy of the enemy fire was also disconcerting. Acting Lieutenant James Johnstone, in the fore control top, thought that two shells landed very close to the forecastle. He later confessed: 'I cannot say for certain but I am strongly of the opinion that the enemy opened fire just by either one gun or possibly two (certainly not a salvo) to obtain the range, these shots fell short by about 100 yards only.'[11] Lieutenant Geoffrey Hampden, in charge of *Sydney*'s after control platform, confirmed that two shells fell within 100yds of their port bow.[12] Glossop promptly ordered Rahilly to open fire then called for full speed. As for the enemy's ranging shots, Glossop conceded that the German rangefinders 'must be marvels of accuracy, or else they had great luck in picking up the range'.[13]

Johnstone was the rate keeper, and had meanwhile obtained the approximate range, inclination and rate, 'the enemy's speed having been estimated at 15 knots and our own at 24'.[14] This information was quickly passed to Hampden by voice pipe, who recorded the closing rate as 500yds per minute. Rahilly opened with lyddite from the port battery just as *Emden* fired a full salvo from her starboard battery. He noted that the enemy salvo was 'very straggly, but appeared to straddle the ship, one shot falling on the starboard bow'.[15] Rahilly was disappointed to see that his first salvo was over, so ordered a down correction of 400yds. Glossop wrote of *Emden*'s gunnery: 'As soon as her first salvo had fallen she began to fire very rapidly in salvoes, the rate of fire being as high as 10 rounds per gun per minute, and very accurate for the first ten minutes.'[16] Shells fell like hail, 'all round the ship, just short and just over, the spray from the splashes often coming on board'.[17]

Assistant Paymaster Eric Kingsford-Smith was near the conning tower, ready to throw the steel chest containing *Sydney*'s secret and confidential books overboard should it become necessary. He later told his mother:

> My word Mummy, I will never forget the sound of shrapnel and other shell shrieking and bursting all around. You seem to hear it coming from a good way off, shortly after the flash from the guns, & then with a sort of whistling shriek it whizzes overhead or to the side & the water it kicks up on hitting the sea goes up about 50 feet.[18]

Kingsford-Smith added, 'It is a ghastly sound & it was continuous, only varied by some of these shells bursting & the sound of countless pieces hitting all round.'

Oberleutnant Witthoeft was observing *Sydney*, and saw 'a flash of orange flame from the other ship as they gave us their broadside': 'We could actually pick up the shells as they came toward us, looking like so many bluebottle flies. They seemed to waver as they neared, and then we lost them as they moaned over us.'[19] The five shell splashes which erupted beyond *Emden* told an unwelcome tale – they were all huge – indicating that the enemy cruiser could fire a full 6in broadside. Fregattenkapitän von Müller was heard to remark, 'We're in for trouble. Those splashes are from a much heavier ship than I had thought.'[20]

It was now imperative that Kapitänleutnant Gaede score damaging hits as quickly as possible. To assist, von Müller ordered Kapitän-leutnant Gropius to alter course to starboard to reduce the range. The alteration in course also helped upset *Sydney*'s gunnery. Leutnant Prinz von Hohenzollern recalled:

In the beginning the Englishman shot badly. Seven or eight salvoes went over, and four or five were short. The short salvoes were a great hindrance to our observation, as the splashes continually came over the ship, obscuring our glasses, and rendering good observation very difficult.[21]

9.40am

Johnstone admitted that it took some time for *Sydney* to find the correct range, all of their early salvoes falling over by 400–600yds. 'This I consider being due to the very long distance we commenced ranging from, and possibly the vibration of the ship travelling at a rate of 24 knots.' *Emden*'s shells, on the other hand, were 'falling short, but as we closed, some of her shots could be plainly heard passing over us'.[22]

Hampden was of the opinion that the enemy shells were passing over *Sydney*'s funnels and his after control platform. He shared the platform, on which the aft rangefinder was mounted, with Petty Officer

Melbourne's funnels and boat deck (looking forward) – the area on *Sydney* targeted by *Emden* on 9 November. The structure at the base of the funnel in the foreground is the after control platform. The No. 2 guns (port and starboard) can be seen in the centre of the photo, and the No. 1 guns (port and starboard) are visible just below the lower bridge wings. (*AWM EN0441*)

Mark Harvey and three seamen, Albert Crosby, Thomas Gascoigne and William Meldrum. According to Hampden: 'At least two & probably three shots from the *Emden*'s third salvo struck the after control on the port side of its deck, but only one seems to have exploded – we were all knocked down & everyone was wounded & the control wrecked.'[23] It was later confirmed that two shells struck the control platform. The first plunged from the sky, narrowly missed the arm of one man, 'scored a deep groove along the whole of one wall', then 'passed through to glance harmlessly off the deck below' without exploding. 'The shell hit nobody, but its impact shook the structure to such an extent that all the men in it were thrown down.'[24]

The second shell arrived and exploded while they were still on their hands and knees. Signalman John Seabrook heard that Hampden 'had a piece taken clean out of both calves of his legs'; one of his men received seventeen wounds in one leg, and another had '7 wounds in his left leg & side & his right eye destroyed'.[25] Miraculously, no one was killed, but Hampden was unable to stand or walk, so Harvey (himself wounded) carried him below for treatment.

Johnstone noted that the action 'became increasingly fierce at a range of about 8,500 yards', and it was about this time that a shell struck the rangefinder on the upper bridge.[26] The 10.5cm projectile severed the rangefinder operator's left leg, sliced through the pedestal near the training wheel (toppling the instrument), then passed through the lower bridge screen on the starboard side without exploding.[27] Able Seaman Albert Hoy, the rangefinder operator, was thrown from his seat, blood spurting from what remained of his upper thigh. The telescope number on the rangefinder, Boy 1st Class Roy Millar, found himself on the deck with the instrument on top of him, but was otherwise unhurt. A witness recalled: 'He got up, shook himself, remarked "Where's my bloody telescope?", which he proceeded to unscrew from the instrument, and looked out for torpedo tracks for the rest of the action.'[28] Sixteen-year-old Millar was extremely fortunate. Had the shell exploded it would have killed him, and probably Glossop and Rahilly as well. Lieutenant Pope was on the lower bridge at the time, and later admitted that had the shell burst, 'it would have finished the control and killed or wounded most of us in the vicinity': 'After this, the signalmen on the lower bridge were ordered down on deck, and I sat in a commanding position on top of the Conning Tower, which is just before the bridge and connected to it by a platform.'[29] Bell-Salter thought that *Sydney* started hitting with her third or fourth salvo. If so, it had no effect on the enemy's fire, and salvoes 'followed at a tremendous pace':

> There was a continuous whir of shells passing over the ship. Of these I noticed a great many that could have only just missed the ship as the splashes seemed to be right alongside ... The majority of the short shots fell amidships.[30]

Garsia was uncomfortably aware that the enemy had found their range, and was shooting well:

> I saw a hit just under No. 2 Port [gun] & a little later a shot grazed the top of No. 1 Starboard then disengaged ... Next I heard a crash & looking aft saw there had been a hit near No. 2 Starboard, but saw no sign of fire. Going forward to Fxle [Forecastle] gun there was now a continual 'Wheeee-ooo' of shots going over & the 'But-But-But' of them striking the water. These I noticed seemed almost alongside the ship.[31]

Garsia then saw Petty Officer Harvey limping forward. Harvey informed him of the casualties on the after control platform, and added that he 'had taken Mr Hampden below'. Garsia could see that Harvey was wounded, but asked him to go aft and check on the situation near No. 2 starboard gun. Owing to a canvas blast screen blocking his view, Garsia was unaware that the gun crew had been decimated.

Two shells were responsible for the carnage.[32] The first, a high-explosive shell, passed between *Sydney*'s third and fourth funnels, exploded on the upper deck, ignited some ready-use cordite charges near the gun, and started a fire in a lifebelt stowage bin. The second was a shrapnel shell, which exploded upon hitting a funnel guy wire, lashing the gun position with hundreds of small steel balls.[33] Able Seaman Arthur 'Tubby' Hooper was the gun-trainer; he felt a stinging pain in his arm, looked down, and saw that a 'hunk of flesh had been torn out':

> When the shell burst it sounded as if a handful of stones had been thrown against the gun. The concussion was terrific. I could not even

85

look round ... Then I felt a terrific heat, and the silence of the crew induced me to look back. I shall never forget the sight. Everything round the gun was on fire, and I looked like being roasted. I made a rush through the flames, and came upon the gun-layer [Petty Officer Lynch], on his hands and knees, crawling out of the fire. I pulled him out of the danger, and, as his clothes were on fire I tore them off him. He had a great hole in his back. Close by the sight-setter was sitting with all his toes torn off one foot, and half the other foot blown off. He was cheerful under the circumstances. I asked him where the gun crew were, as there was not a man to be seen. He replied that he did not know.[34]

Two of the missing men, Able Seamen Bertie Green and Joseph Kinniburgh, were busy dealing with the fire. Green was wounded in the arm and leg, but helped Kinniburgh throw flaming cordite charges overboard. The latter was badly burned in the process, but Green later returned to the gun and remained at his post until he collapsed. Another of the loading numbers, Ordinary Seaman Tom Williamson, sustained severe cordite burns to his face and hands, and a wound to his right thigh. The seventh member of the gun crew, Ordinary Seaman Robert Bell, lay on the deck, barely alive and covered in blood.[35] The sight-setter, Able Seaman Richard Horne, had 'the sensation of my clothes being on fire and of being very wide awake':

> In the rear of the gun we have a tub of water used for sponging out the breech ... so as quick as thought I took off my headpiece and sprang off my seat and splashed myself all over. I looked round and saw my gun-layer laying on the deck crumpled up and the gun's crew gone. I stepped out of the tub of water and quite unconsciously was on my heels. I looked down at my right foot and said to myself 'Little toe shot right off', and then I saw the other. My, I had a peculiar sensation when I saw my foot all smashed up and practically hanging off.[36]

Horne somehow managed to get back to his seat and put his headpiece on, as he 'thought all the time of some orders being shouted through'.

Leading Seaman Bertie Dell heard the shell which grazed the shield of the No. 1 starboard gun, and was relieved to discover that it caused no damage – then he saw the gun-layer, Able Seaman Reginald Sharpe,

6in gunnery practice onboard HMAS *Brisbane*. The tub of water
for sponging out the breech can be seen in the foreground.
(*Author's collection*)

staggering near the conning tower. The shell's driving band had been
ripped off upon contact with the shield, and pieces of the copper band
flew in all directions. One fragment struck Sharpe in the chest, badly
wounding him. Kingsford-Smith didn't see Sharpe because there was a
canvas blast screen between them, but he later saw 'a big red pool &
splats of blood scattered about'.[37]

Sharpe managed to get below without assistance, so Dell took Able
Seaman Duncan McKay aft to help extinguish the fire in the vicinity of
No. 2 starboard gun. Near it they met Williamson and Kinniburgh,
'crawling forward with burns, the latter with clothes smouldering'. They
hosed Kinniburgh down, and then turned the fire hose onto some
burning cordite before rushing back to their posts.[38] A few minutes later
Lieutenant Garsia noticed smoke again rising near the No. 2 starboard
gun, so ran aft to make sure there were no cordite charges at risk. He
found Hooper and Horne on the gun, and Lynch 'lying on deck with a
big wound showing in his back & looking over his shoulder at me':

I saw Horne was bleeding from a wound in the foot. I asked Hooper if
he was wounded. He said 'No', so I told him to do all he could for the

wounded & ran forward again, seeing no cordite charges & the smouldering being unimportant.[39]

Hooper did as ordered, and with the help of Able Seaman William Taylor, carried Lynch below. According to Horne, 'Tubby went away and I was on my own, and I could feel myself going off, so I dragged myself to a hatch nearby and somehow got down it':

> I don't know how I got down [he was helped by Hooper], but I was glad, as I got some water to lay in, I wanted water. Soon after I got down the detailed ambulance party found me and carried me down below to a bathroom, where they cut my clothes off, and bandaged me up.[40]

Another shell had meanwhile struck *Sydney*'s mainmast. Leading Seaman Newman noted that it 'took a nice lump out' of the mast, 'but it wasn't quite big enough to fetch it down'.[41]

The tornado of shells unleashed on *Sydney* resulted in fifteen hits. In at least six cases the shells failed to explode; had they done so, damage and losses amongst key personnel would have been much greater.[42] One of these dud shells, or 'blinds', pierced the waste steam pipe on the fourth funnel before striking the upper deck abaft No. 2 starboard gun and ricocheting overboard. Another struck the hull adjacent to the chief stoker's mess; striking with an angle of descent of 30°, it cut into the ¾in thick plating and then fell into the sea. Newman was particularly impressed by the shell which pierced an engine room grating: 'A shot from *Emden* ploughed its way through a grating, through 2 bulkheads, tore a lump out of the deck of [the] Commander's Cabin, through his chest of drawers & through the ship's side without exploding.'[43] Three other shells exploded, but did not cause any significant damage. One detonated on the armour belt just below the No. 3 port gun, loosening two rivets. The explosion was described as 'rather feeble', but the gun crew was badly affected by picric acid fumes from the explosive. Able Seaman James Stewart heard that the crew immediately lay flat on the deck 'with their heads outside the ship, to get fresh air into their lungs'.[44] The second shell exploded below the waterline on the starboard side, abreast the forward funnel, and left deep scars in the plating. The third shell pierced the port side of the forecastle deck and exploded in the boys' mess. Shipwright White wrote of this hit:

> Every bag and ditty box was riddled with fragments of shell and the usual fire broke out. Luckily there was nobody in this compartment, and the water running over the Fo'castle poured through the hole in the deck and put the fire out.[45]

White added that *Sydney* was steaming at full speed, and the thrust of the propellers was lifting the stern, causing the bows to bite deeper into the relatively calm sea. Consequently, the forecastle deck was continually awash and water was 'pouring down in cascades over the side of the ship' at the breakwater. Spray was also driven over the forecastle gun, drenching the gun crew.

9.50am
By now the first of the wounded had reached Surgeons Darby and Todd. These were the men from the after control platform, and were taken below by a disengaged gun crew. Darby believed he received his first patient, Ordinary Seaman Meldrum, within five to ten minutes of him being hit:

> He had a fractured right leg and 13 shell wounds besides. He was in great agony and I gave morphia and ordered Mullins S.B.S. to attend to the wounds and quickly apply a splint, as by this time a constant stream of wounded men who required urgent attention was being brought below.[46]

Todd received Lieutenant Hampden in the aft surgical station at roughly the same time:

> Within the first few minutes the lieutenant in the after control was brought down on the back of a petty officer [Harvey]. His legs were riddled with shell fragments and his boots were full of blood. While he was being attended to the ship gave a violent lurch and heeled over at a giddy angle. The operating table rolled away and all the fittings fell with a crash. Then the lights went out and we thought we were gone. But it

was only the helm going over while the ship was steaming fast, and a faulty fuse that blew.[47]

After Hampden's wounds were cleaned and dressed, Todd began treating Able Seaman Crosby (slight wound to the left knee), Able Seaman John Butcher (wound in left kidney), Able Seaman Kinniburgh (severe cordite burns to face, hands and forearms), and Petty Officer Harvey (shock and injury to left knee).

Darby's second patient was Sharpe, quickly followed by Able Seaman Gascoigne from the after control platform. Darby noted that Gascoigne 'had various shell wounds in the right leg, thigh, and buttock, and his right eye had been pierced at the same time by a small fragment of shell'. Sharpe, however, needed urgent attention. He was 'bleeding freely, with the apex of the heart beating through a hole in the chest, loud inrush of air through the wounds and marked air hunger'.[48] All Darby could do for Sharpe in the short term was apply pads to his wound, bind it with tight bandages, and administer a large dose of morphia.

Darby then received Lynch and Bell from the No. 2 starboard gun. Both were very badly wounded. Lynch was 'burnt from head to foot' and in terrible agony. A shrapnel ball had pierced his abdomen, left hypogastric area, and exited through the right lumbar region, leaving eight inches of omentum hanging out of the wound. Darby applied dressings and gave Lynch a large dose of morphia. Bell had been shot through the base of the heart and soon died. Williamson and Horne were then brought down, and all available space near the forward surgical station was taken up. Darby gave orders for the stretcher party, some of whom were now giving first aid assistance, to take those already dressed to the wardroom and place them on beds and blankets taken from the officers' cabins.

Glossop had ordered half speed at 9.43am to help his gunnery control personnel find the target, but at 9.45am he ordered full speed again. Rahilly had established the correct range by observation of fall of shot, and a few minutes later it became evident that *Sydney*'s fire was having some effect. *Emden*'s guns gave off a sharp yellow flash each time they fired, but at 9.50am Rahilly observed a 'dark red sustained flash', accompanied by a cloud of smoke – evidence of

Sydney's after 6in gun during gunnery practice. The gun has just discharged and is in full recoil. (*AWM P02613.010*)

a direct hit.[49] *Sydney*'s guns were now ordered to go into independent firing to increase the rate of fire.[50] According to Johnstone:

> Independent firing continued for about a minute. When the Control Officer noticed that the shots from this ship were becoming wild, [he] tried to go into Control again. This was the most difficult thing to do apparently, and it could not be put down to any cause except the general excitement at our guns when the crews observed that they had been hitting.[51]

Sydney's guns were firing on a bearing slightly abaft the beam. This meant that Bell-Salter, observing the fall of shot from inside the conning tower, was subjected to the deafening noise and shattering muzzle blast from the forecastle gun each time it fired. He complained that it got so bad that 'it was very difficult to hear if anyone was controlling the fire'.[52] Rahilly subsequently reported that he experienced 'some difficulty in getting the guns back from Independent into Control firing', and put this down to 'natural keenness' on the part of the gun-layers.[53] They had endured over ten minutes of accurate and sustained shelling, and were eager to pay it back.

The punishment begins

Twelve minutes after fire was opened, von Müller was given a brutal demonstration of the tremendous explosive effect of the British 6in Common Lyddite shell.[54] At 9.50am one of these 100lb projectiles detonated in *Emden*'s wireless room abaft the second funnel. According to Matrose Mayer, the enemy 'had got his range and we received our first hit, which smashed our wireless installation and killed all the personnel'. Mayer added, 'That we had to deal with a much more powerful enemy was now evident.'[55]

The wireless room was completely destroyed and its occupants, Arnold Bieber, Walter Ehlers, Hermann Huster and Paul Wille, were killed and incinerated in the ensuing fire.[56] The hit also resulted in casualties amongst the crews of the No. 3 port and starboard guns, located on the upper deck just below the wireless room. They were caught in the blast zone and flayed with shell splinters and flying debris. Others were also affected by the hit. Fumes and smoke from the explosion and fire were sucked into the port and starboard engine rooms through the air intakes, creating breathing difficulties for the personnel stationed there.

'Simultaneously', wrote Matrose Lochau, another shell exploded on the poop deck, 'blowing some of our gunners clean overboard, and the resulting shower of debris smashed into others'.[57] Oberzimmermannsgast Alfred Reichelt stated that this second shell 'hit the ammunition trunk of Nos. 3 and 4 magazines, and set the poop on fire'.[58] Oberbottelier Johann Ferber managed to send up six boxes of ammunition from the No. 3 (upper) magazine before the hoist trunk was shot away; burning debris then fell down the trunk and started a fire in the magazine.[59] When Maschinistenmaat Peter Hoef was told of the fire he and Zimmermannsmaat Freye left the hoist motor room and went to extinguish it. Heinrich Freye recalled, 'As fire continued to come down through the trunk, the ready ammunition was put back in its place, and a wet blanket placed under the trunk.'[60]

One salvo thus scored two hits on *Emden*, destroying the wireless room and starting a fire on the poop deck which caused burning debris to fall down the ammunition hoist trunk and into the No. 3 magazine. These hits were the first of many. A short time later wrote Lochau, 'an entire salvo seemed to explode almost on top of us. This time it was the

Emden's forward guns and superstructure after the battle. A large section of the breakwater has been blown away by the 6in shell which knocked out the No. 1 starboard gun (left of photo). The bridge and port bridge wing have been completely destroyed by shellfire, but the armoured conning tower remains relatively unscathed. (*Western Australian Museum*)

forecastle.'[61] One shell detonated just in front of the conning tower, blowing away a large section of the breakwater near the No. 1 starboard gun. Witthoeft noted that it 'burst with an appalling noise': 'For the next few seconds everything was strangely quiet. We missed the rapid bark of the forward gun, but in its place came the groaning of the wounded and the dying. It was a frightful mess out there.'[62] The No. 1 starboard gun was damaged and its crew all but wiped out. Several men standing near the No. 1 port gun and the conning tower were also killed or wounded. Otto Mönkediek, inside the conning tower, had his left forearm fractured by a steel splinter which entered the compartment through an observation slit.[63] Splinters also sliced through the thin plating of the bridge, damaging the cabling for the engine room telegraphs and the helm indicator. Arthur Werner heard that the steering gear on the bridge and in the conning tower was put out of action by this hit, and that Obermatrose Büsing was unable to fix it.[64] Von Müller quickly ordered that the ship be steered from Compartment I in the stern, the helm orders being given to that section by speaking tube.[65]

Another shell landed abaft the conning tower, between the foremast and the after end of the forecastle deck. It exploded on the deck above the No. 2 starboard gun, piercing it and showering the gun bay with shrapnel and razor-sharp steel splinters. According to Lochau, nearly all of the gunners on the No. 1 and No. 2 guns were killed by these hits. 'Of the entire complement of my own gun only another man besides myself was left standing.'[66]

Signalgast Hans Lindner survived the hit on the forecastle because he had been standing on the lee side of the conning tower. Realising there were casualties on the No. 1 port gun he, Signalmaat Linnig, Signalgast Gräwe and Matrose Zeidler, 'sprang forward and threw the empty shell-cases and boxes overboard to make room around the gun, and to facilitate the ammunition supply'.[67] While doing so Lindner noticed that the supply of ammunition on the forecastle was being maintained by Matrose Reich and Bäckersgast Franz.

Torpedomaschinistenmaat Paul Köster was stationed below the armoured deck in the motor room for the forward ammunition hoist. He noted that the hoist motor stopped working after the explosion on the forecastle, and discovered that the hoist wires had become twisted. They were quickly untangled and the hoist put back into service.[68] Meanwhile, another fire had started in the ship's office under the poop deck, probably as a result of red-hot shell splinters igniting papers and other combustibles. Heizer Julius Dammann, assisted by Reichelt, tried desperately to extinguish it:

> We fetched the hose from the port engine room, but it was much too short, and the fire main in the auxiliary engine room on the Main

[armoured] Deck was empty [of water]. I now tried to get through the communicating doors of the hatchways and go to the starboard side to use the other fire main, but just as I was going on to the Main Deck, a shell struck us close by, and I ran down the engine room hatchway.[69]

'Closer, Gropius, closer.'

At 9.55am von Müller ordered Gropius to alter course two points to starboard, to 'get closer to the enemy and to obstruct his range-keeping'. Before the order could be carried out he amended it to one point because he could see that the enemy cruiser, 'owing to her superior speed, was already too far ahead of us'.[70] Von Müller realised that if he swung Emden too far to starboard his after guns would be unable to bear on the target.

Von Müller was seemingly unaware of the casualties on his stern guns, or the extent of damage and the fires under the poop deck. It took Hoef and Freye several minutes to extinguish the fire in the No. 3 magazine, after which they returned to their battle positions. Then they got another call:

When we got back to the Motor Room, I received word from No. 4 magazine that it was on fire. Wet blankets were handed into the magazine, and I hurried along the Main Deck to Compartment II to connect the fire hose, which I passed into the magazine.[71]

The hose was destroyed a short time later by another shell hit in Compartment II. According to Hoef, the entire after part of the ship was now full of smoke, so the order was given to abandon and flood the No. 4 (lower) magazine.

The hit to Compartment II started yet another fire in the stern and damaged the steering rodding, as von Müller was informed that the rudder was jammed 15° to starboard.[72] He ordered the hand gear to be manned, and sent Gropius and Büsing aft to take charge of the auxiliary steering position:

Meanwhile the ship, because of the failure of the steering-gear, had swung round about eight points to starboard; any further swing was checked by means of the screws [propellers]. As the fire of our starboard guns had already weakened considerably, I did not alter her course again, but let the port battery come into action.[73]

When Gropius reached the auxiliary steering position (on the forward section of the poop deck), he was horrified to discover that the four men stationed there had been ripped apart by a shell. The twin helm wheels were intact, but the chains connecting them to the mechanical steering rods had been shot away, so Gropius organised a repair party before returning to the conning tower to report the damage.[74]

The slackening in *Emden*'s fire was the result of the No. 1 starboard gun being out of action, casualties amongst the gun crews, and a general shortage of ammunition due to damaged hoists. Bootsmannsmaat Friedrich Heinzelmann was the layer on the No. 3 starboard gun, and he and his men 'continued firing as long as the ammunition lasted'.[75] Matrose Wilhelm Wollburg stated that they fired off all their ready-use ammunition, 'besides 12 boxes brought from the poop'.[76] But with rapid firing, the ammunition was quickly expended. After firing their last shell, Heinzelmann took his men forward to the No. 2 starboard gun and fired off two boxes of ammunition before *Emden* swung to starboard and the gun could no longer bear on the target.[77]

Glossop now thought it time to advise Captain Silver of the situation, and at 9.58am *Sydney* transmitted the message, 'Am engaging the enemy – chasing north.'[78] Ordinary Signalman Gedling was on duty in *Melbourne*'s wireless office and saw the incoming signal; he wrote that *Sydney* 'informed us that the chase was steering North, which would fetch her on us': 'During this time we was [*sic*] preparing to attack should she [*Emden*] come within range, we hoisted our set of silk ensigns to go into action with (these had been presented to the ship by the Citizens of Melbourne).'[79]

Ibuki was similarly adorned. After *Sydney* had earlier sent a wireless message that she had sighted the enemy, the Japanese battlecruiser stoked up for full speed, hoisted her rising sun naval ensigns, and went to action stations in anticipation of battle. Correspondent Phillip Schuler, travelling in *Orvieto*, thought she looked magnificent. 'Lit by the sun's rays, these flags looked [like] blood-red streaks on a background of white. In battle array the cruiser won the admiration of all.'[80] Captain Kanji Kato assumed that he would be ordered to help

Sydney, but Silver merely instructed him to move across and protect the port side of the convoy. *Ibuki*'s officers reportedly wept with frustration and disappointment when they were denied action.

10.00am

Each of *Emden*'s guns crews had started the fight with a quantity of ready-use ammunition, to be replenished with boxes of ammunition sent up from the magazines. The supply arrangements for the No. 3 and No. 4 guns were disrupted when the No. 4 magazine was flooded, and broke down completely when the No. 3 magazine had to be abandoned after the hoist trunk was hit again and the magazine began to fill with smoke and gas. By 10.00am the fires under the poop deck had created a dangerous build-up of smoke and fumes in other compartments. Reichelt ran forward to fetch a smoke helmet from Compartment X, which he used to enter Compartment III (above the No. 3 magazine) to open the scuttles and ventilate it. As he was returning the helmet to Compartment X *Emden* was hit several more times.[81] Lochau noticed that each shell struck with 'a horrible nerve-wracking shriek' before exploding. 'For a second after the deafening noise of destruction everything was ominously quiet. Then the loud groaning of the wounded and dying became audible.'[82]

One of the shells exploded near the ammunition hoist for the No. 2 magazine. According to Feuerwerksmaat Adolf Kruggel, thirty boxes of ammunition were brought up from this magazine before the hoist wires were shot away by splinters. 'The supply was then kept up with the auxiliary gear [block and tackle]'.[83] The hoist trunk for the No. 1 magazine was struck by another 6in shell a short time later. Lochau and Matrose Kugelmeyer were in the process of taking a box of ammunition off the hoist when 'a piercing flame shot out of the pit', horribly burning Kugelmeyer but leaving Lochau untouched. The shell had ripped through the hoist trunk between the *Panzerdeck* and the upper deck. 'Some shells', recalled Lochau, 'passed clean through the surrounding steel structure supporting the foredeck without exploding', tearing away cabling, bursting open lockers, and shattering glass fittings and scuttles.[84]

The hit to the hoist trunk also caused problems for the men below. Wachtmeistersmaat Georg Zimmer and his men had passed up eighteen boxes of ammunition to the forecastle deck, and about ten to the upper deck before the shell 'went through the trunk under the forecastle', wrecking the hoist, causing casualties, and starting a fire in the magazine. The fire was Zimmer's immediate concern. It was quickly extinguished with wet blankets, but he took the added precaution of turning on the flooding sprinklers for five minutes.[85]

The earlier hits to the fore part of the ship triggered a smoke and gas alarm in Compartment XI, to which Zimmermannsmaat Franz Woytakowsky responded. 'As the smoke helmet was aft, I went into the compartment with a mouth protector, and opened two or three of the scuttles'.[86] Shortly afterwards Woytakowsky received a report of water in the upper coal bunker on the starboard side of Compartment VIII, so took four men aft to find the cause. They found several small holes in the outer hull, and plugged them with pieces of wood and oakum.[87]

Woytakowsky then received word of a leak in Compartment XII. It had been discovered by Heizer Kutzmutz of the forward damage repair party, who noticed water trickling past the seals of the door to the refrigerating room in the bow. He tightened up the clips on the door but was unable to make the seal watertight. Woytakowsky knew that it was impossible to stop the leak, as the water was coming in through the cork-filled collision compartment. One of *Sydney*'s shells had evidently exploded in the sea close to the bow and splinters had penetrated the hull plates below the waterline. Woytakowsky instructed Kutzmutz to monitor the flooding then led his men back to the flooded coal bunkers to close the manholes and chutes.

Meanwhile, up on the forecastle deck, Hans Lindner had completed his work around the No. 1 port gun, and had 'returned under the lee of the conning tower':

> Shortly afterwards a second shell killed Matrose Reich. As the ship turned to starboard and the port side came into action, we ran round the foremast to the side that had now become the lee side [starboard]. About half a minute after the ship had turned, we heard from the conning tower that the steering gear which was being worked from Compartment I was out of action.[88]

The shattered remains of *Emden*'s bridge above the conning tower. (*AWM EN0240*)

Lindner had overheard Gropius, who had returned to the conning tower to report that the hand gear was unworkable, whereupon he went aft again to supervise the manning of the No. 5 port gun.[89]

The news that the hand gear was useless did not please von Müller, who was heard to complain, 'Why is there no steering? When this war is over I shall hang the man who designed the steering mechanism.'[90] He was now forced to counter the effect of the rudder as well as steer *Emden* by means of the ship's engines, resulting in a loss of speed each time an engine was slowed or stopped for steering purposes.

Lindner and Linnig were now ordered aft to replace the men killed at the auxiliary steering position:

Linnig and I ran aft, going first to the poop; but as we found nobody there we tried to go below to Compartment I. We found this impossible, as the whole deck under the poop was on fire. Thereupon we ran back to our station. On the way Linnig was killed, just abreast of the Instrument Room.[91]

99

Paul Linnig was probably struck by a splinter from the shell which exploded under the port bridge wing. Von Hohenzollern noted that *Emden* had barely presented her port side when the enemy landed three hits in quick succession. The first exploded on the bridge, blowing the roof (signal deck) off and taking the rangefinder and range-takers with it. The second burst under the port bridge wing. Splinters from this shell cut down Leutnant Zimmermann and the men on the No. 1 port gun, and injured nearly everyone inside the conning tower. According to von Hohenzollern, splinters entered the tower though the observation slits and wounded von Müller, Gaede, Witthoeft and two men: 'The third hit, however, did the most damage, as it caught the ammunition placed ready at fourth port gun, exploded it, and killed and burnt in the fearful flames all the men near it.'[92] At 10.04am another shell exploded near the base of the forward funnel. Under normal circumstances a large hole would have been blown in the casings but the funnel would remain standing. Unfortunately, there had been no time to replace the wire stays after leaving Port Refuge, and the hit caused the unsupported funnel to collapse to port. Maschinist Willy Kampf was stationed in *Kesselraum* IV, directly below the point of impact, and was stunned by the 'violent concussion' when the shell exploded:

> A few seconds later the stokehold was filled with a gas of bluish tint, which we got rid of by using fans and opening the furnace doors. At the same time the starboard athwartship [coal] bunker and the longitudinal bunker began to make water, so we had to isolate the former, and use the port athwartship bunker. The bunker doors, however, were not quite water-tight and some of the water trickled into the stokehold. This was reported in writing and verbally to the transmitting station.[93]

Kampf added that the shell hits were very noticeable in the stokehold by the concussions which followed. 'Once or twice while we were stoking up, the [furnace] flames shot out into the stokehold.'

5

The Reckoning

As soon as the "Sydney" got our range a good deal of
damage was done to the "Emden", and this increased so
quickly that I very soon got the impression that the
"Sydney" had gained fire superiority over us.

Fregattenkapitän Karl von Müller

The dramatic collapse of *Emden*'s forward funnel did not go unnoticed
on *Sydney*. Captain Glossop wrote that it 'went over the side to the
accompaniment of much cheering from our men'.[1] Glossop had also
observed *Emden*'s turn to starboard, and countered it by slowly
swinging *Sydney* to port, thereby increasing the range and keeping his
port battery in action. This meant that *Sydney* would be harder to hit
as the range increased, and the port gun crews, who had their eye in,
could continue hitting *Emden*. Gunner McFarlane, monitoring the
enemy's movements from the upper level of the conning tower, had no
trouble seeing when their shells hit. 'Those bursting on the waterline
gave off greenish smoke; and those hitting the superstructure, black
smoke with a tongue of lurid red flame.'[2] One unidentified German
sailor wrote of *Sydney*'s shells:

> They seemed to drop on the deck in bunches, and as each shell burst it
> sent a tornado of splinters hissing and clanging in every direction. So far
> did these razor-edged steel fragments travel that many people amidships
> were killed by shells bursting on the forecastle or the quarterdeck. There
> was no protection anywhere.[3]

Lieutenant Pope, perched on top of *Sydney*'s conning tower, had a
grandstand view:

> At 10.05 we took the foremost funnel out of her and shortly afterwards
> there was an explosion followed by dense masses of smoke and a raging

101

fire aft. About then she got so enveloped in smoke as to be completely obliterated and our men started cheering and leaving their guns, being under the impression she had sunk. They were induced to carry on with some difficulty (probably most of them temporarily very deaf) and when the smoke cleared away, the *Emden* was seen to be more or less intact, except for one funnel and a fire aft.[4]

The explosion and fire in the after part of *Emden* was caused by two 6in shells which landed on the starboard side of the poop deck. Matrose Lochau felt and heard the explosion, and quickly looked aft:

> The entire poop deck was lifted as if it was cardboard. Suddenly, the whole mass of steel was torn asunder by one or more explosions, with the air pressure alone almost throwing us off our feet. A fierce, fiery column shot up, forcing whole pieces of steel high up into the air, together with parts of our boats and dozens of men who had been stationed on the deck. Next everything was enveloped in thick heavy smoke. A few seconds of stillness followed. I stood frozen and looked at this dreadful scene as if hypnotised.[5]

Fregattenkapitän von Müller assumed that it was 'the blowing up of a part of the ready ammunition'.[6] Matrose Nicolaus Rombach, who had been helping with the ammunition supply for the No. 4 starboard gun, confirmed it:

> There was too large an accumulation of ready ammunition for this gun, and shell boxes were piled up in the wing passages under the poop. I had just been ordered by the gunner to throw the empty boxes and shell cases overboard ... so as to make room around the gun, when an explosion occurred as I was standing in the splinter shelter on the port side.[7]

Miraculously Rombach survived. He was thrown down by the blast and slightly wounded.

The detonation of the ready-use ammunition blew away a long section of poop deck plating and riddled what remained with small holes, so that it looked like the lid of a pepper pot. It was subsequently reported:

Two shells entered and burst under the poop deck, lifting the whole deck up in waves; both guns mounted there were completely put out of action, the entire guns' crews being killed or blown over the side ... One shell burst below and in rear of one of the battery guns; the whole deck was blown up and the gun's crew precipitated into the shield, where they were all killed and horribly mangled.[8]

Obermaschinistenanwärter Bernhard Hülsmann, working in the starboard auxiliary engine room, described the impact of these shells:

Violent explosions were twice heard near Station 21 [Bulkhead 21] and all sorts of things came falling down through the uptake trunk, parts of which were on fire and had to be extinguished with the fire hose brought from the starboard main engine-room. It was impossible to fetch a hose from the Main Deck, as everything was on fire, and the armoured hatch could not be opened sufficiently wide.[9]

When Rombach recovered his senses he noticed that the officers' mess and cabins aft of him were on fire. He could also see that the 'chief gunner, gun's crew and second ammunition man' on the No. 4 starboard gun were dead. As there was nothing left for him to do, Rombach sought shelter below.[10]

The exploding munitions and the subsequent fire knocked out both No. 4 guns and the No. 5 starboard gun. The No. 5 port gun remained intact, but its crew had been killed or blown overboard. In a matter of minutes *Emden*'s port battery was reduced from five guns to two. Bootsmannsmaat Heinzelmann therefore took his men to that side of the ship to assist the crew of No. 2 port gun. All too soon they were down to their last box of ammunition, which had been damaged and could not be prised open.[11]

Maschinistenmaat Hoef now found himself trapped in the stern by the fire under the poop deck. After flooding the No. 4 magazine he had gone aft to close a valve on the fire main, but on attempting to return to Compartment III above the magazines found the bulkhead door 'so hot that it could not be opened'. Hoef and Segelmachersmaat Hasse then tried to fight the fire from Compartment II, but there was insufficient water pressure because of damage to the fire main. As Hoef

The starboard side of the poop deck looking aft, showing the result of the detonation of the ready-use ammunition for the No. 4 starboard gun, and the resulting fire. The raised platform is the after gunnery control, flanked by the No. 5 port and starboard guns. (*AWM P00565.018.001*)

was attempting to isolate the damaged section another shell exploded on the *Panzerdeck*, blowing him down the hatchway. Unable to close the armoured hatch, Hoef joined Assistenzarzt Schwabe and the others in the tiller flat.[12]

After the No. 4 magazine had been flooded Matrose Alfred Weise and Obermatrose Büsing went forward to the conning tower to report that both after magazines had been abandoned. Weise recalled:

I now attempted with Büsing to move some loose cartridges lying on the forecastle and put them under the forecastle, but as a shell had just struck the pinnace and set it alight, we tried to get down on the starboard side. Another shell hit us, killed Büsing, and carried away the starboard hatchway.[13]

10.10am

With the two ships now on opposite courses, von Müller was forced to turn to port and follow his opponent's moves in order to remain in gun range. The turn was accomplished by stopping the port engine, allowing the starboard engine to slew the ship to port. Once *Emden* was on the desired northwest heading the port engine was started again to counter the turn and provide forward thrust. According to Marine-Ingenieur Fritz Andresen, the orders were initially given to the starboard engine room (where Marine-Oberingenieur Ellerbroek was stationed) via the transmitting station. However:

> After the first hits no answer was obtainable from the starboard engine room, although it was clear from the revolution indicator that the engine was working. Orders were then transmitted to the port engine, and thence, with long pauses, to the starboard engine, and the Captain was informed. It was impossible to send a messenger from the transmitting station to the engine room, as the combing of the transmitting station hatch had been bent by a shell ... rendering it impossible for anyone to get out.[14]

Andresen and his men knew that if *Emden* was sunk, they would be trapped in their compartment and drown.

Like the stokers, the men working in *Emden's* port and starboard engine rooms were protected by coal bunkers and the *Panzerdeck* or armoured gratings. They were therefore safe from all but a direct hit by an armour-piercing shell, or from shell splinters passing through gaps in the gratings. They did, however, suffer terribly from the heat, smoke and gas fumes. Obermaschinist Georg Leicht noticed that the electric exhaust fans stopped working shortly after the first hits were received, and this caused the temperature in the starboard engine room to soar to 152° Fahrenheit (66° Celsius).[15] The loss of the exhaust fans also meant that smoke and fumes drawn into the engine rooms via the intakes could not be dispelled.

Ellerbroek acknowledged that there was constant danger from smoke and fumes in the engine rooms, and the working conditions 'sorely tried the men, who protected themselves by holding damp bandages or handkerchiefs up to their faces'. The lack of oxygen also affected the emergency lighting:

An unidentified sailor in the only known photo of one of *Emden*'s engine rooms. (*Paul Nagel collection*)

The candles used for emergency lighting went out at the beginning of the action owing to the concussions caused by the shells. The [glass] globes of the candles and some of the electric light bulbs also burst. The flames of the oil lamps too, became smaller and smaller, and finally went out altogether ...[16]

Compounding Ellerbroek's problems, one of the ship's electric lighting circuits failed and could not be restored. He also lost direct communication with the transmitting station when the starboard speaking tube was destroyed. This meant that orders to him had to be sent via the speaking tube to the port engine room, resulting in delays before the orders were carried out.

As *Emden* steadied onto her northwesterly course the starboard battery came into action again, but only the No. 2 and No. 3 guns were firing. The latter soon stopped, and von Müller noted that the No. 2 gun only managed a few single shots: 'In the meantime the gunnery officer had gone to the guns.'[17] Matrose Johannes Willms was the range receiver operator for the No. 3 starboard gun. He was still at his post when Kapitänleutnant Gaede arrived to ascertain why the gun was no longer firing. Willms could see that the gunnery officer had a wound over his eye, so quickly explained that there was no ammunition, and that the gun crew had gone forward. Gaede and Willms then went under the forecastle to the No. 2 port gun, looking for ammunition. Willms recalled: 'The only remaining box of shells could not be opened. The gunnery officer was then wounded a second time. I accompanied him to No. 2 starboard gun, and got off six rounds. He was then wounded a third time near the ammunition hoist.'[18] Lochau was struggling to maintain the supply of ammunition to the No. 2 starboard gun. Each box of ammunition contained two 10.5cm cartridges and weighed around 50kg, and it was a slow and exhausting process pulling them up the hoist trunk from the bottom of the ship. This caused delays and starved the guns.

Those not hauling boxes of ammunition helped with the numerous wounded. Lochau admitted that most were only too willing to help, for remaining idle gave one time to think. He looked at the men and boys around him, and wondered who would be the next to be killed or mutilated: 'They did not look like human beings – faces and bodies seemed to have turned a yellowish shade, caused by the bursting shells nearby showering us with yellowish powder, which burnt our eyes.'[19] One of Lochau's comrades was watching *Sydney*; he saw the flash of another salvo being fired and shouted a warning. Lochau dashed behind the rope curtain – just before a shell exploded behind the No. 2 starboard gun:

> Immediately after the effects of this explosion we returned to our position at the gun. With terror and sadness we saw that our gunnery officer had been flung across the ammunition tube [hoist trunk]. Both his legs had been severed from his body ... Furthermore, two of our reserve men, who had probably not had sufficient time to find shelter, had been thrown nearby, terribly wounded.[20]

Nothing could be done for Gaede except apply tourniquets to the stumps of his legs, and then drag him and the other wounded away from the gun so that it could continue firing.

Another of *Sydney*'s shells struck *Emden* near the waterline, immediately below the second funnel. Marine-Ingenieur Hugo Haaß recalled that it exploded with such force in the upper coal bunker that the square chute being used to supply coal to *Kesselraum* II 'was almost made into a round one'. When he removed it, he noticed that the starboard upper bunker was taking in water.[21] Heizer Heinrich Hülsbusch had a miraculous escape. He was in the top of the bunker, trimming coal, when the shell burst below him; the blast rendered him unconscious, but he was otherwise unharmed. 'When I came to again, the bunker door was open and I scrambled to the starboard wing passage, where I found a wounded seaman, whom I carried with the assistance of one of my mates to the port stoker's bathroom.'[22] Maschinistenmaat Karl Jürgens noticed that the electric lighting remained on, and the exhaust fan and pumps continued to work, but the concussion caused two boiler insulation lagging plates to fall off. The stokehold also started to make a little water, which 'ran down from the upper bunker through the coal chutes'.[23]

Everyone wondered how much more punishment *Emden* could take. Lieutenant Bell-Salter perhaps thought that she was done for, as he called Lieutenant Commander Finlayson into the upper level of *Sydney*'s conning tower 'to see *Emden* on fire'. Finlayson discovered that the Germans were far from finished. 'I observed *Emden* almost obliterated by whitish smoke, the upper part of her wireless masts alone being visible, & she appeared to be turning in our direction.'[24]

By 10.15am *Emden*'s gunfire had become so ineffectual that Glossop decided to allow the range to reduce so he could attempt a torpedo shot. The opportunity presented itself a few minutes later when the German cruiser was seen to be on a converging course. Von Müller was trying to reduce the gun range, but he and Oberleutnant Witthoeft were also hoping to fire a torpedo.

10.20am

Leutnant Prinz von Hohenzollern was waiting in *Emden*'s torpedo flat for just such an opportunity. Unable to see what was happening, he and his men had been listening to the enemy shells exploding on and around their ship, and wondered if they would ever get the chance to use their torpedoes. The waiting was not made easier by the smoke and gas fumes which entered their compartment. At 10.20am *Emden* took a raking hit on the *Panzerdeck* above them. According to von Hohenzollern, the explosion was so powerful, and the concussion so great, that Torpedoobermaschinist Pyttlik, 'an unusually big and strong man', measured his full length on the floor plates. 'It was so comical that, in spite of the seriousness of the position and the fight for life or death, we could not restrain our laughter.'[25]

Diensttuender Maschinistenoberanwärter Gustav Schepputat believed that the shell split the *Panzerdeck* near Station 75, allowing water and gas to enter the torpedo flat:

I reported to the transmitting station that there was a leak in the starboard side of Compartment X. With the assistance of the men in the torpedo compartment the rivet holes and smaller rents were plugged up. Hammocks and blankets were used for the purpose, and the frame had to be shored up on both sides. After a short time we reported to the transmitting station that the flow had been stopped as well as possible. The water in the room was about 5 centimetres deep, and gradually rose to 10 centimetres.[26]

Von Hohenzollern was more worried about the gas fumes. He and his men applied their cotton-waste nose and mouth pads then released some of the compressed air from the torpedo charging reservoir. This helped to expel the fumes, but when von Hohenzollern ordered the port auxiliary engine room to start the air pumps to replenish the reservoir he received no response. He assumed that the port auxiliary engine room had been hit, and reported this to the conning tower.[27] At 10.25am von Hohenzollern received the order 'Ready starboard tube'.

Glossop was obviously aware of his opponent's intentions, but had no qualms about letting the German cruiser close with *Sydney*, as he too was getting ready to launch a torpedo. McFarlane wrote:

> I received the order to run out the torpedo bars. This was done after some slight difficulty with the port bar, due to the high speed at which the ship was travelling. Orders were received to torpedo the enemy & directors were set & [torpedo] gyroscope angled towards her.[28]

According to Bell-Salter, the range received in the conning tower was less than 5,000yds. As the distance between ships was reducing every second, McFarlane decided to improve his chances of a hit by ordering the fast setting on his torpedo.[29] Beset with other problems, he failed to consider that the range might actually be greater than 5,000yds:

> Due to *Emden* & *Sydney* repeatedly altering course for gunfire, it was most difficult to get a promising shot with a torpedo; for as fast as the gyroscope was angled to bring the Director Sight on or near the enemy, *Emden* altered her bearing by a large number of degrees.[30]

McFarlane opted to leave the torpedo gyroscope set for 10° left; it was then a matter of waiting until *Emden* became aligned with his director sight:

> Presently a possible shot presented itself and by turning the ship slightly to port, sight came on and torpedo No. 16 was fired from the port tube ... Range 4,600 [yards] ... The torpedo took up its depth well and started on its course; but I then lost sight of it altogether, due to *Sydney* turning to starboard immediately after firing.[31]

The torpedo failed to reach the target.[32]

Glossop had ordered a hard turn to starboard to increase the range and reduce the risk of *Sydney* being torpedoed. Witthoef watched in despair as his target turned, presented her stern, and steamed away.

Von Müller ordered a matching turn to starboard, as he 'wanted to make a second attempt to get within torpedo range':

I was not, however, able at first to send through the exchange [transmitting station] to the starboard engine the order 'Stop the starboard screw.' I therefore sent the message orderly, Matrose Werner, twice along the deck to the engine-room skylight to call down the necessary orders.[33]

With *Sydney* heeling under full rudder, Lieutenant Garsia realised that their starboard battery would soon be in action. This was confirmed when he received the order 'Starboard Guns'. He now discovered that the gun-layer of the No. 1 starboard gun, Able Seaman Sharpe, had gone below hurt. Garsia at once ordered Petty Officer Atkins to take over as gun-layer on S-1 then went to check on his forecastle gun:

I found in training round [from port to starboard] there had been trouble with [the] training rack, so ran to hoist & called down for an Armourer. Chief Armourer [Sam Perry] came up & put matters right.
On return to S-1, I met a group of men cheering & waving their caps. Some called out to me 'She's gone Sir.' I ran to the side & could see no sign of her or anything likely to obscure her, so called out to the men to turn out the Lifeboats. A moment later someone called out 'She's still firing', & guns crews immediately closed up, & then I could see the tops of her masts showing above some yellow or very light coloured smoke.[34]

Glossop later reported that *Emden* 'disappeared in the smoke for about five minutes', and 'most of our men thought she had sunk and cheered heartily, but soon got back to their guns when she appeared out of the smoke and started firing again'.[35]

10.30am
Von Müller's turn to starboard allowed his port battery to bear on *Sydney*. Two guns were brought into action, but it was all for nothing as their shells fell well short of the target. Von Hohenzollern wrote of their plight:

111

Sydney's remaining gun-layers, December 1914. Standing, left to right: Able Seaman Hoar, Chief Petty Officer Lambert, Petty Officer Bertie Atkins. Sitting, left to right; Petty Officer Etheridge, Petty Officer Newham, Petty Officer Young. (*AWM A03400*)

At many guns there was now only a single man, who served his gun in fear of death. The faithfulness and heroism of these men was most evident. The heroes kept their posts to the bitter end. Several worked imperturbably in spite of severe wounds, among them a Bootsmannsmaat who had had his right arm shot away. This warrior continued to serve his gun with the arm remaining to him, as if nothing had happened to him.[36]

The warrior was Joseph Ruscinski, the reserve layer on the No. 2 port gun, and it was actually his left forearm which had been mangled by shell splinters. The No. 3 gun was being served by Heinzelmann, Wollburg and Willms, having gathered up all available ammunition to bring it into action. Bootsmannsmaat Heinzelmann later reported, 'Subsequently seven more rounds were fired from the No. 3 port gun, till no more ammunition was to be had anywhere.'[37]

All of *Sydney*'s guns remained intact, and presently Lieutenant Rahilly turned his starboard battery on *Emden*. The No. 2 starboard gun was now manned by the crew from the No. 2 port gun, under the leadership of Chief Petty Officer Arthur Lambert. Rahilly was impressed by Lambert's actions, and noted that he and Petty Officer Atkins 'layed their own guns and also their opposite numbers, thus firing throughout the action, shifting from side to side quickly and coolly'.[38] The only cause for concern was the forecastle gun, which became increasingly sluggish and would not return to its correct position after recoil.[39] When the electric firing circuit failed to close, Petty Officer Young fired the gun by percussion, enabling him to join in each broadside. Salvo after salvo was now fired at *Emden*, but the 'Swan of the East' was proving to be a tough bird to kill.

Although *Emden*'s upper decks resembled a charnel-house, the boilers and engines remained intact, giving von Müller some hope that he might yet get within torpedo range of his opponent. All he needed was one lucky, speed-reducing hit on the enemy cruiser. Von Müller was a professional naval officer, and it was a matter of honour that he fight his ship as long as he could. For others it came down to duty – duty to the Kaiser; duty to the Fatherland; duty to their families; duty to their dead and dying comrades; duty to themselves. According to Matrose Mayer:

> Blood was flowing in streams on deck and terribly mutilated corpses were laying about ... I myself had only a few unimportant injuries ... Hartmann came towards me to give me an order, but he had not opened his lips yet when a shrapnel [shell] came bursting over us between the tower and the bridge. Hartmann fell and I got a shell splinter on the right hand which broke the centre knuckle ...[40]

Nothing could be done for Hartmann, so Mayer went to help the men pulling up a box of ammunition from the No. 2 magazine:

> We all lent a hand and had the box half way up when another bird came just in the middle of us. The tow [rope] was shot through and the box fell down again. All the men were dead or terribly mutilated. Only one sailor and myself left over, but both wounded. A piece of shrapnel tore

113

a big piece out of my back and another piece of shrapnel went through my right leg.[41]

The pain proved too much and Mayer passed out. When he regained consciousness he found that he had to crawl through the remains of the dead to reach shelter.

Just after Wilhelm Hartmann was killed, a shell exploded on the skylight above the starboard engine room. Ellerbroek noted that the room 'at once filled with smoke, fumes and steam'. In addition, floor plates were dislodged by the concussion and fell into the bilge, and several men were injured by splinters which entered through the armoured grating.[42] Conditions quickly became so bad that Ellerbroek ordered the engine stopped and the room abandoned. As soon as the smoke and fumes dissipated he and his men re-entered the room to assess the damage: 'It turned out that a shell had damaged the lubricator on the cover of the High Pressure cylinder, causing steam to escape at each stroke of the piston. An unsuccessful attempt was made later to stop up the opening with a wooden plug.'[43]

Most of the lubricating oil cups on the cylinders were torn off, and the discharge pipe from the main compressor to the hot well tank was pierced by a shell splinter – causing hot water to pour into the engine room. Orders were given for the compressor to be isolated and the engine started again, with lubrication being carried out by hand. The situation was far from ideal, and the noise of escaping steam made voice communication almost impossible.

Obermaschinist Georg Keller, stationed in the starboard engine room hatchway, had just opened the hatch to receive an order when the shell struck the skylight. He was wounded by a splinter to the right side of his head, and thrown against a bulkhead by the blast: 'As my right knee and thigh swelled up at once, it was only with great difficulty that I was able to stand upright, and standing on my right leg caused me great pain.'[44] Keller was subsequently employed relaying orders from the port engine room, and manning a fire hose to help suppress steam and fumes in the starboard engine room.

Diensttuender Maschinistenoberanwärter Peter Henseler had been in the hatchway with Keller, but escaped injury and climbed through the hatch when the starboard engine room was abandoned. He had orders to close a number of valves on the upper deck, but was knocked off his feet by another shell which struck the ship near the engineer's store: 'Picking myself up again, I ran down the hatchway to the port engine. As communication with the starboard engine had ceased [owing to having been temporarily abandoned], I received orders from Obermaschinist Dressler to try and re-establish the connection'.[45] Direct access between the two engine rooms was prevented by another shell hit. According to Heizer Theodor Körver, the shell exploded on the *Panzerdeck*, bending the connecting doors leading to the engine rooms out of shape, and blocking the hatchway with two corpses.[46]

At 10.34am *Emden*'s foremast was struck by a shell. *Sydney*'s carpenter, Edward Behenna, saw the mast come down 'very gracefully, partially wrecking the bridge in its fall'.[47] Bell-Salter also observed the hit, and reported that the shell exploded on the foremast 'level with the bridge, bringing it down and causing chaos around the bridge & fore peak'.[48] Torpedomaschinistenmaat Ernst Püschel, stationed in *Emden*'s torpedo compartment, described it as an explosion followed by a 'creaking, splintering, bursting of iron and steel, followed by a hard metallic thud'. The entire ship shook with the impact. Püschel shouted into the speaking tube, 'What's happening? What's going on?' The reply from the conning tower confirmed that the foremast had taken a direct hit and had fallen to port, throwing Leutnant von Guérard and Signalgast Theodor Metzing into the sea. 'Mast and rigging', Püschel was told, 'are dragging in the water alongside the ship.'[49] More hits followed. Bell-Salter noted that *Sydney* was now 'sending in a rain of shell, but many seemed to go over'.[50]

Boy 1st Class John Ryan was one of those tasked with keeping *Sydney*'s guns supplied with ammunition. The 16-year-old had been lugging shells from the ammunition hoist below the bridge to the forecastle gun for nearly an hour, and Able Seaman Stewart could see that the lad was 'tiring somewhat':

He could just manage to carry the 100-pound projectile from the ammunition hoist to the gun, but he hadn't the strength to heave it into the gun. The Officer in charge of the gun took the projectile from the lad each time and loaded the gun.[51]

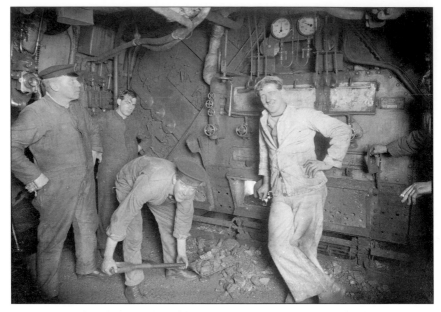

One of *Sydney*'s stokeholds in quieter times; the stoker standing
second from the left is Henry Wilson. He was a 17-year-old
Ordinary Seaman at the time of the action. (*AWM EN0171*)

Garsia was grateful when Stoker McGowan, without orders, came up
from below and assisted with loading the gun.[52] Stewart spared a
thought for those below decks, working in *Sydney*'s shell rooms and the
gunnery transmitting station:

> In a little confined space down below the water line, known as the
> Transmitting Station, about 6 men and boys sat with their ears close to
> voice pipes passing on the ranges sent down by the Gunnery Officer.
> And what were the thoughts of these men, who sat sweating in a
> temperature of 140°, with no news of the fight reaching them, we do not
> know. But, we do know they worked quickly and calmly, monotonously
> passing up gun ranges.[53]

The stokers and engine room personnel were also working under
extreme conditions, and the electrical artificers were in constant
demand. McFarlane was told that the engine room fans tripped with

every salvo, forcing the artificers to tie the circuit breakers closed. As for *Emden*, he noted that she now only had one gun firing – 'one of those right aft'.[54] Incredibly, despite the choking smoke and intense heat, someone had brought the No. 5 port gun back into action.

10.40am

At 10.40am Glossop finally informed *Melbourne* that *Sydney* was in action by transmitting the message, 'Am engaging the enemy briskly'.[55] A minute later Glossop noted the collapse of his opponent's second funnel. Marine-Ingenieur Haaß, in *Kesselraum* II, felt the violent concussion when the shell struck the funnel, and was informed that some of the lagging plates on No. III port boiler had fallen off as a result of the explosion. The boilers, though, remained undamaged:

> There were no leaks in the boiler pipes. Only one of the water gauges, that on No. II starboard boiler, burst, and a new [sight glass] frame was put in its place. No inconvenience was caused by the starting [shifting] of some of the floor plates.[56]

The failure of the electric lighting on the starboard side, and a few lights on the port side, was a hindrance, as it necessitated the use of oil lamps to observe the water gauges. Smoke and gas also started to build up in the stokehold, forcing Haaß and his men to hold caps, cotton waste or handkerchiefs up to their faces.

Despite the fact that his ship was shot to pieces and was burning in several places, von Müller remained focused on his opponent. The two ships were again on a slightly converging course, so he decided to try to get within torpedo range:

> My order was 'Everything you can get out of the engines'; but even at this second attempt my opponent would not let me get nearer than 5,000 to 5,500 metres. Our engines could now only attain a rate of 115 to 120 revolutions, which means a speed of 19½ knots, probably because the funnels had been shot away, and the furnace doors had, in consequence, to be left open to avoid danger from gas and smoke; further, one or two boilers had ceased functioning during the action.[57]

Another hit and rising water in *Kesselraum* III were responsible for the loss of two boilers. Haaß, unable to ascertain if the boiler room had sustained damage, ordered Obermaschinistenmaat Handel to investigate. 'He came back and reported that No. V port boiler was out of action.'[58] According to Heizer Bernhard Unger, who was stationed in *Kesselraum* III, a 'heavy shell' struck the *Panzerdeck* above No. V port boiler. The shock caused several water-pipes on the boiler to burst, so the fire was drawn, the accumulated steam vented to atmosphere, and the boiler shut down.[59]

The shell had penetrated the hull near the waterline and entered the lower coal bunker before exploding on the *Panzerdeck*. This and earlier hits allowed water to enter the hull, causing the ship to list to port. Maschinist Josef Tull was carefully monitoring the water in *Kesselraum* III, and it soon reached a critical level: 'Owing to the list of the ship the water was over the floor-plates on the port side. After a short time the bilge was also full of water, and the port boiler could no longer be used.'[60] Tull ordered that the fire be drawn from No. IV port boiler, and the boiler shut down as a safety precaution.

Emden's No. 5 port gun was now silent again, forcing von Müller to decide on his next course of action. He could press on until his ship was sunk, or he could try to save what remained of his crew:

> As it was now impossible for me to damage my opponent in any way further, I decided to put my ship, which was badly damaged by gun-fire and burning in many places, on the reef in the surf on the weather-side of North Keeling Island and to wreck it thoroughly, in order not to sacrifice needlessly the lives of the survivors.[61]

Von Müller promptly ordered a 180° turn to starboard for a reversal in course. As *Emden* swung away from *Sydney* she became hidden behind a curtain of smoke and steam, and thus enjoyed a brief respite from the constant shelling.

During the earlier lull Surgeon Darby received a message from Glossop to recover a wounded man on *Sydney*'s upper bridge. Darby ordered the forward stretcher party to collect him while he went aft to check on the wounded in the wardroom, and to see how Todd was coping. He now returned to the No. 1 theatre and found that the stretcher party had brought down Able Seaman Hoy from the upper bridge. Darby was informed that it had been a very difficult task, but with the aid of a Neil-Robertson folding stretcher, the patient had been recovered with no great loss of time. This was true, but Kingsford-Smith wrote that it was unfortunate that 'the poor chap had to lie for 25 minutes without attention before a stretcher party could come to him': 'I had to go up to the Captain shortly after & the fore control was simply soaking in blood. It must have been an inch deep on the deck & pieces of flesh and bone were over everything.'[62]

Darby noticed that Hoy's left leg had been 'shot away at its junction with the body, and was a horrible sight. He had lost a tremendous amount of blood and was almost dead on arrival below':

I sent for Surgeon Todd and got the patient's clothes cut away rapidly, and had him placed on the operating table. We then administered one pint of normal saline subcutaneously and started to trim up the stump, which consisted of a ragged end of skin, fascia, muscles, nerves, and vessels, longer anteriorly than posteriorly. In fact there was scarcely enough flap left to cover the stump. After having made a few cuts in clearing away the ragged ends, the patient died.[63]

Darby stated that it was hopeless from the outset, and that Hoy 'must have lost a fatal amount of blood in a few seconds during a hot period of the engagement, when nothing could be done for him'.

Lieutenant Johnstone was meanwhile trying to follow *Emden*'s movements. He reported that nothing could be seen 'except a cloud of smoke, and it was impossible to see in which direction the enemy was heading'.[64] According to Rahilly, *Emden* was 'completely hidden except the top of the mainmast', and once again 'many people cheered and shouted that she had sunk'.[65] Able Seaman Stewart heard others yelling 'She's gone! She's gone!' and was amazed by their reaction:

A rush by the guns crews near the lifeboats was made and these men, who had seen some of their shipmates killed and badly wounded less than an hour before, were now stuffing their serge jumpers and flannels into the shell holes in the boats in order to help save the *Emden*'s

119

wounded from being drowned. Just as the boats were fully manned, the *Emden* appeared out of the steam and started to blaze away again.[66]

Only one gun was firing. McFarlane couldn't determine if it was the No. 1 or No. 2 starboard gun, but he thought it must have a damaged sight because the shells 'fell from 600 to 1,000 yards short'.[67] It was the No. 2 gun, now manned by Bäckersgast Henkes. Glossop responded by reducing speed, turning *Sydney* to starboard, and unleashing his port battery. Only three guns fired. The forecastle gun couldn't be swung around in time (its voice pipe had become caught in the rolled-up canvas gun cover), and the No. 1 port gun suffered a misfire. Garsia discovered that the gun crew, in their haste to load, had forgotten to insert a cordite charge into the breech.[68]

Henseler was meanwhile trying to carry out the order given to him by Obermaschinist Dressler. He attempted to enter *Emden*'s starboard engine room via the shattered skylight, and after much effort, managed to open the hatch in the upper armoured grating on the port side: 'The steps between the armoured gratings had been shot away. The hatch in the lower armoured grating [on the starboard side] opened easily, and so I got to the engine. When I got there the engine was running "Full speed astern".'[69] Henseler discovered that communication between the port and starboard engine rooms had already been re-established, and that von Müller's order for the turn to starboard had been carried out. A short time later the order 'Full speed ahead' was received.

10.50am

'About fifteen minutes after the mast had fallen', recalled Torpedo-heizer Georg Pörrer, 'a shell hit us on the starboard side at Station 79.'[70] Schepputat thought that the hit was closer to Station 78, as water, smoke and gas fumes entered the torpedo compartment. 'There was a hole in the hull measuring about thirty centimetres in diameter, through which the water poured.'[71] Von Hohenzollern's men frantically shoved hammocks into the hole to stem the inflow of water. Püschel lamented, 'It was no use. Our flood-control timbers were broken like matches. We tried everything and still the water kept coming in.'[72]

Andresen felt the impact of the shell and heard the initial damage report via speaking tube. A short time later he heard, 'Ten centimetres of water in the Torpedo Compartment, and rising slowly.' Andresen quickly ordered that the forward steam bilge pump be started to drain the water.[73] Maschinist Kampf, in *Kesselraum* IV, received the order to start the pump, but the water continued to rise. Kampf believed that the suction pipe was probably blocked with debris, as the valve on the bulkhead between the stokehold and the torpedo compartment was open, but no water came through it.[74]

Another 6in shell had meanwhile exploded above the *Panzerdeck* near the starboard engine room. Maschinistenmaat Hans Harms, already 'covered from head to foot with black mud' (wet coal dust) from an earlier hit, noted that the intermediate pressure cylinder on the engine 'suddenly began to blow, and a cloud of steam was seen in the skylight'. A shell splinter had damaged the lubricating cock on the top of the cylinder, causing steam to escape with each upward stroke of the piston. Steam was also escaping from the intermediate pressure receiver. This created breathing problems as the steam, 'in escaping above, drew the gases with it from below'. The low pressure cylinder was also damaged, as hot water 'continued to pour on to the engine, causing us great inconvenience'. Other shells, stated Harms, exploded in the starboard coal bunkers, causing 'violent concussions' in the engine room.[75]

Ellerbroek was alert to the danger of noxious gas, and detailed one of his men to spray the engine room with a hose to keep the fumes down. Maschinistenmaat Alfred Klages had a similar problem with smoke in the starboard auxiliary engine room. 'However, we were able to remain ... as we kept on sprinkling with the fire hose.'[76] Conditions in the port auxiliary engine room were worse. Just prior to the turn to starboard, Maschinistenmaat Diedrich Wesemann felt several violent shocks as shells struck *Emden*. These caused the wires behind his switchboard to short-circuit, but more alarming was the thick smoke which poured down the discharge trunk – forcing the abandonment of the room.[77] Oberheizer Karl Reche and several others left via the armoured hatch. Finding their passage aft blocked by fire, they went forward, through the port auxiliary coal bunker, to Compartment VI. According to Heizer Hans Forst, they were then ordered to Compartment X, where they heard cries for help coming from the torpedo compartment below.[78]

11.00am

Due to *Emden*'s list to port, the water on that side of the torpedo compartment was now above knee level. Realising that the risk of gas poisoning was also increasing, von Hohenzollern ordered his men out. The armoured hatch, however, refused to open. The torpedo loading hatch now represented their only chance of escape, but it was bolted shut. One man was hoisted above the port torpedo tube to loosen the securing nuts while others shouted for help. Their calls were heard by Reche and Forst, and as the nuts were undone they withdrew the securing bolts so that the hatch cover could be removed, enabling von Hohenzollern and his men to escape. None were prepared for scenes of carnage and destruction which awaited them. Püschel saw wounded everywhere, crying out for help:

> We clambered over the smouldering wreckage to the stoker's showers, for we were plagued by a terrible thirst. Luckily we found some dirty bath water and slurped it greedily. I pushed my head through a porthole and saw the destroyed foremast dragging in the water. Leeward, I saw huge water spouts raised by enemy shells.[79]

Von Hohenzollern was equally shocked:

> In the waist I found a number of wounded, who were being bandaged by Oberhoboistenmaat Wecke, and who quickly told me how things looked in our beloved *Emden*. Going farther along the upper deck I then saw for myself a frightful amount of damage, everywhere dead and severely wounded men – everywhere groaning and moaning and plaintive cries for help.[80]

Most distressing for von Hohenzollern was the realisation that he could do little to help.

Von Hohenzollern picked his way through the debris and dismembered bodies in search of Oberleutnant Geerdes, and found him in the fore battery under the forecastle deck. Geerdes had been hit in the head and leg, but motioned von Hohenzollern towards the mortally wounded Gaede:

Gaede was lying at the port gun breathing his last breath, dying fully conscious, for he still recognised me. His uniform was red with blood. He dozed while he was thanking me for the words of comfort I gave him, and was then carried onto the forecastle, where he soon afterwards closed his eyes for ever. His body was committed to the sea, according to seamen's custom.[81]

Emden's collapsed funnels, as seen from the leading edge of the poop deck. The forward funnel has fallen to port and the centre funnel leans against it. The outer casing of the after funnel has folded over itself and is bent to port (the inner casing has fallen out or been removed). The engine room skylight is located below the elevated compass platform. (*AWM P00565.020.001*)

Those present no doubt believed that Gaede's soul went straight to Heaven, because his body had left *Emden* – now the epitome of Hell.

Emden was still under heavy fire, and Matrose Werner had the unenviable task of relaying von Müller's orders to the engine rooms. This involved running back and forth along the upper deck from the conning tower to the engine room skylight, all the time exposed to shells, splinters and flying debris. Werner recalled:

> About 20 minutes before the ship was run ashore, I was sent to the engine room to order the starboard engine to be stopped. I shouted the order down through the skylight, and it was also repeated by several others. I returned to the conning tower and thence to the port engine. The order to stop the port engine was also received below.[82]

Obermaschinistenmaat Jaguttis was continuing to monitor the port engine and its steam gauges. At approximately 11.00am he received the order 'Stop port engine', followed a short time later by 'Utmost possible speed'. According to Jaguttis:

> As the steam pressure did not rise above 170 lbs to the square inch, it was only possible to maintain a speed of 21 knots, and at times I could not keep her up to that on account of knocking in the cylinders. The vacuum gauge showed .85 lbs. The condenser must have been slightly damaged. Smoke and gas fumes prevented our ascertaining the damage in the port auxiliary engine-room. Sometime later the Engineer in Charge [Ellerbroek] was ordered to go to the bridge. This message was received by the starboard engine-room.[83]

Von Hohenzollern believed that the enemy now realised that von Müller intended to beach *Emden*, as they 'tried to sink us by an increased rate of fire'.[84]

After turning *Sydney* to starboard, Glossop adjusted his course and speed in order to remain off his opponent's starboard quarter. Such a position was good for spotting and great for shooting. *Emden* was on fire amidships and aft, trailing a huge plume of black and white smoke, and steaming through a forest of shell splashes. Rahilly initially thought that *Emden* was trying to pass around the western side of North

Keeling Island, apparently with the intention of sheltering behind it. 'We went full speed to try to cut her off, and it was soon evident that she was sinking rapidly and making for the island.'[85] Johnstone continued to observe *Emden*, and noticed that *Sydney* was scoring hit after hit, 'with little or no response from the enemy'.[86] Stewart saw it all. 'At eight minutes past eleven, a beautiful broadside from *Sydney* practically swept the *Emden*'s upper deck and knocked her 3rd and last funnel over.'[87]

11.10am

When Glossop realised that *Emden* was going to reach North Keeling he reduced speed and swung *Sydney* to port to keep the enemy under observation and under fire. Finlayson chanced another look from the upper level of the conning tower:

> I saw *Emden* heading for the beach, all 3 funnels and her foremast down, and on fire fore and aft ... No. 2 Starboard gun still firing, though at very long intervals, as if only one or two men were left at the gun, and had to look for ammunition.[88]

It was an accurate assessment of the situation onboard *Emden*. Nikolaus Henkes remained on the No. 2 gun, but the ammunition supply had broken down again. The block and tackle at the top of the hoist trunk for the No. 2 magazine had been shot away, and the surviving ammunition carriers were busy dragging the wounded to shelter. Feuerwerksmaat Adolf Kruggel therefore ordered four of his men to climb up the hoist trunk and assist with the supply of ammunition to the guns. Heizer Cornelius Nagels was one of them:

> I was ... ordered to go with Heizer Gurak up the trunk and rig up another tackle, with which we hoisted one box, taking it to No. 2 starboard gun, which Bäckersgast Henkes was serving. On the last round being fired, a shell hit the ship forward, disabling the gun's crew and throwing me to the deck.[89]

Bell-Salter saw both enemy shells, which he believed were shrapnel, fall well short of *Sydney*.

Kruggel now began to worry about the amount of water in the No. 2 magazine, and estimated that it was 30cm deep on the port side.[90] Paul Kutzmutz was also alarmed by the level of water in the refrigerating room: 'By tapping on the bulkhead I made out that the refrigerating room was half full of water (ie about one metre deep). In the bilge of the refrigerating machinery room the water was up to the platform deck.'[91] The water was entering the machinery room though popped rivet holes in the hull plating. Kutzmutz tried to plug the holes, but the water 'continued to come in, in streams as thick as a man's finger'.

Steuermannsmaat Plötz was trapped in the transmitting station with Andresen. There was 10cm of water in their compartment, but more worrying was the strong smell of gas coming from the main deck and torpedo compartment speaking tubes. Plötz had no idea what was happening on the upper deck, but he knew that command and control was still functioning because a few minutes earlier the conning tower had ordered that the starboard engine be stopped. He would soon find out why.[92]

6

Beached and Done For

Shortly before grounding, which happened about
11.15am, I had both engines stopped; immediately after
the impact I ordered 'Full speed ahead' again so as to jam
the ship on the reef as thoroughly as possible.

Fregattenkapitän Karl von Müller

Emden grounded on the windswept southern reef of North Keeling
Island at 11.11am. Marine-Ingenieur Andresen was initially unaware
of this, but felt the 'sudden jerk' of impact just before he received the
order 'Open Kingstons and draw fires' from the conning tower.[1] He
quickly relayed this order to the port engine room, where it was
supposedly understood and passed on to the starboard engine room
and the boiler rooms.[2] Marine-Ingenieur Haaß, in *Kesselraum* II, had
no idea that *Emden* was aground, and thought that the shock he felt
through the floorplates was caused by the impact of a large shell or a
torpedo. Upon receiving the order 'Abandon ship', he instructed his
men to turn on the fire extinguishing gear for the boilers and leave the
stokehold.[3]

Just before *Emden* ran onto the reef a messenger entered *Kesselraum*
IV and informed Maschinist Kampf that everything on the upper deck
was 'shot to pieces and out of action'. Kampf recalled:

Almost at the same moment a concussion of considerable duration was
felt, and through the voice pipe came the message 'Ship is aground.
Open the Kingstons, all hands on deck.' At the same moment flames
shot out of both furnaces into the stokehold. Within a short time the
stokehold was full of gas fumes and had to be abandoned, on doing so
we connected up the fire extinguishing gear on both boilers. The branch
pipes on the main [steam pipe] were not opened, as it would have
reduced the pressure and made it harder to put out any fires on deck.[4]

Maschinistenmaat Klages complied with his orders to flood the starboard auxiliary engine room by opening all the cooling water valves. Maschinistenmaat Harry Hellwege carried out similar scuttling action in the port engine room; he unscrewed the connection in the cooling-water pipe, 'thus letting the water run into the engine-room'.[5]

Obermaschinistenmaat Jaguttis also received the order to open the Kingston valves and draw fires from the boilers, but he did not understand it, 'and on my asking for an explanation the reply was unsatisfactory'. He therefore sent two of his men to make inquiries. When they returned to the port engine room and reported that the ship had run ashore, Jaguttis knew what he had to do:

> I stopped the engine and ordered the cover of the condenser to be removed, and I also opened the pressure reducing valve. I then abandoned the engine room with the rest of the men and got out through the skylight, as the hatchway was impassable.[6]

Emden, ten days after the battle; men from HMS *Cadmus* can be seen inspecting the aft guns, which remain trained on their last action bearings. (*Western Australian Museum*)

Jaguttis was less prepared for what awaited him when he emerged from the skylight:

> On deck the ship was on fire amidships and aft. As the Captain had given the men leave [permission] to jump overboard, the report got about aft that we were to do so, whereupon I and 10 or 15 others jumped into the water and reached the shore safely.[7]

Captain Glossop witnessed *Emden*'s grounding, and at 11.12am he had the message 'Enemy beached herself to save sinking' transmitted. Previous wireless transmissions had been in code, but this one was *en clair* so that all ships in the convoy could understand it.[8] Although high on the reef, *Emden* still had her ensign flying from the top of the mainmast. Lieutenant Commander Finlayson wrote that in consequence, 'three or four well directed salvoes went into her, causing her to get well alight abaft the bridge'.[9] Lieutenant Rahilly believed that the salvoes silenced the enemy's 'sole remaining gun in action', but acknowledged that *Emden*'s ensign was still flying when Glossop ordered 'Cease Fire' at 11.15am.[10]

Emden was stuck fast on a coral reef about 100m from shore. The white sandy beach, fringed with cool and inviting coconut palms, appeared tantalisingly close, but the surf and a treacherous undertow prevented all but the strongest swimmers from reaching it. Those who did make it ashore, cut and bleeding from contact with sharp coral, discovered that it was far from paradise. There was no fresh water, and the small atoll was inhabited by thousands of nesting birds, ticks and aggressive land crabs.

Even after the firing ceased, some men had no choice but to try their luck in the surging water. When Marine-Oberzahlmeister Woytschekowsky, Assistenzarzt Schwabe and Maschinistenmaat Hoef emerged from Compartment I they found their way forward blocked by smoke and flames. The sea represented their only chance of survival, so they jumped overboard. Schwabe managed to reach the beach, but was badly injured when a wave threw him onto rocks.[11]

Matrose Lochau was one of the lucky ones. He was thrown overboard when *Emden* ran aground; one minute he was on the ship, the next he was struggling in the water. When he surfaced, gasping for air, he saw that his ordeal was not over:

> There was the huge grey hull of the *Emden* not far away. The bombardment was still in progress ... Many white fountains, big and small, sprang up all around me from the many splinters and exploding shells, reminding me of the chance that I could be hit by one of these.[12]

Lochau then realised that *Emden* was jammed on a reef, and that he was between ship and shore. Rather than risk certain death by returning to the ship, he decided to try for the beach. This proved harder than it looked. The waves pushed Lochau towards shore then dumped him on the rocks and sharp coral. Before he could gain a handhold the undercurrent pulled him down and dragged him out

Sydney sets off in pursuit of *Buresk*. Guns crews pose for the camera while a repair party (right) prepares to patch the shell hole in the forecastle deck. The displaced roll of canvas awning around the upper bridge and the hole in the lower bridge wing screen (left) shows the path of the shell which destroyed the forward rangefinder. (*Sea Power Centre-Australia*)

beyond his starting point. Cut and bleeding, and with his clothes torn to shreds by the coral, Lochau surfaced again near *Emden*'s stern, more dead than alive.

After regaining his breath Lochau struck out towards the ship and saw others in the water doing the same. He then realised that the enemy had ceased fire, and a welcome silence replaced the mind-numbing crash of exploding shells: 'Quite unexpected, I found near me in the water a boatswain's mate, a giant of a fellow, muscular and powerfully built, struggling to keep afloat; he hailed me and asked me in between puffs of breath to assist him to reach shore.'[13] Lochau swam across to the Bootsmannsmaat and saw that he had a bad wound to his arm. It was Joseph Ruscinski. Lochau pushed a piece of floating wood towards his injured shipmate, and was in the process of helping him towards shore when a wave broke over them. Once more Lochau was forced under, but this time the sea was merciful and deposited him on the beach.

Glossop now left *Emden* to pursue a merchant ship which had appeared during the action.[14] He informed Captain Silver of this with the signal, 'Enemy beached to save herself from sinking. Am pursuing her merchant collier.' Glossop still wasn't entirely sure which enemy ship he had been fighting, but at 11.30am he had the signal '*Emden* beached and done for' transmitted to *Minotaur*.[15]

No one was more thankful for the lull in proceedings than Surgeon Darby, who wrote:

> Cease fire sounded at 11.15am after we had been working two solid hours in confined atmosphere, and a temperature of 105 degrees F. The strain had been tremendous, and S.B.S. Mullins, who had done wonderfully well with me, started off to faint, but a drink of brandy saved him, and likewise myself. Our clothes were saturated with blood and perspiration, and altogether it had been a terrific two hours of high tension.[16]

Darby returned to the wardroom to check on the eleven cases there, and found most of them restless and groaning in agony. Fresh doses of morphia were administered, and iced water, soda water and brandy were given as thought fit. Darby continued:

Our constant attention was now taken by two cases, Lynch and Sharpe. Normal saline was administered, in the first case subcutaneously, in the latter intravenously; wounds were all re-dressed, and all methods of reducing shock tried. Lynch was hopeless from the first, and died two hours after being wounded, after going through much pain. Sharpe somewhat improved after the saline, but air-hunger was pronounced and he complained of constriction round the chest, and tried to remove the bandages. There was oozing of blood from the wound and pulse was very weak. The other cases were not quite so urgent but many were in considerable pain and all that could be done was temporary until operative interference could be carried out.[17]

As soon as his sick berth staff could be spared, Darby ordered that the sick bay be rigged up as an operating theatre with all despatch. This took some time, and required an enormous amount of work because the sick bay had been flooded with water from a damaged fire main. Darby was, however, realistic, and wrote:

It was found impossible to do any operative surgery until the following day for numerous reasons, nor was it considered advisable on account of the condition of the wounded. The sick bay staff were too done up to get the theatre ready, with instruments and dressings sterilised for the first day, and neither Surgeon Todd nor myself was in a fit state to undertake operations until we had rested.[18]

The ship being pursued by *Sydney* was *Buresk*. Gunner McFarlane believed that she 'had stood off watching the fight, and appeared to contemplate obstructing if a favourable opportunity offered'.[19] At the start of the action *Buresk* had tried to assist *Emden* with gunnery observation reports, but she was now in full flight, and as *Sydney* closed, she hoisted the German naval ensign. According to Finlayson, 'She stopped on being signalled to do so & hauled down her Colours when the Captain signalled her.'[20] Glossop subsequently reported:

Although I had guns on this merchant ship at odd times during the action, I had not fired, and as she was making off fast I pursued and overtook her at 12.10, firing a gun across her bows, and hoisting

132

International Code Signal to stop, which she did. I sent an armed boat and found her to be the SS *Buresk*, a captured British collier, with 18 Chinese crew, 1 English steward, 1 Norwegian cook, and a German Prize Crew of 3 Officers, 1 Warrant Officer and 12 men.[21]

Glossop hoped to save *Buresk*, but Kapitänleutnant Klöpper had ordered the Kingston valves to be opened and the spindles bent so they couldn't be closed again. By the time the boarding party under Lieutenant Bell-Salter took possession of the collier she was deemed to be beyond salvage. At 12.45pm, Bell-Salter flag-signalled to *Sydney*, 'Ship is filling fast.' Twenty-three minutes later he reported that the ship was listing. At 1.20pm Glossop ordered Bell-Salter to abandon *Buresk*.

At 1.30pm *Sydney* started embarking *Buresk*'s crew and the boarding party. Glossop then hastened the collier's end with a salvo of four 6in shells. Chaplain Little wrote that it was an awful sight watching the shells burst 'in great clouds of black smoke, lit up with long tongues of lurid flame'.[22] Engine Room Artificer James Dardel believed that one or more shells failed to explode, as they 'went right through her and went for miles on the other side'.[23]

Just after 2.00pm Glossop set course for North Keeling. The pace was slow, between 5 and 7 knots, because *Sydney* was towing two of *Buresk*'s lifeboats. Glossop planned to use them to recover several men seen in the water earlier; it was thought that they had been blown overboard from *Emden* during the action. Glossop's concern for survivors of the battle did not end there. Shipwright White wrote that it was 'only after taking the prisoners from *Buresk* that we were certain that the ship we had just fought was the *Emden* and not the *Königsberg*'.[24] Supplied with this information, Glossop began writing a letter to his vanquished foe in the hope of avoiding further bloodshed:

> H.M.A.S *Sydney*,
> at sea
> 9th November, 1914

Sir,

I have the honour to request that in the name of humanity you now surrender your ship to me. In order to show how much I appreciate your gallantry, I will recapitulate the position.

(1) You are ashore, 3 funnels and 1 mast down and most guns disabled.

(2) You cannot leave this island, and my ship is intact.

In the event of your surrendering in which I venture to remind you is no disgrace but rather your misfortune, I will endeavour to do all I can for your sick and wounded and take them to a hospital.

> I have the honour to be,
> Sir,
> Your obedient Servant,
> John C. T. Glossop.
> Captain

The Captain,
H.I.G.M.S. *Emden*[25]

One of *Buresk*'s lifeboats alongside *Sydney* on 9 November; the man closest to the camera, holding a pair of binoculars, is Chaplain Little. (*AWM P11611.049.001*)

Unfortunately, when Glossop questioned Klöpper, he was told that von Müller would never surrender.[26]

Miraculously, the men in the water were spotted at 3.45pm, whereupon the *Buresk* boats were slipped so that the survivors might reach them. *Sydney* then went to general quarters and proceeded to close with *Emden*.[27] Bell-Salter wrote: 'When we left, the *Emden* was lying [with] bows well aground, mainmast standing, her colours flying, and a fire raging aft. She was still in much the same condition when we returned about 4pm, fire being less.'[28]

Wreck or warship?

Emden's survivors had been left to their own devices for over four hours. This gave them ample time to render the guns inoperable, burn confidential books and papers, put out fires, assist with the wounded, and watch mortally injured comrades die. It also provided Fregattenkapitän von Müller with sufficient time to clarify the status of his ship. He and his remaining officers and men knew that *Emden* was a wreck and incapable of further action, but by leaving the Imperial German Ensign flying from the mainmast von Müller was, in effect, declaring that *Emden* was still a ship of war. Admittedly, he did have more pressing matters to deal with.[29]

After *Emden* ran aground and *Sydney* departed, the able-bodied survivors were able to take stock of their situation. It was not good. The ship was a shambles, there were numerous fires burning above and below decks, and wherever one looked there were scenes of death and destruction. Many continued to carry out their orders and duties, some turned to assisting the wounded and those trapped below, whilst others started looking for water, personal belongings and missing comrades.

Leutnant Prinz von Hohenzollern was very anxious for the safety of his friend, Oberleutnant von Levetzow, who had been in charge of *Emden*'s after guns, but the collapsed funnels, fires and debris blocked his passage aft. His first duty, however, was to report to von Müller; 'He was visibly glad to see me again safe, for he had believed that the torpedo flat had been hit far worse that it had.' Von Hohenzollern noted that he and von Müller looked a mess, 'with our faces sooty and blackened, and our uniforms lemon-yellow with the effects of shell explosions'.[30] The 23-year-old prince then began helping with the wounded and searching for missing men.

Andresen also reported to von Müller, via the speaking tube to the conning tower, and stated that he and his men were trapped in the transmitting station. Torpedomaschinistenmaat Paul Köster heard their frantic knocking, found that the hatch coaming was bent over the hatch, and then fetched Zimmermannsmaat Woytakowsky who forced the hatch open.[31]

After dousing the fires in his boilers and ensuring that no one remained in *Kesselraum* IV, Kampf helped several wounded men before putting out a fire on the upper deck. He then turned his attention to the ship's guns, which had to be rendered inoperable lest they fall into enemy hands. Kampf went from gun to gun, removing breech blocks and recoil pistons, and throwing the parts into the sea.[32]

One of Kampf's men, Heizer Karl Lange, went forward after leaving the stokehold and heard cries for help coming from the No. 2 magazine. Heizer Karl Blümel was one of those trapped. He and his comrades had tried to open the armoured hatch, but water poured into the magazine, so they closed it and shouted for help.[33] Lange called for assistance, and with the aid of several others and a rope, 'hauled up all the men from below through the [ammunition] trunk'.[34]

Obermaschinistenmaat Peter Blauenburg was the last man to be pulled from the No. 2 magazine. After climbing out of the hoist trunk he was ordered to flood the magazine to help safeguard the ship. He did as instructed, but then went back down the trunk to check the water level. Blauenburg was alarmed to discover that the magazine was only half flooded because *Emden* was sitting so high on the reef. 'While I was there I noticed that the magazine was slowing making water; consequently the adjoining spaces must have been full of water.'[35]

Maschinistenmaat Harms escaped from the starboard engine room via the hatch in the armoured grating on the port side, and the skylight:

> On coming on deck on the port side everything was enveloped in smoke and my eyes were quite blinded. Suddenly I saw that the water at the door between the hammock boxes was about up to the armoured deck, and that several of my shipmates were jumping overboard with mess tables, benches and hammocks. I undressed, and as I noticed that the

ship had a list to port, I went over to the starboard side. This was now the weather side, and it [the breeze] made things pleasanter to bear. I now realised for the first time that we were no longer in the open sea, but had run ashore.[36]

About an hour later von Hohenzollern took a few men below in an effort to get aft, but found their way blocked by fire. They then tried the opposite gangway, and found it full of coal. Climbing over the coal, they managed to reach the ship's laundry, where they discovered two of the ship's Chinese washermen, dead on the deck:

> From here we tried to get further aft, but had to give up and return to the fore part of the ship, on account of the unbearable heat, glowing metal, and the water which had quickly run in. We discovered a few wounded, however, and brought them up to the others.[37]

Before returning to the upper deck von Hohenzollern decided to check the torpedo flat. He had the loading hatch cover removed again and saw that the compartment was full of water. Two shells from *Sydney*'s final salvoes had exploded on the waterline on the starboard side, blowing large holes in the plating and opening the torpedo flat to the sea. He and his men had got out in the nick of time.

The wounded made their way to, or were carried onto the forecastle deck. Marine-Stabsarzt Luther did what he could for them, but a shortage of medical supplies and trained assistants meant that treatment was reduced to applying tourniquets and bandages to stem the bleeding. When these ran out, bed linen and table-cloths were torn into strips and pressed into service. Luther's biggest problem was the sheer number of patients. There were about two dozen seriously wounded and double that number with lesser wounds. Luther could not tend to everyone, so many had to fend for themselves, tearing strips off their own uniforms to cover or bind wounds. When von Hohenzollern clambered onto the forecastle he was shocked to see a new battle developing:

> The severely wounded men were tended with the greatest care, and in a few hopeless cases morphia had to be given to lessen the terrible pain.

As soon as we had treated one patient and left him for the next, he was at once assailed by gulls. This was a kind of gull known as '*Döskoppe*', and they hovered over the helpless cases and attacked their eyes. These unpleasant birds were killed off as far as possible with cudgels and short-range pistols.[38]

Thirst only added to their misery. It was unbearably hot, and there was little shade and no water.

The water tanks above the *Panzerdeck* had been shot away during the action, and the small quantity of water left in the pipes had already been consumed. There was ample water in the main fresh water tanks located below the now submerged torpedo flat, but the water could not be pumped out because there was no steam for the pumps.[39] All hope now rested with the men who had made it ashore. It was thought that there might be water on the island, or at the very least, enough coconuts to provide a mouthful of milk for everyone. Unfortunately, every attempt to pass a line from ship to shore with floats and a line-throwing rifle failed. In desperation, two men volunteered to swim ashore with lines tied around their waists; they nearly drowned in the attempt and had to be dragged back to the ship.

Matrose Mayer lamented that time 'went away slowly'. He was nevertheless kept busy making sure the 'vultures' did not attack the wounded. 'They expected tit bits, but were so daring that you could catch them with the hand.'[40] Mayer added, 'It was almost quiet now excepting the moaning of the wounded and the explosions of one of our shells now and again.'[41] Just before 4.00pm his attention was drawn to *Sydney*, now returning from her pursuit of *Buresk*. Von Müller was also watching the cruiser:

> As she had two boats in tow, we imagined that she intended taking the survivors on board. When a fairly long distance from the *Emden* the boats were cast loose and the *Sydney* steamed past the *Emden*'s stern at a distance of about 4,000 metres.[42]

No one could understand why the enemy cruiser had slipped the boats, or why she was keeping her distance. It should have been obvious – Glossop was guarding against a possible hostile reception.

Klöpper's comment that von Müller would never surrender, coupled with the fact that *Emden*'s ensign was still flying from the mainmast, forced Glossop to adopt a cautious approach. He had to assume that *Emden* remained armed and dangerous, and that von Müller intended to continue with the fight, given the opportunity. McFarlane understood the situation, and wrote that Glossop kept *Sydney* 'well out' in case *Emden*'s 'torpedo tubes were still intact'.[43]

Glossop attempted to clarify the situation by signalling to *Emden*. At 4.10pm he ordered John Coleman, his Chief Yeoman of Signals, to hoist the signal 'Will you surrender' in the International Code, this being R-N-G-O-M-R. Steuermannsmaat Plöst, Obersignalgast Schwarz and Signalgast Lindner, stationed on *Emden*'s shattered bridge as lookouts, saw *Sydney*'s flag hoist, but did not understand it. This was because *Sydney* was two miles away, and Lindner and Schwarz could only make out three of the signal flags. These made no sense, and they couldn't consult *Emden*'s signal books because these had been destroyed. Von Müller focused his binoculars on the enemy cruiser and couldn't understand the signal either, but ordered Schwarz to respond.[44]

McFarlane, observing *Emden* though his binoculars, saw a man (Schwarz) waving a red flag. From *Sydney*'s bridge it could be seen that he was flag signalling in Morse, 'What signal. No signal books.' At 4.20pm *Sydney* replied, in Morse, 'Do you surrender.' This signal was not acknowledged, and no response was forthcoming. Five minutes later *Sydney* signalled, 'Have you received my signal.'[45] Once again the signal was ignored.[46]

Glossop had had enough. At 4.30pm he ordered Rahilly to open fire. Leading Seaman Newman recalled: 'Captain gave the order open fire & aim for the foot of the Mainmast. The port guns fired 3 salvoes but owing to the amount of previous firing done by them, they were a little out ...'[47] Von Müller was unprepared for this fresh onslaught, and later wrote:

When the *Sydney* had passed our stern and lay aft on our starboard quarter, she opened fire again unexpectedly with several salvoes, by which several of my men were killed or wounded, and fresh fires were started. I again gave the crew leave to abandon ship if they could swim

139

and wanted to, as I did not know how long the *Sydney* would go on firing, and this seemed the only possibility of escape.[48]

Mayer was equally surprised. 'Instead of sending us help, they sent us shells.' But he, at least, understood why. 'The *Sydney* was firing ... [because] on our one and only mast which was already very shaky, was still our War flag':

> The tow [halyard] had been shot away and none of us could pull it down. The first rounds tore away a portion of the bridge. Some others went over the deck and struck land. After that several rounds hit the middle of the ship and killed a lot of people. The Commander [von Müller] now gave the order 'Abandon Ship'.[49]

Harms was below, putting on a clean uniform, when he heard the shells explode. He tried to climb to the upper deck, but was forced back by others seeking shelter. 'While firing was continuing, I heard someone in the battery shout "All hands abandon ship." I then saw many of the men jump overboard through the open scuttles.'[50]

One of *Emden*'s stokers, Max Schuhmacher, was on the port side of the upper deck just before *Sydney* opened fire:

> I saw Maschinistenmaat Schneider swimming about in the water and heard him shouting for help, so I threw him some mess tables and hammocks. Suddenly, owing to the explosion of some shells, I was hurled into a corner near the hammock locker. I picked myself up again and fetched some hammocks out of No. 2 locker. On some more shells exploding I jumped overboard.[51]

Schneider drowned, but Schumacher managed to cling to his hammocks, 'on which I was carried up and down for a long time until I lost them in the surf'. Finally, 'by great exertions', he reached the shore.

Obermaschinist Keller was amidships on the starboard side, and in the line of fire. He quickly ran around to the port side and was 'thrown against the seaman's head [lavatory] by a sudden concussion of air':

After several more shells had found their mark, I tried to get into the [coal] bunker near the galley, but had nothing to hold onto as the [deck] plates around the coaling hatches were too hot. I then jumped overboard near No. 2 port gun with all my clothes on, and kept myself up for about 15 minutes by holding on to a rope's end, until I was pulled on board again by Oberheizer Stechmeyer and others who let down hammock nets and a rope's end.[52]

Diensttuender Maschinistenoberanwärter Henseler also had a lucky escape. He was in the petty officers' mess under the forecastle when the shelling resumed:

I heard the firing and [felt] the shock of the shells as they struck the ship. When a shell crashed through the Warrant Officer's lavatory, there was a panic and the cry was raised: 'Abandon ship'. Some of the men jumped into the water from the hatch. I took off my boots and sat down on the hatch. Suddenly in the crush I was pushed overboard. I tried to swim ashore, but could not do so owing to the heavy surf, and held myself up, like several others, by clinging to the foremast which was lying suspended in the water.[53]

Some men were unable to hold on and drowned, but Henseler was eventually hauled back onboard with the aid of a rope.

Lochau was sound asleep on the warm sand of North Keeling when the shelling resumed. Disturbed by an earth-trembling explosion and a shower of sand and pebbles, he sat up and saw *Sydney* firing another salvo at *Emden*:

As I watched, I could see how every gun flashed forth a piercing flame which was immediately surrounded by a ring of smoke as they sent shells across. Those that missed whizzed fairly low above my head. In quiet disbelief I rubbed my eyes. Then a sudden explosion quite nearby, throwing up high columns of sand and dust, uprooted palm trees and hurled them through the air like matchsticks.[54]

Lochau tried to get below the trajectory of the shells by crawling down the beach towards *Emden*. The after part of the ship was still burning, and the setting sun was providing an eerie backlight to the horrific scenes being played out before him. His comrades, in their white uniforms, looked like ghosts as they surged forward onto the forecastle deck to escape the shelling. Hellwege was amongst them. He was below the bridge when the firing resumed, and decided that it would be safer on the forecastle.[55]

Rahilly fired three salvoes from *Sydney*'s port battery before the ship was turned to bring the starboard guns into action. He was just about to resume firing with the starboard battery when Glossop ordered him to cease fire. McFarlane noted that 'a little while after, a white flag was visible flying from *Emden*'s forecastle'.[56] Bell-Salter recalled the sequence of events somewhat differently. He believed that a 'flag of truce' was displayed before firing ceased, but both officers agreed that a man was 'then sent aloft to strike their Colours'.[57] It was von Müller's faithful runner, Arthur Werner:

> Some of the wounded cried out to us to haul down our flag. The captain looked at me and I knew where my duty lay. In hopes that the *Sydney* would be able to see my intentions I deliberately climbed up that side of the ship facing her. In the meantime she had ceased firing, which was just as well for the task I had in hand.
>
> As I reached the mast on the aft deck, I saw that the halyards were burnt through, so that I would have to clamber to the top of the mast itself, not such a simple task at 40 metres. This task was not made any easier by the fact that the shrouds were also burnt or torn, but somehow I managed to reach the top. On trying to loosen the flag I noticed that the knots had tightened considerably so that I could not do so by hand and as I had no knife I was obliged to use my teeth. Eventually I got the flag free and with it tied around my waist descended in all haste.[58]

Werner then reported to his captain and requested permission to keep the flag. Facing capture, von Müller was determined that *Emden*'s ensign should not fall into enemy hands. He ordered Werner to burn it.

Satisfied that *Emden* no longer posed a threat, Glossop turned away to collect the *Buresk* boats. These were taken in tow at 5.00pm, and a few minutes later two Germans were plucked from the sea. Shipwright White recalled:

As we neared the *Emden* we saw two men in the water, one wounded and the other supporting him in a lifebuoy. Like one man, our lads applauded them, the wounded German in broken English thanking us very much. Two of our men jumped over after them and they were soon aboard us. It was only a little incident, but one of which I was a very proud witness.[59]

It was nearly 6.00pm before *Sydney* reached *Emden*, and Glossop was starting to worry about the time:

It was now getting late in the afternoon, and as it was essential that Cocos Island should be visited as soon as possible to see if a party had been landed there, it was impracticable to take the survivors off that night. However, one of the boats from the *Buresk* was sent over manned by a German officer and crew taken from the collier, with a supply of food and water, and a promise of assistance next day on the understanding that the survivors would give their parole while on board the *Sydney*.[60]

The officer was Leutnant Fikentscher, and from him, von Müller learned for the first time that his opponent was the Australian cruiser *Sydney*.

Glossop now set course for Direction Island, fourteen miles to the south, to ascertain the condition of the wireless and telegraph stations. He hoped to arrive before dark, but was delayed by the rescue of another *Emden* sailor. White wrote of this:

The sun was setting as we steamed away. About four miles from North Keeling Island we heard a cry from the water, a night lifebuoy was immediately released, and a lifeboat's crew was called away. They picked up an unwounded German who had been in the water about eight hours.[61]

Shortly after being rescued the man collapsed and became unconscious. Darby noted that he had 'been in the shark-infested sea for nine hours, and was brought round after much trouble.'[62]

After supper all available officers and men were piped aft for the burial at sea of the bodies of Petty Officer Lynch, Able Seaman Hoy

143

and Ordinary Seaman Bell. According to White: 'This was a ceremony that will always live in my memory; the faint whirr of the propellers, the darkness and the calm of the mighty deep, and the lantern throwing a soft glow upon the Chaplain's face and the prayer book he was holding.'[63] White noticed that after the service everyone moved off to their night defence stations 'speaking not a word'.

Later that evening *Sydney*'s wireless operators picked up the distinctive sound of a German wireless transmission. This caused Glossop to wonder if another enemy warship was in the vicinity. *Königsberg* was reportedly operating in the Indian Ocean, and as her current location was not known to Glossop, he had to act accordingly: 'Having heard a Telefunken note on the wireless while approaching Cocos, it was not considered advisable to anchor there for the night and the ship stood off and on until daylight'.[64]

Glossop had another problem. One of the rescued Germans divulged that *Emden* had landed an armed party on Direction Island to destroy the wireless and cable stations. He stated that there were forty-three men in the party, and that they were armed with rifles and four Maxim machine guns.[65] Putting men ashore in darkness to deal with these Germans was considered foolhardy, so Glossop decided to wait until morning when, covered by *Sydney*'s guns, two boats would go in under a white flag. Finlayson was to command one boat, and Lieutenant Cavaye would be in charge of the other. It was hoped that the Germans could be induced to surrender, and so avoid further loss of life.

Unknown to Glossop, the birds had flown. Earlier that day, when Kapitänleutnant von Mücke realised that *Emden* might not return, he began looking at his options:

With our four machine guns and twenty-nine rifles we could, for the time at least, have prevented the English from making a landing on the island, but against the fire of the English cruiser's heavy guns, which would then have been directed against us, we would have had no defence whatever. Taking everything into consideration, therefore, we could do no more than defer the surrender of a position that, from the outset, it had been impossible to hold. Moreover, confinement in an English prison was little to our taste.[66]

Von Mücke and his men prepare to leave the Direction Island
jetty. *Ayesha* can be seen at anchor in the background. (*Western
Australian Museum*)

Not wishing to become a prisoner of war, von Mücke decided to
commandeer the only sea-going craft available. According to
Maschinistenmaat Härttrich: 'The First Lieutenant watched the fight
from the roof. As both ships disappeared on the horizon he said –
"Probably no more ships will come back, we will get this sailing ship
ready (he pointed to the *Ayesha*) in order to escape being made
prisoners".'[67] Von Mücke immediately went out to inspect the three-
masted schooner anchored in the lagoon. The 97-ton *Ayesha* was
owned by John Clunies-Ross, and had been employed on the copra run
to Batavia until a regular steamship service made the vessel redundant.
Ayesha's master warned that the little ship was old and rotten, and
would not survive a long journey, but von Mücke thought otherwise.
Upon returning to shore he ordered Leutnants Gyssling and Schmidt to
take a party to the schooner and prepare her for sea.

145

Superintendent Farrant and his staff thought the Germans quite mad risking their lives in such a decrepit boat. They also warned of British and Japanese warships in the vicinity, and tried to talk von Mücke out his foolish enterprise. Von Mücke recalled:

> When, in spite of all these warnings, we remained firm in our purpose, and continued the work of getting the *Ayesha* ready for sea, the sporting side of the situation began to appeal to the Englishmen, and they almost ran their legs off in their eagerness to help us.[68]

Stores, provisions, blankets, spare clothes, and even advice on currents, wind and weather conditions were readily given to the Germans. There was genuine friendship in the assistance offered, just as there was genuine relief that the Germans were leaving, for Farrant and his men were keen to repair their equipment and re-establish communications with the outside world.

At 5.45pm the lookout on the roof was called down and there was a rapid move towards the jetty. Robert Saunders was almost sad to see the Germans go: 'There had not been a single untoward incident throughout the day – a job of work had to be done & they did it. It wasn't of their choosing, but as they said, the "Fortune of War".'[69] He added that everyone looked upon von Mücke's party as brave men going to their fate.

The wireless and cable station staff gathered on the jetty and gave von Mücke and his men three cheers as they pulled away. On reaching the schooner the sailors in the cutters clambered aboard then secured their boats aft while the steam pinnace passed a tow line to the bow. At 6.00pm the shrill sound of a bosun's whistle carried across the water, whereupon the Germans could be seen mustering aft. Von Mücke wrote: 'I made a short speech, and with three cheers for the Emperor, first in command, the war flag and pennant fluttered up to the masthead of his Majesty's latest ship, the schooner *Ayesha*.'[70] With that, the anchor was raised and the steam pinnace took *Ayesha* and the two cutters in tow. Von Mücke then climbed to the top of the foremast so that he could guide the pinnace around the shoals and reefs. Saunders wrote of their departure: 'As the ship's head turned round the officer in command mounted the rigging & taking off his helmet, gave the lead to his men for three hearty cheers, which were replied to as lustily by all on shore.'[71] At 6.15pm Saunders caught his last glimpse of *Ayesha* and the Germans, 'threading their way thru the narrow & intricate exit from the lagoon'. In the last rays of the setting sun he saw the tall figure of von Mücke, silhouetted against the sky, directing the movements of the pinnace. It was, he wrote, a 'scene to us at least who had witnessed the events of the day, indescribably moving.'

7

Rescue

At last the morning arrived. I don't think any one of us had any sleep. There was nothing to be seen of the "Sydney". Finally she appeared on the horizon towards midday. Never has an enemy been expected with such longing.

Matrose Nicolaus Mayer

The night of Monday, 9 November had also been one of uncertainty for those onboard *Emden*. Fregattenkapitän von Müller was unaware that his landing party had escaped, so continued to worry that if Kapitänleutnant von Mücke vigorously defended his position and inflicted casualties on *Sydney*'s landing party, the enemy might not be too keen on rendering assistance afterwards. Even if *Sydney*'s captain did fulfil his promise of help, a heavy swell could prevent rescue boats coming alongside *Emden*. It was thus a case of waiting for the dawn and hoping that Tuesday would bring salvation.

Leutnant Prinz von Hohenzollern recalled that each man made himself as comfortable as possible under a beautiful tropical night sky, 'with the particular sign of the southern hemisphere, the Southern Cross', watching over them.[1] Few got any real sleep. All were tormented by thirst and hunger, and their slumber was disturbed by the cries of the badly wounded and the warning shouts of the sentries when fires reignited.

It was much the same for those who had made it ashore. Matrose Lochau had a particularly restless night, plagued by mosquitoes, thoughts of the battle, and the constant moaning of Assistenzarzt Schwabe for water. Obermaschinistenmaat Jaguttis had a slightly better night, having spent the afternoon of 9 November assisting his comrades, collecting hammocks which had washed up, and looking for coconuts. On Tuesday morning he returned to the beach and found Schwabe and Torpedoobermaschinist Pyttlik. 'The latter was dead, and the former was carried by me and several others to our camping ground.'[2]

Morning rounds on *Emden* revealed that several of the injured had succumbed to their wounds during the night. Von Hohenzollern checked on one sailor who had been very badly burned during the action. 'The unfortunate man suffered frightful pain. It was over now.'[3] Another officer discovered men who had bled to death – and worse: 'In many parts of the ship we found carbonised bodies of men who had stood at their post to the last. We hoisted the distress signal and were anxiously looking for passing ships.'[4] The two-flag distress signal was displayed at the top of the mainmast in case *Sydney* did not return; it was hoped that the signal might attract the attention of a passing ship which would stop and rescue them.

There was also a renewed effort to make contact with the men on the beach. Von Müller considered using the *Buresk* boat, now riding the waves off *Emden*'s stern, but decided not to risk this precious resource. Once again they tried to float a line ashore, and when this failed Maschinistenmaat Harms volunteered to swim:

I had a thin signal halyard tied round me, but the weight and the length of it kept pulling me under. The men on board also noticed that it was entangled round a hammock which was drifting about in the water. This prevented me from getting any further, and I let go the line. I was now caught by the high surf and dashed backwards and forwards against the coral reefs, but with much exertion I managed to get into smooth water and was finally dragged ashore by Torpedooberheizer Maaß.[5]

Von Hohenzollern had meanwhile taken the opportunity to look for von Levetzow, and found him near the mainmast. His friend, identifiable only by a small metal Oberleutnant's star in the ashes, had been incinerated.[6]

It had been an equally long night for Captain Glossop. He tried to sleep, but there was much on his mind, and he thought that he might have got one good hour at best. Glossop rose at 5.15am and found the sea empty of ships and, disappointingly, land. He had wanted to arrive off Direction Island at first light, but it wasn't until 6.05am that land was sighted.[7]

Sydney, still towing the other *Buresk* lifeboat, reached Port Refuge at 8.00am, anchored, and then lowered two cutters with the armed landing party. According to Stoker James Kirby, the boats carried thirty-five men and two officers, and 'on nearing the landing stage the people from Cocos Island all gathered there & gave the armed party cheer after cheer'.[8] Superintendent Farrant was amongst those on the jetty, and he informed Lieutenant Commander Finlayson that *Emden*'s landing party had sailed the previous evening in the *Ayesha*. Farrant was promptly taken to *Sydney* so that he could make a full report to Glossop.

Farrant told Glossop that the telegraph cable to Perth had been cut, but his men had already re-established communications with Batavia, and it was thought that the cable to Rodrigues Island was also intact. Upon hearing that von Mücke's men had scuttled Farrant's work boat, Glossop offered him the *Buresk* lifeboat to help with cable repairs. Glossop then asked if he could borrow the company doctor to assist with the expected large number of *Emden* wounded. The super-intendent accepted the offer of the boat, and when he returned to shore put Glossop's request to Dr Ollerhead. Harold Ollerhead was more than willing to go, and two other company employees, Robert Cardwell and Frank Ross, also volunteered their services.[9]

At 8.45am, having confirmed that von Mücke's party had indeed escaped, Finlayson signalled to *Sydney*, 'There are no Germans here,' and added that he was coming off with the doctor and his two assistants.[10] The islanders had lavished drinks, cigarettes and coconuts

Sydney, anchored off Direction Island on the morning of 10 November. (*AWM P11611.037.001*)

on Finlayson's men, and as the boats pulled away they sang 'For they are Jolly Good Fellows' and 'God Save the King'. Kirby and the other oarsmen felt obliged to respond, so 'we laid on our oars & gave them three cheers'.[11]

The landing party began to re-embark at 9.30am, and thirty minutes later Glossop weighed anchor and set course for North Keeling. Shortly after departure Glossop cleared lower deck so that he could address the men. Shipwright White recalled:

> His words were to the effect that, we were gathered together to thank Almighty God for the victory vouchsafed to us. He thanked us one and all for the assistance given. He could not select anyone for special mention, but if there was one class he must speak about, it was the boys.[12]

Glossop acknowledged that some of the lads had only recently joined *Sydney*, but they had borne their baptism of fire coolly and had performed splendidly.

Surgeon Darby was meanwhile dealing with the wounded. After supervising the conversion of the sick bay into an operating theatre, he had Able Seaman Sharpe carried in: 'He had had a restless night and from his dyspnoea [laboured breathing] and the oozing of blood it was obvious that there was much blood in his pleural cavity. His colour was also bad, likewise his pulse.'[13] Surgeon Todd administered the chloroform and then Darby, assisted by Ollerhead, commenced the examination. This revealed that a metal fragment the size of a sixpence (19mm in diameter) had entered Sharpe's chest via the right armpit. It had 'tracked downwards and forwards to the left, through the pleural cavities, finally emerging through a large ragged hole just below the apex of the heart'. Darby wrote:

> A piece of the sixth rib had been carried away leaving a gaping wound. This wound was enlarged, a piece of the rib removed, and a search was made for bleeding points. This search could not be prolonged owing to the patient's condition, so I swabbed out the blood from the left pleural cavity and a considerable amount of gauze was inserted therein and a tight binder and pad then applied. The patient was removed to the only bed left in the sick bay and saline given subcutaneously.[14]

151

Darby then turned his attention to Lieutenant Hampden, who had multiple wounds. His left leg had been pierced by a shell fragment which left a 'jagged sinuous hole through the calf' just below the knee; his right calf was similarly pierced, 'leaving a large ragged hole, charred at the edges', with the fragment deep in the muscles. There was another deep hole in his right thigh, and numerous smaller wounds to his buttocks and back. Darby thought it unwise to cut and look for the shell fragments, 'because more harm than good would have been done', so cleaned, plugged and dressed the wounds, and had Hampden taken to his cabin.[15]

Due to the need to steam at slow speed while Darby performed his surgery, it was 11.10am before *Sydney* reached *Emden* – now seen to be flying a distress signal. The navigating officer, Lieutenant Pope, could not find a safe place to anchor close to *Emden*, so *Sydney* was stopped well clear of the reef while the cutters were lowered, then manoeuvred as required.[16] Lieutenants Bell-Salter and Garsia were in charge of the boats, and one was rowed across to *Emden*. Garsia wrote:

> *Sydney* stopped opposite *Emden* & lowered both cutters. I went in one of them to *Emden* with orders from the Captain to inform Captain von Müller that if he gave his parole, the Captain was prepared to take everybody off the *Emden* onboard the *Sydney* & take them straight to Colombo.[17]

As Garsia approached the stranded cruiser he noticed that her stern was very low in the water, and that there was a sizeable swell, but the rollers did not break until opposite a point well before the mainmast. He thought it possible that 'given a boat-rope from right aft' his cutter would be able to 'ride alongside the port side aft with the bow of the boat to seaward'. Nevertheless, the risk of the cutter being damaged by striking the spars and projections from the ship's side was great: 'However, in the lulls characteristic of a surf, boarding *Emden* was not difficult & willing hands hauled me up onto the Quarterdeck, where I was received by Captain von Müller in the presence of Lieutenant Witthoeft & others.'[18] It was fortuitous that von Müller, like many of his officers, could speak English, but when he received Glossop's message he questioned the meaning of the word parole. This was

Emden, viewed from *Sydney*'s quarterdeck on 10 November. One of *Sydney*'s cutters can be seen approaching *Emden*'s stern. (*Sea Power Centre-Australia*)

quickly sorted out. As von Müller understood it, Glossop was prepared to embark all of *Emden*'s surviving ship's company if he would give his word that none of them would commit a hostile act against *Sydney* while they were onboard.[19] At 11.45am Garsia signalled to *Sydney*, 'The Captain agrees to give parole. There are 150 including 30 wounded, 15 difficult cases.' Glossop replied, 'Start and bring over some wounded at once.'[20]

Garsia wanted to tranship the badly wounded first, but they needed to be strapped onto stretchers and lowered over the side. He therefore signalled to *Sydney* for some Neil-Robertson stretchers and a quantity of rope before allocating slightly wounded and unwounded men to his and Bell-Salter's cutters. Arrangements were also made for the *Buresk* lifeboat to be loaded with men and rowed to *Sydney*. Once unloaded, the boats were sent back with the stretchers and water.

Garsia found the Germans badly in need of water, so had the casks in the cutters hauled on deck and broached. Matrose Mayer was overjoyed by this thoughtful act. 'They brought water with them. We all got water to drink. Never has any drop of water been finer than this one.'[21] Garsia then took the opportunity to salute von Müller before remarking, 'You fought very well, sir.' Von Müller was taken aback, and replied, 'No.' Garsia walked away, but presently von Müller approached him and said: 'Thank you very much for saying that, but I was not satisfied. We should have done better. You were very lucky in shooting away all my voice-pipes at the beginning.'[22] Garsia left it at that, but was then told of the men on the island. At 12.20pm he signalled to *Sydney*, 'There are 20 men onshore, so what shall we do about them.' Glossop replied, 'Men onshore will have to wait until ship goes round the west side where the entrance of the lagoon is.'[23]

The return of the cutters with the Neil-Robertson stretchers allowed the first of the seriously wounded to be sent away at 12.47pm. Garsia admitted that it was a difficult task getting them into the boats:

When the officer (usually myself) watching for the rollers saw there was a lull he would give the word & the stretcher was lowered vertically over the side, to be seized at the foot by three of the [boat] crew ... and hauled into the boat. Unfortunately it was sometimes impossible to get some of the bad cases into the boat without causing them much suffering.[24]

Von Hohenzollern was impressed with the seamanship displayed by *Sydney*'s boat crews, and thought they showed 'great ability by keeping the boats in such a position that they were not dashed against the ship's side'.[25] Darby subsequently reported:

The transhipping was an exceedingly difficult and painful undertaking, as there was a large surf running on the beach where the *Emden* went ashore, and she was so much of a shambles that the shifting, collecting and lowering of the wounded into the boats was necessarily rough. They were hoisted on board us in cots and stretchers by means of davits, but there were no such appliances on the *Emden*.[26]

Initially, a boatload consisted of three badly wounded and six uninjured Germans. Later, by careful arrangement, four cot cases were taken in each cutter. The work of the boat crews in fending off, assisting the wounded and accommodating them in the pitching cutters wasn't made easier by the gruesome surroundings. Engine Room Artificer Dardel recalled: 'Good Lord, it was a sight I'll never forget ... There were bodies floating about in the water all round us, some with awful wounds, and sometimes you would see a leg or arm or head or something.'[27] The human flotsam would soon be claimed by the sharks. They had been frightened off by the shelling, but were now starting to return, hungry and inquisitive.

After the first boatloads of wounded had been sent away Garsia took the opportunity to look around the shattered warship:

> The whole of the ship abaft the mainmast is burnt right out, presenting a spectacle of gaping holes & torn & twisted iron. The remains of an officer almost completely incinerated [von Levetzow] were lying just abaft the mast. Progress along the fore & aft bridge was blocked by [the] after funnel which had fallen nearly vertically to port. The starboard waist was also blocked with wreckage. The port waist remained the only way open & progress along it was indescribably revolting. The fore bridge proved to be a mass of tangled & twisted iron, apparently inaccessible & no reason apparent to scale it. The Conning Tower & Forecastle appeared practically untouched & here a lot of men, wounded & unwounded were gathered. At this point the German Doctor approached me & asked me if I would signal for some morphia.[28]

Garsia readily agreed. He tried to signal *Sydney* from *Emden*'s forecastle, but received no response, so was forced to make his way aft again to make the request. The signal was then acknowledged, and resulted in the dispatch of Dr Ollerhead with a medical party. Ollerhead later told Darby that the scenes on *Emden* were truly awful:

> Men were lying killed and mutilated in heaps, with large blackened flesh wounds. One man had a horizontal section of the head taken off, exposing mangled brain tissue. The ship was riddled with gaping holes and it was with difficulty one could walk about the decks, and she was gutted by fire.[29]

Leading Seaman Newman found dead crewmen 'lying in all directions & positions'. In one corner of the port battery he saw 'a pile (pieces of humanity) covered up with coal bags ... The stench from the burnt & half burnt bodies was awful'.[30]

One *Sydney* officer, possibly Bell-Salter, wrote of a particularly shocking sight. An *Emden* sailor had been blasted against the side of a gun shield, 'and it was just as though the whole outline of a man had been pasted by a crude artist upon a black grey tablet'. He added, 'Limbs were everywhere, and one officer coming up from below was seen to stoop and throw the dismembered fragments of men overboard before giving orders.'[31] Stoker Arthur Johnstone encountered von Hohenzollern, who pointed to von Levetzow's burnt body on the poop deck, and said, 'My friend there he officer.' Johnstone recalled:

> The body – at least skeleton – he pointed to had once been an officer. His two shin bones showed that both feet had been shot away, one arm was missing and the hand of the other arm was missing. I expect he had fallen there when wounded and had been unable to get away, and so had been burnt to death.[32]

Kingsford-Smith didn't board *Emden*, but he heard harrowing tales from those who did:

> The decks were simply strewn with heads, arms & legs & were simply swimming with blood. All the guns were out of action & around some, whole gun crews had been blown to bits, & pieces of them were splattered on the gun mechanism ... Down below the officers' quarters & Captain's Cabin were simply unrecognisable, being shot to pieces & pieces of bodies were scattered everywhere.[33]

Sydney had fired 670 rounds of 6in shell, most of them common Lyddite, and a good number had detonated on or inside *Emden*. Glossop later reported that had he known the appalling effect these high-explosive shells had on exposed personnel he 'might have left her after the first half hour'.[34] The wounded now being embarked in *Sydney*, wrote Todd, were a piteous sight:

> They had lain for over twenty-four hours with no water and scarcely any attention, for the *Emden*'s fresh water tanks had been badly holed.

Survivors gather on *Emden*'s poop deck as the *Buresk* lifeboat pulls away from the burnt-out stern. The No. 4 and 5 port guns remain on their final forward bearings, and a large shell hole can be seen in the hull just below the crumpled third funnel. (*Western Australian Museum*)

As they came aboard they were laid in rows along the waist and starboard passage, for the sick-bay and wardroom were already full. Some had arms and legs shot off short, some were riddled with holes, and two had their faces gone.[35]

Darby was equally shocked by their condition, noting that their wounds were nearly all foul, putrid, and crawling with maggots.[36] In cases where large blood vessels of the arm or leg had been opened, 'we found tourniquets or pieces of spun yarn, or a handkerchief or a piece of cloth bound round the limb above the injury':

In some cases, I believe the majority, they had been put on by the patients themselves. One man told me he had put one on his arm himself. They were all in severe pain from the constriction and in all cases where amputation was required the presence of these tourniquets made it necessary to amputate much higher than one would otherwise have done. But no doubt their lives had been saved by the tourniquets.[37]

157

Matrose Paul Engel had an injury to his right leg and a deep chest wound. Someone had tied a kimono in a knot, plugged the wound with it, and kept it in place by tying a piece of cord around his chest.[38]

Darby also saw men who were burnt from head to foot, one was deaf and dumb, and several were stone deaf in addition to other injuries:

> The worst sight was a poor fellow who had his face literally blown away. His right eye, nose, and most of both cheeks were missing. His mouth and lips were unrecognisable. The tongue, pharynx, and nasal cavity were exposed, part of his lower jaw was [gone] and the soft tissues were severed from the neck under his chin, so that the face really consisted of two curtains of soft tissue hanging loosely from the forehead, with a gap in the centre, like an advanced case of rodent ulcer [skin cancer].[39]

The wound was also stinking and foul, 'with copious discharge'. The unfortunate man was Matrose Heinrich Sellmeyer. Darby wrote that the case was so bad he immediately administered a large dose of morphia, and after cleaning and dressing the wound, had the patient removed to the upper deck to die. Darby was amazed when he was later seen to get up and walk around. The miracle was short-lived, and as there was no chance of him surviving, Sellmeyer was given a larger dose of morphia.

Darby discovered another facial injury that was just as bad. 'Practically the whole right side of the face was completely blown away. His temporal, pterygoid, and maxillary regions were deeply exposed and the temporo-mandibular articulation was entirely removed.' Darby heard that *Emden*'s doctor had given up hope for the man, and was not going to send him to *Sydney* until Ollerhead insisted on his evacuation. Ollerhead's intervention saved Johann Plotha's life.[40]

The main problem with the wounded was where to put them all. Darby later confessed, 'I was at my wit's end ... I had no beds [&] no blankets for many of the poor devils.'[41] Although the wardroom was already full with *Sydney*'s wounded, he managed to squeeze in six Germans. One of them was Matrose Mayer:

We were received with the greatest respect. I myself was put into the wardroom which had been transformed into a hospital. Here too were berthed the wounded of the *Sydney*. We were at once properly bandaged and were well treated as far as circumstances allowed ... next to me lay a sailor of the *Sydney*, he had his right foot blown away. He bent himself towards me and gave me his hand.[42]

Nicolaus Mayer shook hands with Richard Horne. This and other examples of humanity prompted Dardel to write that the Germans 'were all very decent chaps & our own men made friends with men whom they were trying to kill 24 hours before'.[43] The bed crisis was eased slightly at 3.00pm when Sharpe died, freeing up the cot in the sick bay.[44]

Garsia and Bell-Salter had meanwhile returned to *Sydney*, having been relieved on *Emden* by Lieutenant Cavaye and Gunner McFarlane.[45] At 3.55pm *Sydney* signalled to Cavaye, 'How many more are there to come over.' He replied, '50 after this boat load.' At 4.12pm Glossop had another signal sent to *Emden*, addressed to von Müller. It read, 'I am sending whaler for you.' Cavaye responded, 'Captain would like to burn a little of the deck with dead bodies on & would rather come off in last boat.'[46] Von Müller was permitted to light his funeral pyre but Glossop, no doubt aware of the state of the cutters after carrying so many wounded, insisted on sending a clean boat for him.

Cavaye should have kept a closer watch on von Müller, as he had an ulterior motive for wanting to light a fire on the upper deck. According to von Hohenzollern, other fires were surreptitiously lit below decks, near the partially flooded forward magazines. It was hoped that the fires would spread, touch off the magazines, and blow *Emden* to pieces.[47] Von Müller wrote: 'I was the last to leave the ship; before doing so I had, with the help of a few of the officers, petty officers, and crew, fired the forward part of the ship in the 'tween-decks and the battery deck, after pouring over it turpentine and oil'.[48] Von Müller's arrival on *Sydney* at 4.55pm aroused considerable interest. One eyewitness recalled:

When von Müller came aboard Captain Glossop saluted him. Von Müller seemed momentarily at a loss as to know what to do. However, he stood erect and returned the salute and then shook hands – not a word was spoken. They both turned around and Glossop, with his arm on von Müller's shoulder, guided him below to our captain's quarters down the hatchway.[49]

Todd described the German captain as a 'tall, fair, blue-eyed, sparsely built man of pleasant mien, but his manner and bearing clearly showed traces of his awful experiences':

> All through the action he had remained in the conning tower with fires all around, his men rapidly falling, and his ship being battered under his feet; and then he came aboard the *Sydney* up her starboard after gangway to find his enemy apparently undamaged for no shell had landed near this part of the ship at all.[50]

Glossop took von Müller to his cabin, where he was to be accommodated, so that he could wash and put on clean clothes. Matrose Werner later discovered that *Sydney*'s captain gave up his day cabin for von Müller, and that Glossop had shifted into his sea cabin on the bridge – 'the gesture of a perfect gentleman'.[51] Von Hohenzollern described similar treatment for himself and the other officers:

> We washed in the officers' bathroom, put on fresh underclothes and tropical uniforms, which had been placed at our disposal by the English officers, and then received a hearty supper. How good it tasted can be imagined when I say that we had been hungry for 35 hours. Still better was the well-cooled beer.[52]

Just before sunset Ordinary Signalman Arnold Mellor saw von Müller on *Sydney*'s quarterdeck: 'He was obviously suffering great mental anguish and fatigue. Turning aft, he went and rested himself against the ensign staff, and after gazing at the *Emden* in the distance, buried his face in his hands.'[53] *Sydney* was at this time about a mile and a half to the west of *Emden*. Earlier that afternoon the survivors on shore were signalled to move around to the western side of the island, where they would be picked up. 'Unfortunately', wrote Garsia, 'they went the wrong way,' so when *Sydney* reached the intended recovery position there was no sign of the Germans. It was decided to land a signal party in *Sydney*'s gig, and Leutnant Schall and several of his men in the *Buresk* lifeboat. When these two parties safely reached shore Garsia was ordered to follow in the whaler. By this time it was quite dark, and he thought that getting ashore would be 'almost a matter of luck':

> When halfway in a big roller broke right over the boat, filling her with water. Petty Officer Newham just as this happened let go the anchor & paid out the grapnel, undoubtedly saving the boat from being broached to. Unfortunately the rocks stove in some of the timbers. The bowman soon had the painter [rope] ashore which was taken round a coconut tree & with the help of hands ashore the boat was dragged up high & dry.[54]

In the middle of this drama the *Buresk* lifeboat was seen pulling away from the beach with a load of survivors; amongst them was Lochau.

Exhausted, sunburnt, and desperately thirsty, Lochau barely understood what was happening to him. He was aware that fellow Germans had rescued him, and that they had brought water, but his mind couldn't process the sequence of events which culminated in his deliverance. Lochau's arrival onboard *Sydney* was equally confusing to him:

> I have vivid recollections of dozens of eyes staring just at me ... Then an officer, apparently becoming aware of my helplessness, got hold of my arm and indicated the direction in which I was to proceed along the deck, where guards formed a passage on each side.[55]

Lochau was received by his comrades, given a blanket, and allocated a place in a row of sleeping men. Nourished by a mug of tea with a dash of brandy, he quickly fell into a deep slumber. That night Heinrich Sellmeyer drifted off into eternal sleep.

Garsia was under the impression that there were no badly wounded Germans on North Keeling, but at 7.12pm he received a signal from *Sydney*, instructing him to send two of his best hands to assist an injured man along. This man was apparently trying to reach Garsia's position from the direction of *Emden*'s wreck. A short time later Garsia was informed that there were two wounded survivors on the western side of the island, so he signalled *Sydney* that he was prepared to stay ashore for the night. He then took three men and commenced a clockwise sweep of the shoreline. They encountered two of Schall's men on the northern side of the atoll, who reported that there were four wounded on the beach near *Emden*. Garsia instructed one of his men to return to the whaler with the two Germans, and then continued on with Able Seamen Jones and Warburton.

Forced to detour around the lagoon, the trio spent several hours wading through knee-deep water and pushing through thick scrub infested with roosting birds before Garsia conceded that he was lost. Taking a bearing on a star, they headed due south and eventually found their landing place and a welcoming campfire. After ascertaining that *Sydney* would pick them up in the morning, Garsia, Jones and Warburton joined the sleeping forms on the sand around the fire.[56]

After recovering his gig and the *Buresk* lifeboat, Glossop ordered that *Sydney* be steamed very slowly to the north to give Darby a more stable ship for his surgery. Operations had commenced at 6.00pm Tuesday, and continued until 4.30am Wednesday. The first case was Matrose Adolf Kunkel, whose right foot had been almost severed by a shell splinter. Darby wrote that the German surgeon, Dr Luther, assisted by Ollerhead, and with Todd as anaesthetist, amputated the leg midway between the knee and the ankle. The second case was 19-year-old Ordinary Seaman Meldrum, who had been waiting a day and a half in considerable pain for his surgery. According to Darby:

> This boy had over thirteen separate shell wounds, most of them very severe. They involved the right thigh, buttock, leg, and foot. Both bones were fractured two inches above the ankle and in addition there was a large area blown out of his left groin, exposing the femoral vessels and spermatic cord. It looked at first as though we would have to amputate, but we decided to give him a chance, and after cleaning up the wound with soap and water, hydrogen-peroxide and iodine, and removing the metal accessible, iodoform drains were inserted and the leg put up in a back and side splint.[57]

It took Darby and Ollerhead two hours to complete the work, after which Meldrum was placed in the Commander's cabin with a personal carer. By this stage Luther was so fatigued that he broke four syringes without successfully giving a hypodermic injection, so was sent away to rest. Darby, Ollerhead and Todd then operated on Able Seaman Butcher. He had a shell wound in his back 'the size of a half crown, just below the last rib on the left side'.[58]

> Earlier in the day he had retention of urine and a catheter was passed drawing off almost pure blood, so evidently the fragment had lodged in, or passed through, the kidney. The patient had had a good deal of pain and haemorrhage, but apart from a pale colour he was very fit.[59]

Darby tried to find the shell fragment with a probe, but even after enlarging the wound could not locate it. Fearing he might carry infection deeper into the wound if he kept cutting, Darby decided to insert a drain and wait a few days to see if Butcher's condition improved.

Surgery was suspended at 12.30am because the assisting sick berth ratings were exhausted and had to be sent to bed. Darby, Ollerhead and Todd rested for thirty minutes then, with the help of three volunteers, cleaned and restocked the theatre before recommencing operations. The next case was Feuerwerksmaat Heinrich Steinfurth, whose right leg was mutilated and fractured below the knee. The wound, wrote Darby, was horribly offensive and alive with maggots, gangrene had set in, and infection was spreading up the veins to the thigh:

> There was a tourniquet round his leg just above the knee, and though the man must have lost a good deal of blood, his condition was very fair considering all things. Under chloroform it was decided to amputate above the knee ... [60]

Darby had difficulty finding the large arteries, as they did not bleed freely on loosening the tourniquet, but the surgery went reasonably well and a satisfactory stump was obtained. At 4.00am Steinfurth was put to bed in the sick bay with two German sailors watching over him, but he began to kick the stump about on coming to, and had to be tied down. Darby gave Steinfurth a large dose of morphia then 'retired to rest after a cup of Bovril at 4.30 am':

> No sooner was I in bed than I was called up to the sick bay to this case, and found him pulseless. Strychnine was administered and heart massage and artificial respiration tried without success. It was most disappointing and I was unable to decide whether he had died from shock or from morphia poisoning.[61]

Darby thought that it might have been the latter, as he had had disappointing results with previous patients, and had increased the dose for Steinfurth.

Sydney returned to North Keeling at 5.45am and lowered a cutter with a party to assist Garsia before proceeding to Direction Island to land Ollerhead and his assistants.[62] Darby instructed his sick berth staff to tend the less seriously injured while he thanked Ollerhead for his help and saw him off:

> I cannot lay too much stress on the great assistance so generously afforded by the Eastern Extension Co's Surgeon. He was always cheery and energetic throughout the 24 hours he was with us and he kindly left behind some instruments, lotions, and dressings, which were most useful to me in after treatment.[63]

Sydney departed Direction Island for North Keeling at 8.30am, but stopped again twenty minutes later for the burial at sea of Steinfurth and Sellmeyer 'in accordance with British customs', and in the presence of *Emden*'s ship's company.[64]

When *Sydney* reached North Keeling at 9.45am, von Müller was disappointed to see *Emden* still intact. He now had to rely on the sea to destroy his ship, and took comfort in the fact that occasionally waves could be seen breaking over the poop deck: 'The ship was lying with two-thirds of her length actually on the reef. The heavings and concussion caused by the swell to the after-part of the ship were so violent that it seemed as if she must break in two in a comparatively short time.'[65] *Sydney* steamed past the wreck and stopped off the western side of the island at 10.00am to recover the boats and Garsia's party.

Garsia had woken just after dawn on Wednesday, and set off a short time later with all but three of his men to collect the wounded Germans reported near *Emden*'s wreck. They took an improvised stretcher and a quantity of coconuts. Leutnant Schall was with the wounded, and upon Garsia's arrival he eagerly seized the coconuts and cut them open for their milk. He told Garsia that the wounded had been crying to him for water all night. Schall then showed him where Schwabe lay. Garsia was informed that he had died the previous afternoon when, very thirsty, he insisted on the men giving him salt water to drink, 'after which he went insane & died in a terrible state':

> As soon as the four wounded had been refreshed with coconut milk, one was placed on the stretcher & sent back & another could walk between two men. While waiting for two stretchers to be sent from *Sydney* I went along [the] beach to a point opposite *Emden*. The shore, in addition to wreckage, had some half-a-dozen dead bodies lying washed up. These were covered up as best we could. A species of red land crab with which the ground is infested in hundreds, made this the least we could do.[66]

The cutter sent ashore from *Sydney* at 6.00am was under the command of Bell-Salter. It carried water, hot chocolate and stretchers, and shortly after landing, Bell-Salter had the latter taken to Garsia, who wrote:

> The stretchers now arrived & some very welcome hot cocoa, which after the wounded had had their fill, was not unwelcome to those who had been ashore for the night – Lieut Schall in particular. Telling off 4 men per stretcher to work in reliefs, we started back for the landing place.[67]

One of the stretcher cases was Bootsmannsmaat Ruscinski who, besides his shattered arm, had a large wound to his left thigh. He had also lost a great deal of blood, and the odds of him surviving the journey to *Sydney* were not good.

Upon reaching the landing point Garsia was pleased to see that Bell-Salter had worked out how to get nearly everyone off in the one seaworthy boat at their disposal. The wounded were carefully loaded into the cutter, and with several able-bodied men clinging to the outside, it was rowed to a point beyond the surf. A long rope trailed back to the whaler, which Garsia and four men now launched before clambering in. The cutter took up the slack, pulled the slowly sinking whaler safely through the surf, and then the men hanging onto the outside of the boat were helped in. Signalman Seabrook claimed that the exercise was not without its humour:

> Garsia was clad only in a shirt; he had given up all the rest of his clothing for bandages, slings, etc for the *Emden*'s wounded. His return to the *Sydney* in the bow of the boat, where the wind played all sorts of tricks with his shirt, gave the sailors a great deal of amusement.[68]

The hoisting of the boats commenced at 10.00am; thirty-five minutes later *Sydney* got underway and set course for Colombo. Having recovered all of the surviving *Emden* officers and men, a head count of the prisoners was then undertaken. There were eleven officers (including von Müller), one surgeon, eight warrant officers, and 180 men. Of these, one officer (Marine-Ingenieur Stoffers) was dangerously wounded, and thirty-eight men were seriously wounded. Another six officers and thirty-two men were injured to a lesser degree.[69]

The men were found places on *Sydney*'s boat deck while the officers were accommodated in the flat outside the wardroom. According to Todd, 'To those who were badly wounded our people gave up cabins.'[70] At 10.50am the Germans were given a jarring reminder of how they came to be captives on an enemy ship. *Sydney*'s aft and starboard guns had been loaded on the afternoon of 9 November, but the order to cease fire was given before they could be discharged. Glossop now had the guns fired to clear them. The deafening roar silenced all conversation, and the acrid smell of burnt cordite caused many to recall the horrors of the battle.

One of the German officers discussed the action with Garsia, and alleged that *Sydney* had fired on the white flag. Garsia disputed the claim:

> I at once took the matter up, and the torpedo lieutenant [von Hohenzollern] and an engineer both said emphatically, 'No, that is not so; you did not fire on the white flag.' But we did not leave it at that. One of us went to the captain, and he got from Captain von Müller an assurance that we had done nothing of the kind, and that he intended to assemble his officers and tell them so.[71]

Sydney's honour was restored.

Marine-Ingenieur Stoffers died at 1.00pm on 11 November. In addition to the burns and wounds to his chest and head, he had been suffering from pneumonia for six weeks. Von Hohenzollern heard that he 'could not take food, and his breathing became steadily worse. He died fully conscious ... having been served faithfully up to his death by his servant Dehorn.'[72] August Stoffers was buried at sea at 2.06pm.

The wounded from North Keeling placed an additional strain on *Sydney*'s medical staff. Darby had been working through the morning in anticipation of their arrival. Much of his time was taken up with Able Seaman Horne. He admitted that this and many other cases should have been done much earlier, but it would have taken at least six fully manned operating theatres to have dealt with them. As for Horne:

> This Able Seaman had the distal half of his left foot shattered by a bursting shell. Besides [this] there were numerous fragments buried in the tissues of the left leg and thigh. The outer side of the sole of the right foot was furrowed down to the metatarsals, and one toe was carried away. With Surgeon Todd as anaesthetist and S.B.S. Mullins as assistant we cleaned up the wounds, which were by now quite offensive, with hydrogen-peroxide, alcohol and iodine, removing metal where possible, and draining the wounds. The left foot was amputated at the transverse tarsal articulation, sufficient sound tissue having been obtained from the sole to make quite a satisfactory covering. The case took some time owing to the number and state of the wounds.[73]

The next case was Able Seaman Gascoigne. This time Luther performed the duties of anaesthetist, and Todd assisted Darby. Gascoigne had a hole in his left buttock, another in his left hand, numerous small shell wounds in his right leg, and a shocking eye injury. A tiny steel splinter had entered his right eye through the upper lid, carrying a minute fragment of bone into the eye and disintegrating it. Darby wanted to leave the surgery to a specialist in Colombo, but the eye became inflamed and swollen, and a large amount of pus collected in the orbit, so he decided to remove the organ:

> On account of the antiquity of the Service eye instruments it was impossible to remove the eye through the optic nerve, so I had to be

content with cutting away the anterior portion of the globe, syringing out with weak antiseptic, and draining the orbit with Iodoform gauze. This temporary treatment saved any spread of the infection to the meninges, and the patient did well.[74]

Darby then operated on a German sailor with a mutilated left forearm:

Bellies of muscle had herniated through the skin, and both large [blood] vessels had been severed. A tourniquet placed on the lower third of the arm had saved the patient from bleeding to death, but necessitated amputation of the arm.[75]

According to Dardel, the patient was a 'poor little boy', about seventeen years of age, and it was quite obvious that he didn't want his arm removed: 'The German doctor told him he'd die if he didn't have it off, and so he wouldn't see his mother again. The boy looked for a while and then said, "Take it off. I want to see Mother again."'[76] The patient was August Benthien. Darby reported that he 'refused operation at first, but eventually consented on the advice of his messmates and the German surgeon'. With Luther again acting as anaesthetist, and with Sick Berth Steward Mullins assisting, Darby performed a circular amputation of Benthien's upper left arm.[77]

Bootsmannsmaat Ruscinski was the next to go under the knife. Darby described this case as similar to the previous, only his forearm was even more damaged. Assisted by Todd, Darby performed a circular amputation in the middle of the left arm. The surgery proved difficult, 'owing to the great muscular development of the arm', but a satisfactory stump was obtained which healed well. Darby took a personal interest in Ruscinski, made inquiries, and wrote:

He had managed to get a tourniquet placed round his arm and was later blown overboard. He succeeded in swimming ashore through the surf and was brought off to this ship after being ashore for 40 hours. Besides the above injury he had a large septic flesh wound of the left thigh ... By the time he got to us all his wounds were in a shocking condition, and were crawling with large maggots. The patient was weak from loss of blood and exposure, and his life was saved on shore by our party who gave him coconut milk through the night. His constitution was wonderful and his stature and physique were magnificent. He appears to have been the only man on the upper deck saved.[78]

The person credited with saving Ruscinski's life on North Keeling was Boy 1st Class John Payling. He was the only one nimble enough to climb the palms to obtain the coconuts. Shipwright White stated that the 16-year-old came back from the island with his chest, arms and legs 'skinned through his efforts in climbing coconut palms to obtain the nuts for drink for the wounded'.[79]

Darby reported that the remainder of 11 November was occupied 'cleaning up and dressing wounds and putting up fractures, most of them under anaesthesia'. He went to bed at midnight, having worked for over forty hours without sleep.[80]

Emden survivors onboard the transport *Armadale*, which took them from Colombo to Australia for internment; Joseph Ruscinski is sitting on the right, with Adolf Kunkel in the centre. (*AWM P05194.009*)

8

Prisoners

The feeling that we were prisoners of war was repugnant,
but the English officers took every trouble to mitigate our
position and make us for a time forget it. They brought us
book, cigars and cigarettes.

Leutnant zur See Prinz von Hohenzollern

Sydney's ship's company spent the afternoon of 11 November cleaning
the guns, tidying up, and attending to the needs of the wounded.
Captain Glossop was also kept busy, but found time to write his diary
entries for this and the previous day. *Sydney*, he wrote, had 'wounded
lying about everywhere & very little for them to lie on in most cases',
and was 'not a fighting unit in any sense'.[1]

That *Sydney* could not clear her decks for action if required was a
major concern, and had prompted a request for assistance on 10
November. The following day Vice Admiral Jerram advised Navy Office
in Melbourne of *Sydney*'s signal, and his response. 'In compliance with
request of *Sydney* 10th November, for Medical Assistance Cocos Island,
Empress of Asia is on her way there and will arrive 14th November.'[2]
Jerram knew there was no longer any real threat to the convoy because
he had been informed that *Königsberg* was blockaded up the Rufiji
River in German East Africa. He nevertheless ordered *Hampshire* and
Empress of Russia to join the escort. *Empress of Russia* was subsequently instructed to rendezvous with *Sydney*, and *Melbourne* was
ordered to proceed independently to Colombo, leaving *Ibuki* to
shepherd the convoy until *Hampshire* arrived (on 13 November).[3]

Thursday, 12 November dawned with *Sydney*'s below deck passages
and upper deck crowded with prisoners and wounded. One man did
not live to see the day; at 5.45am Heizer Emil Scheller succumbed to
his wounds. Surgeon Todd attended his committal to the deep four
hours later, and was quite moved by the experience:

The ship was hove to, and the body, sewn in a hammock and weighted, was covered with the German flag. Then all hands mustered aft, the Chaplain read the burial service and while the buglers sounded the Last Post the body was lowered into the sea.[4]

The burials also affected Fregattenkapitän von Müller. Todd noted that for a couple of days he scarcely spoke, but stood right aft and gazed out to sea. 'This was the end of all his striving – his ship gone, his men mostly dead or wounded and himself a prisoner of war.'[5]

Surgeon Darby, for his part, was still trying to save the lives and limbs of von Müller's men. One in particular, Oberleutnant Geerdes, was being carefully watched for infection as he had two serious wounds:

He had his right cheek turned down as a flap from the level of the upper lip, in addition the mandible was fractured and a piece of skin, fascia and muscle the size of a large plate was blown clean out of the middle of the anterior surface of the left thigh.[6]

According to Chaplain Little, the surgeons 'extracted a piece of either coal or charred wood the size of a cherry' from his broken lower jaw.[7] Darby was more worried about the thigh wound, which was so bad that Marine-Stabsarzt Luther wanted to remove the leg: 'But though there was much destruction of tissue, and the wound was very foul, I refused to allow him to do so, and after events proved the wisdom of this, as the wound cleaned up and the limb was saved.'[8]

Sydney was now maintaining a steady 16 knots as she steered a northwesterly course towards Colombo. By midday the ship was 428 miles south of the equator, and the weather, which had been fine and hot, was becoming muggy and unsettled. With rain threatening, Glossop ordered the canvas awnings to be rigged to give the prisoners on the upper deck some protection from the elements. At 1.30pm there was a torrential downpour, causing Glossop to write that the awnings proved useless against tropical rain, which also increased the humidity: 'Tea at 3.45, a terribly wet hot day, the damp tropical heat & the smell from the wounded most nauseating. Walked on bridge for an hour, had a talk with various gunlayers, walked around the deck with Darby.'[9]

Glossop told Darby that *Sydney* was scheduled to meet *Empress of Russia* the next morning, and that the *Buresk* crew and a number of the prisoners were to be transferred to her for passage to Colombo. Priority was to be given to the wounded, so that night Darby and Luther sorted out which cases they would send off.[10]

While the two surgeons decided who would go and who would stay, Glossop, von Müller and Lieutenant Rahilly attempted to reconstruct the movements of *Sydney* and *Emden* on the morning of 9 November. Glossop wrote in his diary that he and von Müller were 'getting on splendidly', but plotting the courses of the two ships during the action was proving 'most difficult'.[11]

At 11.27pm *Sydney*'s lookouts sighted *Empress of Asia*. The two ships had been in wireless communication during the day, and the auxiliary cruiser was now instructed to take station close on *Sydney*'s starboard beam so that messages could be exchanged by signal lamp. *Empress of Asia* complied, and then signalled, 'Hearty congratulations for ridding the sea of that ship. Hope the captain was saved and that the wounded are doing well.' Glossop was unimpressed with the execution of the signal, and responded with, 'Your deck signalling is disgraceful,' before having the following sent:

> *Emden* an utter total wreck very inaccessible on North Keeling Island. Sanitary conditions will render her unapproachable for some time ... Her wireless gear and torpedoes might be examined and form useful information. Be prepared for a shocking sight.[12]

Chastised for her poor signalling, but warned of the likely state of *Emden*, *Empress of Asia* then turned away and set course for Cocos.

The ship Glossop really wanted to meet up with appeared at 6.35am on 13 November. *Sydney* reduced speed, and at 8.25am *Empress of Russia* took station two cables (405yds) off her starboard beam. Both ships stopped at 10.05am, and shortly thereafter the transhipment of five *Emden* officers, four warrant officers (all wounded), sixty-six men (most of them wounded), and eighteen Chinese seamen ex-*Buresk* began.[13] Fortunately the sea was calm, but it still took the best part of two hours to transfer everyone in ship's boats. Darby wrote: 'We sent over all the cases who could walk and about 25 to 30 cot cases. But for the fact that we had to wait for our cots to be returned in order to send over more patients, the work would have been finished much quicker.'[14] Darby, having been informed that the auxiliary cruiser had two surgeons but only one sick berth attendant, decided to keep back all of *Sydney*'s wounded and the severest of the Germans. Von Müller was to remain onboard as Glossop's guest.

Matrose Mayer was one of the cot cases. When he was lowered into a lifeboat he was surprised to find three armed French sailors in charge of it. Their animosity towards him, a sworn enemy, was obvious. *Empress of Russia*'s crew was part British but mostly French, and Mayer correctly guessed that he and his comrades would receive no favours from the French matelots:

> After some difficult manoeuvring, we got alongside the *Empress of Russia* ... I was hoisted on top with the boat and put over the side. I was quietened down a little when English sailors noticed me. The usual handshake of the English sailor shows his good heartedness. Only those three Frenchmen bore testimony that we were enemies. They received defenceless wounded with side arms in their hands.[15]

The last of the selected men were sent off just before midday, at which point *Sydney* got underway, leaving the auxiliary cruiser to recover her boats and follow. *Empress of Russia* caught up with the Australian cruiser at 3.00pm and took station off her starboard beam.

Glossop and Darby were pleased with the outcome. Although they still had over a hundred prisoners onboard, there was more space for them, and both officers were able to get on with their duties. That afternoon Glossop started writing up his official Letter of Proceedings, and began reading the action and after-action reports of his officers and warrant officers.[16] Darby was able to devote more time to the cleaning up and the care of the wounded. A fresh supply of blankets had been obtained from *Empress of Russia*, allowing *Sydney*'s bedding and blankets, now 'horribly filthy, foul, and offensive', to be thrown overboard. Darby then began removing dressings and examining the wounds of the earlier cases.[17]

At 8.00pm Glossop had *Sydney*'s position, course and speed transmitted to *Hampshire*, *Melbourne* and *Orvieto*, adding that

British and French ratings on *Empress of Russia* carry away a wounded *Emden* sailor. Another German, strapped into a Neil-Robertson stretcher, waits in the lifeboat. (*Author's collection*)

Empress of Russia was in company. He went to bed two hours later, but had another disturbed night; woken at 2.00am, he couldn't get back to sleep, so got up and waited for the dawn. After breakfast

Glossop applied himself to letter writing, and in the afternoon he completed the track chart of the action, believing he had 'finally got it fairly accurate'.[18]

At 4.00pm on 14 November Glossop sent a wireless message to *Orvieto*, requesting her midday position, course and speed, so as to enable him to plot the current position of the convoy. The requested information was provided by Captain Gordon-Smith, who had taken charge of the convoy following *Hampshire*'s departure with thirteen transports the previous morning.[19] Gordon-Smith, realising that *Sydney* would overhaul his slow-moving convoy later that night or in the morning, added, 'We should be glad if you would pass between our lines with your crew on deck.' Glossop understood that Gordon-Smith wished *Sydney* to be cheered by the troops as she passed through the lines of transports, but was sensitive to the feelings of von Müller and his men; he replied: 'Thank you very much indeed but we would rather there was no demonstration on account of all the wounded & prisoners onboard. If you kindly agree to this I will steam between 1st & 2nd Divisions.'[20] Gordon-Smith responded, 'Quite agreeable to your suggestion. Was under the impression prisoners transferred to *Empress of Russia*. Orders issued no demonstration.'[21]

The lights of the convoy were sighted at 3.15am on 15 November, whereupon *Empress of Russia* took station astern of *Sydney*. Fifty-five minutes later they drew level with the rear of the convoy and were challenged by one of the transports. In reply to 'What ship', *Sydney* signalled '*Sydney* and *Empress of Russia*'. It was a very dark night, and Glossop decided to steam down the starboard side of the convoy rather than risk a collision by passing through it. At 4.40am he signalled to *Orvieto*, 'Regret I must pass in the dark in order to be in [Colombo] in time.' The convoy flagship responded with a message from Major General Bridges. 'From GOC to Captain. On behalf of all Australian Imperial Force I heartily congratulate you on the service you have rendered by your successful action.' Glossop replied, 'Thank you very much.'[22]

It took *Sydney* over an hour to reach *Euripides* at the head of the convoy, at which point Glossop sent a personal message to Lieutenant Robert Massie, Adjutant of the 4th Australian Infantry Battalion. It read, 'Hope you are alright.' Glossop knew the young officer's influential parents, and had been a guest at their home in Sydney on numerous occasions. At 7.10am Glossop received a congratulatory message from Captain Kato. Glossop knew that if *Ibuki* had been on the port side of the convoy on 9 November, she would have been the ship ordered to the Cocos Islands. In which case, in all likelihood, they would now be celebrating a Japanese victory. Glossop humbly replied, 'Many thanks. The fortune of war fell to me.'[23]

Sydney and *Empress of Russia* pushed on at 16 knots and reached Colombo three hours later. Glossop waited at the breakwater for the pilot, but when one failed to appear he took *Sydney* into the crowded harbour. Major James McCarroll, of the Auckland Mounted Rifles, was on the New Zealand transport *Star of India*, and witnessed her arrival:

> About 10.30 HMAS *Sydney* came in and passed close to us. We all stood to attention and no cheering. We could see all the German prisoners onboard, it must have been a sight for them to see what they missed. The shot holes in the *Sydney* were plainly seen, so they had something to show.[24]

Leading Seaman Newman noticed that nearly every ship in the harbour had hoisted a signal of congratulation, and despite the request that there be no cheering, the troops on one transport gave voice to their jubilation 'after the ice had been broken' by the crew of a merchant ship.[25] Mayer, onboard *Empress of Russia*, was annoyed by the cheering, but astonished to see so many ships:

> The harbour was full with men-of-war as well as merchant ships. The names of the men-of-war were *Hampshire*, *Melbourne*, Russian cruiser *Askold*, a few older ships, a Japanese armoured cruiser and to these were added the *Sydney* besides some 30–35 transport vessels with Australian troops ... They made a big noise as we entered. They had good cause to as the way was now free. We wished them God Speed and soon a meeting with German infantry.[26]

Todd heard similar comments from the prisoners on *Sydney*. One, seeing Australian and New Zealand troops for the first time, remarked,

'Poor wretches, they will all soon be killed. They will never stand up to our Prussians.' Others were amazed by the sheer size of the troop convoy, which was visible on the horizon, and expressed disgust that *Emden* had missed such a prize target. According to Todd, they kept saying, 'If only we could have got amongst them with our torpedoes!'[27]

Darby wrote that by this time the wounded in his care were in a fairly clean condition, though most of their wounds were 'more or less septic'. *Sydney* was filthy and stank. This, he reported, was due to the foul wounds and the hot damp climate, which increased the rate of decomposition of dead tissue. 'We arrived Colombo 10.00am Sunday morning, and after much delay from the shore the Military took over the wounded, depositing them in the Military Hospital till that was full, and then sent the overflow to the Civil Hospital.'[28] Darby sent Engineer Lieutenant Commander Coleman, Lieutenant Hampden, eight *Sydney* ratings, and nine of *Emden*'s wounded ashore for admission to hospital.[29] Von Müller and the remaining prisoners were then transferred to *Empress of Russia*, pending their dispersal to other ships for onwards passage to Malta.

The perfect host till the end, Glossop accompanied von Müller on his short journey to *Empress of Russia*. Before leaving *Sydney*, von Müller thanked Lieutenant Garsia for rescuing his men, shook hands, and then saluted him. Garsia thought it 'very nice and polite' of von Müller, and later wrote, 'I think, acting under their rules, he and his crew refused to give parole after their arrival in Colombo, but he conscientiously observed it while in the *Sydney*.' Garsia considered Prince von Hohenzollern a 'decent enough fellow. In fact, we seemed to agree that it was our job to knock one another out, but there was no malice in it.'[30]

According to von Hohenzollern, it was around midday when they were sent across to *Empress of Russia*:

We had scarcely assembled on deck when the first officer of the *Empress of Russia* came up to us and read an order from the War Office by which the King of England returned to us officers and subordinate officers our swords. This was in so far meaningless, as we had no swords with us, but doubtless the order was intended as an honour for the *Emden*, and as such it greatly pleased us.[31]

The 'order' had actually emanated from the Admiralty. On 11 November it had sent a telegram to Vice Admiral Jerram, which read: 'Captain, officers and crew of *Emden* appear to be entitled to all the honours of war. Unless you know of any reason to the contrary, Captain and officers should be permitted to retain swords.'[32] The First Lord of the Admiralty, Winston Churchill, wrote that this honour was bestowed upon von Müller and his officers, despite all the harm *Emden* had done, because they had performed their duty 'without offending against humanity or the laws of sea war as we conceived them'.[33]

Mayer thought it was about 2.00pm when he was put on a stretcher and lowered into a boat for transfer from *Empress of Russia* to shore: 'At the pier there was a whole crowd of people. Black and Whites. Naturally the Military were well represented. The crowd received us with quiet respect and everyone of us was stared at as if we had been wonders of the other world.'[34] Mayer heard that the superstitious locals regarded *Emden* as a 'Ghostship', and believed that she could sail underwater like a submarine.

At 5.00pm Glossop had *Sydney*'s ship's company paraded on the quarterdeck so he could thank them for their efforts, 'reading out also the long list of congratulatory telegrams'. He then retired to his cabin for a brief rest before the Australian government's official correspondent, journalist Charles Bean, came onboard to obtain an account of the action with *Emden*. At 7.30pm Glossop had his dinner, rounding off a long day and an equally long week. He then enjoyed 'a pint of champagne', after which he 'turned in & slept like a log'.[35]

Sydney had reached Colombo with only 247 tons of coal in her bunkers, so 16 November was spent coaling, cleaning and replenishing ship.[36] Evening leave was granted to the Port Watch that afternoon and to the Starboard Watch the following day. Todd wrote that the ratings, upon going ashore, went straight to their chosen hotels, 'where they traded lies for beer'.[37]

There was no such joy for the surviving officers and men of *Emden*'s ship's company. Forty-seven were in hospital, and the others, including eighteen lightly wounded and the *Buresk* prize crew, had been transferred to transports for passage to Malta.[38] Von Müller, von Hohenzollern, Luther, Leutnant Fikentscher, and forty-eight men were embarked in *Orvieto*, whilst Oberleutnant Witthoeft, Marine-

Sydney, coaling at Colombo on 17 November; some of her 6in guns have been dismounted for maintenance. (*AWM PS0322*)

Stabsingenieur Ellerbrock, and forty-two men were sent to *Omrah*. The remainder were embarked in the New Zealand transports *Arawa*, *Hawkes Bay*, *Maunganui* and *Tahiti*.[39]

Private Arthur Wilson, of the Wellington Infantry Battalion, wrote that thirty were put on his ship, *Arawa*. 'There was no trouble getting volunteers as guards for these prisoners, for they had hatbands and canteen tokens marked EMDEN. I said they had them. They were soon souvenired.'[40] Matrose Lochau discovered that there was similar interest in souvenirs on *Orvieto*, and cap ribbons, uniform buttons and personal items were willingly exchanged for cigarettes. The prisoners travelled in the transports as far as Suez, where they were transferred to HMS *Hampshire* for the final leg of their journey to Malta.

The prisoners might have left *Sydney*, but evidence of their stay, and the smell, remained. Darby was concerned about the 'insanitary and dangerous' state of the ship, as conditions were ripe for an outbreak of disease, but he could not begin cleaning the affected compartments until coaling was completed. Glossop fully understood the need to clean and disinfect the ship, and despite orders to proceed to Malta after coaling, delayed sailing for twenty-four hours until this could be carried out.

The extended stay in Colombo was not without its advantages, as it gave Glossop more time to host and pay calls, visit his wounded in hospital, and grant more leave to the ship's company. He was especially keen to see Lieutenant Massie, and was able to invite him onboard for breakfast when *Euripides* entered harbour on Tuesday morning. Massie was accompanied by the famous Australian poet and balladist, Andrew 'Banjo' Paterson, who was travelling with the convoy as a war correspondent for *The Sydney Morning Herald*. Massie had offered to take Paterson to meet Glossop, as he felt sure he might 'get some stuff that the other correspondents wouldn't get'. They found *Sydney*'s captain relaxed and happy to talk about the *Emden*. Paterson wrote of Glossop's opening comment:

> Well, Massie, I had a lot of luck didn't I? Fancy her coming to Cocos just when we were right on the spot, and fancy just having the luck to be on that side of the convoy. If I'd been on the other side, then I wouldn't have got the job. Of course I had the speed of her and the guns of her, but if our people hadn't served the guns properly, or if she'd dropped a shell into our engine-room, we might have been sent to the bottom instead of her.[41]

Glossop then went on to describe the action, *Sydney*'s casualties, the incident with the flag when he signalled *Emden* to surrender, and the appalling condition of the enemy ship after the battle: 'She was a shambles. Blood, guts, flesh, and uniforms were all scattered about. One of our shells had landed behind a gun shield, and had blown the whole gun-crew into one pulp. You couldn't even tell how many men there had been.'[42] The son of the Vicar of Twickenham had seen what modern guns and shells could do to a ship and her crew, and was clearly horrified. He ended the discussion with the remark, 'I've seen my first naval engagement, Massie; and all I can say is, thank God we didn't start the war.'

Coaling was completed at 2.00pm on 17 November, enabling Darby to put his cleaning party to work:

> The corticene decks of the Ward Room, Sick Bay, and starboard corridor had to be scraped as they were thick with marine glue which had been

unavoidably fouled by dressings and discharges from wounds. All these places were then scrubbed out and next day the Colombo Health Authorities were brought off and they sprayed out with Cyllin [disinfectant] the whole of the living places of the ship.[43]

Sydney sailed for Aden on the morning of 19 November. Darby hoped that he and his assistants might now be able to enjoy a well-earned rest, but they had to perform another operation the first day at sea. Able Seaman Thomas Bent also had to be cared for. The 18-year-old had taken ill after the battle, and was diagnosed with 'pulmonary trouble, which may have been accelerated in its progress by the stress and excitement of the fight'.[44] Bent was put ashore at Aden for admission to hospital, and was subsequently invalided back to Australia.[45]

Darby's final duty in relation to the *Emden* action was preparing his report on the conduct and performance of his medical team. That *Sydney* had been placed in a highly unusual predicament was acknowledged in his eleven-page report:

> It would be very difficult to imagine a more trying set of circumstances for the medical staff of a cruiser and an action where so many wounded would be rescued. Had the *Emden* sunk before she reached the beach our work would have just halved itself, as many wounded must have drowned.[46]

Darby also conceded that treating and caring for so many patients would not have been possible without the invaluable services of Surgeon Todd, the great assistance given by Dr Ollerhead, and the work performed by *Sydney*'s medical personnel and volunteers. Regarding the latter, he made a point of mentioning Petty Officer John Donnelly, Master-at-Arms Francis Holley, Able Seamen James Hill and Herbert Holmes, Officers' Steward Fred Tilbrook, Ship's Steward William Sweetland, and Cook's Mate John Fulton for their efforts. Darby was also unstinting in his praise of Sick Berth Steward Thomas Mullins, 'whose endurance and energy were wonderful'.

Darby's medical team was tested because Karl von Müller put the welfare of his men before personal pride. A lesser man would have fought his ship until it was sunk for the sake of his personal honour, and that of the Kaiser and the *Kaiserliche Marine* – in which case few would have survived. After *Emden*'s ability to fight had been all but destroyed by battle damage and casualties, von Müller realised that his duty lay with saving as many of his men as possible.

Emden started the battle with a complement of 318 officers, men and civilian personnel. Of these, 136 were killed, drowned, or died of wounds.[47] Von Müller reported that of the 182 survivors, one warrant officer, three petty officers and seventeen men were severely wounded, whilst two officers, two warrant officers, nine petty officers and thirty-one men were wounded to a lesser extent. These men survived because of von Müller's decision to run *Emden* ashore on North Keeling Island. Had he not done so, very few would have lived to see their families and their homeland again.

The prospect of spending part of their lives as prisoners of the British was, however, a bitter pill to swallow. The main body reached Malta on 6 December. Lochau recalled, 'It was to be the end for us as far as the war was concerned, for we were interned as prisoners-of-war.'[48] Von Hohenzollern believed it the worst day of his life: 'We officers were taken in a cart to the Verdala Barracks, where we were to spend the next long period. The men and subordinate officers were separated

Emden sailors, guarded by armed marines from HMS *Hampshire*, stand (left) and sit in the cruiser's pinnace after being taken off the transport *Orvieto*. (*AWM PS0249*)

from us and taken to Fort Salvatore.'[49] He noted that he and his fellow officers entered Verdala Barracks just after 6.00pm. 'The huge, heavy gates shut behind us and our captivity proper began.'

The ones who got away

While von Müller and his fellow survivors were contemplating life as prisoners of war, Kapitänleutnant von Mücke and his men were doing their best to avoid a similar fate. Before leaving Direction Island on the evening of 9 November, von Mücke told the cable station staff that he planned to sail *Ayesha* to German East Africa. This was a ruse. Once they were clear of the reefs and shoals and far enough out to sea, the steam pinnace crew was embarked and the boat cast adrift; von Mücke then set course for the Dutch East Indies.[50]

The wisdom of trying to cross 700 miles of ocean in an unseaworthy schooner was soon brought into question. Von Mücke noted that *Ayesha* leaked badly, and an examination of her bottom boards revealed rotten wood. The canvas sails weren't much better, and tore at the slightest provocation. Water, however, was the main problem. The sea water in the hold couldn't be pumped out because the rubber packing in the bilge pumps was missing, and the drinking water in three of the four fresh water tanks was found to be contaminated. The pumps were made serviceable by replacing the rubber packing with rag soaked in oil, but the shortage of drinking water was serious.

Ayesha had been provisioned with cases of bottled seltzer water before leaving Direction Island, but von Mücke wanted to keep this supply for an emergency. If they had to abandon ship the bottled water could be taken into the two cutters still in tow. The plan changed when one of the cutters was cut loose after smashing into *Ayesha*'s stern, and completely unravelled a few nights later when the second boat tore itself free in a heavy swell. This left two small jolly boats, capable of holding just five men between them. A work party had meanwhile drained and cleaned the contaminated tanks, and one was partially refilled with rainwater collected during a tropical downpour on 13 November. As they travelled further to the northeast more rain fell, easing the water crisis.

Progress was slow, and the days passed even more slowly. All that really mattered though was that they were not seen and intercepted by an enemy warship. There was some concern on the morning of 21

November when smoke was sighted to the northwest, but the vessel, be it warship or freighter, failed to spot *Ayesha*. That afternoon a strong northwesterly breeze sprang up and good headway was made.

Von Mücke had been heading in the general direction of Batavia because the charts found on *Ayesha* were limited to the Cocos–Batavia run, but on 22 November he began steering for Padang on the west coast of Sumatra. At 2.30pm a navigational calculation indicated that they were seventy nautical miles southwest of Seaflower's Channel, an eight-mile-wide passage between the islands of Siberut and Sipura, and eighty miles southwest of Padang. The old Dutch trading port was the preferred destination for several reasons; *Ayesha* was presumably not known there; Leutnants Gyssling and Schmidt were familiar with it; a German consul was stationed there; and there was a good chance that a German ship or two, possibly even a damaged *Emden* (von Mücke was unaware that she had been destroyed), might be found in the roadstead.[51]

Von Mücke expected to sight Siberut or Sipura on 23 November, so that morning the rifles, machine guns and pistols were readied for use

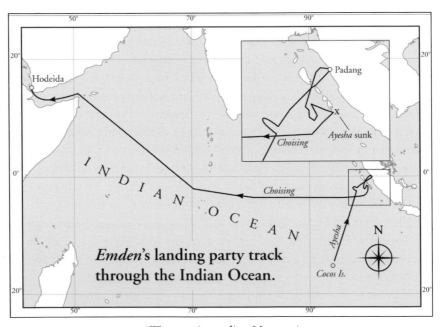

Emden's landing party track through the Indian Ocean.

(*Western Australian Museum*)

Ayesha under full sail. (*Sea Power Centre-Australia*)

in case an enemy warship was encountered. The precautions proved unnecessary. Vice Admiral Jerram believed that *Ayesha* was trying to reach German East Africa, and had ordered *Empress of Russia* (now free of *Emden* prisoners) to search for her and *Exford* in the Maldives and Diego Garcia. When the auxiliary cruiser failed to find the schooner Jerram wrote, 'I think it is just possible that *Ayesha* may never be heard of again ... I am informed that she makes 4 ft. of water a day when sailing and that both the pumps are out of order.'[52] He had not taken into account German improvisation and determination, or considered the possibility that they had sailed off in the opposite direction.

Ayesha's lookout spotted land at 10.10am on 23 November, the navigation proving excellent, but it took all day to reach the entrance to Seaflower's Channel. By this time a lack of wind and gathering darkness forced the planned passage of the channel to be postponed until the next morning. It took another day to reach Sumatra. On 26 November they were becalmed within sight of Padang. That afternoon *Ayesha* was spotted and approached by the Dutch destroyer *Lynx*, which took a great deal of interest in the schooner. Uncertain of her intentions, von Mücke had his battle flag readied for hoisting. As

Ayesha was armed and crewed by naval personnel, he considered the schooner an auxiliary warship in the service of the *Kaiserliche Marine*, and was not going to give her up without a fight. Fortunately for all concerned, *Lynx* made no attempt to challenge or stop them.

Unfavourable winds and currents prevented *Ayesha* reaching Padang until 27 November. When von Mücke was certain that he was in Dutch territorial waters, he had the German naval ensign hoisted to declare *Ayesha*'s nationality and status. Just before midday they embarked a pilot, which prompted *Lynx* to close and investigate. Von Mücke had the ship's company paraded to salute the Dutch warship, and was pleased to see that *Lynx* 'at once returned our salute in like manner'.[53]

Three hours later, when *Ayesha* was nearing the harbour, von Mücke signalled to *Lynx* that he wished to go aboard and speak with her captain. On doing so he learned of *Emden*'s fate, and was told that *Ayesha* would probably be prevented from leaving Padang.[54] Shortly after von Mücke returned to *Ayesha*, the harbourmaster arrived in a small steam tug. He directed the schooner to anchor well outside the harbour, but von Mücke wanted to get closer to the German freighters he could see inside the harbour, and through trickery and bluff managed to do so before anchoring:

> As soon as the *Ayesha* lay at anchor, I sent my senior officer, Leutnant Schmidt, on shore to report our arrival officially, and to make my wishes known to the authorities. At the same time, the German consul was asked to come on board. Furthermore, I announced that, in accordance with international custom, no one would be allowed to come on board without the permission of the [German] government authorities, nor would anyone from the ship be permitted to go ashore.[55]

Nevertheless, boats from the German ships came out to greet the *Emden* men. The crews announced that they were from *Kleist*, *Rheinland* and *Choising*, and gleefully threw over gifts of cigars, cigarettes, tobacco and pipes, wine, eggs, fruit, newspapers and clothing.

The following morning von Mücke was informed that the Dutch authorities considered *Ayesha* not to be a legitimate warship, but a prize of war, and that he and his men should allow themselves to be interned. In response von Mücke made an official protest through the German consul:

> I am submitting a protest against this [prize of war] designation and demand that the ship be treated as a warship. All conditions of a warship are met by her. There are only members of the Imperial German Navy on board; the crew is therefore militarily organised. The officers on board are all in the active Imperial Navy and are in the Imperial Navy's official list. The *Ayesha* flies the pennant of a German naval commander and the battle flag of the German empire. The question of how I came into possession of the ship and by what right I am its commanding officer are matters of German domestic concern, and in explaining this turn of events I am only responsible to my superior officer.[56]

Von Mücke added that he had entered Padang because his ship was unseaworthy and he needed provisions and water. As soon as these deficiencies were corrected, he intended to put to sea again.

Water and provisions, including ten live pigs, were delivered to the schooner that evening, and the German consul covertly supplied von Mücke with money. He also slipped him a note, which read, 'I will cruise until 20 December at 3° 20' S, 99° 20' E. The rendezvous will be within a 20-mile radius, depending on wind and current.' The consul had secretly arranged for *Choising* to meet *Ayesha* some 160 nautical miles southwest of Padang.[57]

Von Mücke had been hoping to obtain charts of the local waters, but the Dutch authorities refused to provide them. They also refused to supply clothing, soap, toothpaste and toothbrushes, as it was believed that these would increase the military strength of the ship's company.[58] These items were now of little consequence, for von Mücke had decided to leave Padang under cover of darkness. At 8.00pm the steam launch which had brought the water and provisions took *Ayesha* in tow, and pulled her out of the harbour. Sails were then set and the schooner glided away into the night.

Waiting outside territorial waters was a small boat with two men from the German cargo liner *Rheinland*. They sighted *Ayesha* just after 2.00am, and started rowing towards the schooner. By 2.30am they were within hailing distance, and insisted on being taken aboard. Von

Mücke was surprised when naval reservists Leutnant zur See der Reserve Franz Wellmann and Obermaschinistenmaat der Reserve Erich Schwaneberger requested permission to join the ship's company.

Another surprise awaited them the following night as they approached Seaflower's Channel. The lights of a warship were spotted at 2.30am, and a short time later the vessel began exchanging lamp signals with another ship. Von Mücke feared they were British or Japanese warships, so strove to reach Dutch waters again off Siberut Island. He was very relieved when the second ship steamed away and dawn revealed that the remaining vessel was Dutch. The coastal defence ship *De Zeven Provinciën* proceeded to shadow *Ayesha* until she had passed through the channel and was outside territorial waters.

Von Mücke now set course for the rendezvous position. Light winds or none at all prevented *Ayesha* reaching it until 14 December, but the passage was not without incident. A ship was sighted on 9 December and, thinking it was the expected freighter, von Mücke altered course towards her. The vessel promptly turned away and steamed in a wide arc around the schooner. An initial exchange of signals relating to their navigational position led to the vessel requesting the name of the schooner. Von Mücke did not wish to give this information as he suspected the vessel was British, but he couldn't ignore the request:

> So we took four flags that happened to be at hand, arranged them one above the other, tied a knot in the two upper ones, so that no one could tell what they were, and then hoisted the signal in such a way that it was half hidden by the sails.[59]

The vessel responded, 'I have seen your signal but cannot make it out,' before steaming off.[60]

Von Mücke was therefore apprehensive when another ship was sighted near the rendezvous position on 14 December. This vessel proved to be the 1,657-ton Norddeutscher Lloyd freighter *Choising*. Originally assigned as a supply and coal ship for *Emden*, she was now to serve as a transport for von Mücke and his men. Rough seas prevented an immediate transhipping of weapons and personnel, so *Ayesha* and *Choising* headed southeast in search of better weather. It was not until 16 December, near the island of South Pagai, that the transfer was effected. Von Mücke had grown fond of *Ayesha*, and was saddened to have to scuttle her, but before doing so he took as souvenirs her figurehead and the ship's wheel. *Ayesha* sank at 5.00pm, her service to the landing party being acknowledged with three hearty cheers.

Choising then steamed southwest while von Mücke and his officers discussed destination options with her master, Captain Minkwitz. Tsingtau was out of the question because it had fallen to the Japanese on 7 November. The logical destination was German East Africa, where they might join up with local forces or *Königsberg*, but von Mücke abandoned this idea when told of fighting there, and reports that the cruiser was either sunk or bottled up in the Rufiji River. The decision of where to go remained unresolved until they read of the declaration of war between Britain and Turkey in an old newspaper. Another report mentioned a battle between British and Ottoman troops at Cheikh Saïd, near the island of Perim at the entrance to the Red Sea.

A cautious course was therefore set for the Red Sea. Once there, von Mücke hoped to land in Ottoman territory and return to Germany through Turkey. He and Minkwitz chose a path well south of the equator to avoid storms, and away from the regular shipping lanes to avoid detection. British ships were expected to be encountered in the Red Sea, so while en route *Choising* was repainted to resemble the Italian ship *Shenir*. To complete the disguise a replica Italian flag was made, and the ship's name and port of registration (Genoa) was painted on the stern.

Von Mücke was led to believe that the Turks had extended the Hejaz Railway (which ran from Damascus to Medina) to the holy city of Mecca, and that an extension to Hodeida (Al Hudaydah) in Yemen was under construction. If this was true, and the extension had been completed, it might be possible to board a train at Hodeida and reach Constantinople (Istanbul) via Damascus. Von Mücke decided to aim for Hodeida. If the line extension was not yet complete, he would try to obtain charts of the Red Sea so that *Choising* could continue to Djidda (Jeddah); he and he men would then trek overland to Mecca.

Choising reached the Strait of Bab el Mandeb at the southern entrance of the Red Sea on 5 January 1915. Von Mücke 'counted with certainty' a meeting with patrolling British warships in the narrow waterway, so had a supply of food, water, weapons, ammunition and medical supplies stowed in the four largest boats in case of emergency. The landing party, which now included *Choising*'s surgeon, Dr Heinrich Lang, and a junior officer, Leutnant zur See der Reserve Johannes Gerdts, was divided into four and allocated a boat so that some might escape if the ship was stopped. Enemy warships were sighted, but *Choising* slipped through the narrows that night and disembarked von Mücke and his men near Hodeida at dawn on 9 January.[61]

As they were rowing towards the port a French cruiser was spotted at anchor. Von Mücke assumed that Hodeida was in enemy hands, so ordered the boats to veer away and land further south. Once ashore he discovered that the local Arabs were pro-German and that Hodeida was occupied by Turkish troops. Maschinistenmaat Härttrich wrote, 'The Arabs would not believe at first that we were Germans; one small English speaking Arab helped us. We were at last in the land of our friends.'[62] Two months to the day since their escape from Direction Island, *Emden*'s landing party had finally reached friendly territory. At midday, surrounded by hundreds of excited Bedouins and Ottoman soldiers, the detachment entered Hodeida. That afternoon, following a very welcome meal, von Mücke discussed the next phase of his journey with the civil and military authorities.

The travel-weary German naval officer was dismayed to learn that the rail extension did not exist, and that the British were maintaining a blockade across the Red Sea north of Hodeida. The only way forward was across country, and it would take at least a fortnight to gather together sufficient camels, horses, handlers, guides and provisions for the two-month journey to El Ula (Al-'Ula) on the Hejaz Railway.[63] Of some consolation, the enforced wait would allow his men to rest and reclothe, as some were sick and many were wearing only the tattered remnants of their uniforms. That night von Mücke fired prearranged signal rockets, informing *Choising* that she should proceed to Massawa.[64]

Von Mücke and his men departed Hodeida on 27 January, mounted on a motley collection of horses, mules and donkeys; provisions and baggage were carried by camel train. Their initial destination was Sanaa (Sana'a), in the mountains to the east. The inland route via Sanaa was favoured in order to avoid marauding bands of Arabs who opposed Turkish rule, and to skirt the Holy Land where infidels were not welcome. The mountains also offered a cool respite from the

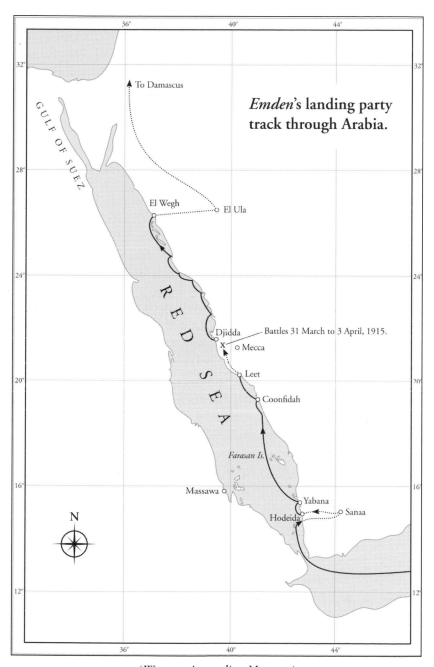

Emden's landing party track through Arabia.

(*Western Australian Museum*)

191

scorching heat of the coastal strip and the desert. Three men, too ill to travel, remained in Hodeida in the care of Dr Lang. The caravan, escorted by Turkish gendarmes, travelled at night and rested during the heat of the day, but progress was slow due to numerous instances of men falling off their steeds and the time lost catching and remounting them. They reached Sanaa on 6 February after a difficult climb through the foothills and a two-day rest in the mountain village of Menakha (Manakhah).[65]

The landing party was warmly welcomed at Sanaa, and rode into the city to the tortured strains of 'Deutschland, Deutschland über Alles', which the garrison band almost managed to play. This was unexpected, as was the official resistance to the onwards passage of the Germans. Von Mücke was informed that no camels or riding animals were available for the next phase of his journey, and that he and his men were required to remain in the city to strengthen the garrison. Emden's first officer accepted that he couldn't go on without transport, but refused to stay and be subordinate to the local Turkish commander. He resolved to return to Hodeida as soon as everyone was sufficiently rested. Unfortunately, increasing sickness amongst his men and the need to secure funds for the return passage delayed departure by a fortnight.

Now mistrustful of the Turks, von Mücke decided to make his own travel arrangements. While the main body retraced their steps towards Hodeida, he and an advance guard rode ahead to purchase two native sailboats (sambuks). These were sailed to Yabana (Al-Jabana), a small bay to the north of Hodeida, while von Mücke checked on Lang and his three patients; they were instructed to join the main body outside the city and meet him at Yabana on 14 March. Von Mücke wrote:

> On the fourteenth of March, at five o'clock in the afternoon, my fleet sailed from Yabana. The Imperial war flag flew proudly at the masthead of my flagship, and with three cheers for his Majesty, the Emperor, we began our onward journey.[66]

Their departure went smoothly and without enemy interference because von Mücke had leaked word in Hodeida that he intended to sail from another bay further south.

Von Mücke had hired an interpreter, a pilot with knowledge of the reef-fringed coastal waters, and local fishermen to sail the boats. The second and larger sambuk carried the sick – men suffering from malaria, dysentery and typhus – and was under the command of Gerdts. The two craft separated that night for their attempt to run the British blockade the next day, but no enemy warships were sighted and they were safely reunited on 16 March.

Disaster struck the following night when Gerdts' sambuk struck an inshore reef and began to sink. Miraculously, no lives were lost, but von Mücke had to dump most of his water and food in order to embark everyone in his boat. In the morning his best swimmers recovered two machine guns, a few pistols and some of the ammunition from the submerged sambuk. Their luck changed for the better when a strong southerly breeze began blowing; the wind filled the sails of the dangerously overloaded sambuk and pushed it up the coast at a good pace. That evening they reached Coonfidah (Al-Qunfudah).

At Coonfidah von Mücke was able to charter a larger sambuk so that everyone could be safely carried in the one boat. There was also space for a Turkish government official and his wife who were trying to get to Constantinople. After a hot meal and a brief rest they pushed on to Leet (Al Lith), which was reached on 24 March. This was as far as they dared go by sea as it was reported that Djidda was blockaded by British warships. Several days were therefore spent at Leet sourcing camels, straw mats (for protection from the sun), and water and food for an overland journey. One man was not able to continue. On the morning of 27 March Matrose Wilhelm Keil died of typhus; he was subsequently taken offshore and buried at sea.

The trek through the desert commenced on the evening of 28 March. Von Mücke was pleased to have an escort in the form of a Turkish officer and seven gendarmes, and the traditional 'hostage' – the district sheikh whose presence prevented attacks by his tribesmen. This protection did not safeguard the caravan against attack by bandits and thieves, and the camels and their cargoes were a tempting prize. Von Mücke therefore took added precautions:

We kept to a route that follows the coast, close by the sea. This entire region is considered unsafe, robbery and attacks upon passing caravans being the order of the day. From the time we left Leet, our rifles were therefore kept loaded, and ready to shoot.[67]

There were no untoward incidents, and on 31 March the caravan reached a watering hole a day's march from Djidda. Waiting there was another Turkish officer and seventeen gendarmes who had brought more camels, a supply of water, and greetings from the military and civil authorities in Djidda. Von Mücke reasoned that if this small party of armed police had come through from the city, then surely a heavily armed body of fifty-two Germans could travel the same route safely. He was wrong.

The caravan, now made up of over a hundred camels tethered nose to tail by a 4m length of rope, resumed its journey at 4.00pm. The route took von Mücke and his men away from the coast and into country consisting of sand drifts overgrown with tufts of grass. Later that night some Bedouins were spotted on the right flank, riding quickly in the opposite direction. Von Mücke didn't like the look of it. The caravan was an easy target in the bright moonlight, so he decided to split the long line of camels into two columns and warned his men to be on the alert. As the hours passed and nothing happened von Mücke began to relax:

> The officers were riding at the head of the caravan. When the first signs of the coming day began to appear behind the mountains that rose on our right, from out of the flat surface of the desert, I supposed that all occasion for anxiety was now passed, as Bedouins never make their attacks by daylight. So I slung my rifle across my saddle, unbuckled my heavy cartridge belt, and rode slowly down the line to see whether everything was in order.[68]

He was halfway back, in the middle of the two columns, when he heard a loud whistle, followed by a volley of shots. The muzzle flashes, clearly visible in half-light of dawn, indicated that the hostile riflemen were in the dunes to the front of the caravan. Von Mücke and several men dismounted and ran forward to assist those returning fire, and to help bring two machine guns into action; a few bursts from these momentarily silenced the enemy fire, which had been heaviest on the left forward flank.

The lull in the firing allowed the Germans to pull their camels down to make them less of a target, and to find better firing positions. The enemy riflemen, estimated to be about 80m away, soon began shooting again, and as the light improved several hundred more Arabs could be seen on the surrounding dunes. Without waiting for orders, those sailors with rifles fixed bayonets.

Von Mücke was wondering how he might deal with such odds when a junior rating asked him when they were going to storm the enemy positions. The question made von Mücke realise that the immediate threat was the Arabs to his left front. With that he ordered his men to their feet and they charged the enemy positions, clearing first the left, then the front, followed by the right flank. Fifteen Arabs were killed as they tried to flee, and many others were wounded. One enemy rifle, of British manufacture, was recovered.

The bayonet charge had the desired effect. The enemy was pushed back and the hostile fire was reduced to an occasional long-range shot. Upon returning to the caravan von Mücke discovered that one of his men had been wounded, as had a number of his Arab camel drivers. Several camels had also been shot. More disturbing, the seventeen gendarmes who had joined the day before were now missing, evidently having ridden off when the shooting started.

Von Mücke decided to leave the established caravan route and head towards the sea, visible in the distance to his left. This meant a longer march, but he would be able to secure his left flank by hugging the coast. For added protection he instructed Gerdts to take ten men armed with rifles and form an advance guard 150m ahead of the caravan, which was now arranged in six columns to make it more compact and easier to defend. Nine riflemen under Gyssling were to provide left and right flank protection, and ten under Schmidt would form a rear guard. As before, two machine guns were carried near the front of the caravan, and two towards the rear. Leutnant Wellmann and those men armed with pistols were tasked with protecting the sick and the wounded.

Thus arranged, the caravan started moving again. Ten minutes later they came under fire again. The shooting was wildly inaccurate, so they tried to keep moving, but when a report came from the rear that one of the camels carrying a machine gun had been shot, von Mücke was forced to halt the caravan. Schmidt had already set up a defensive

195

position around the dead camel, and presently the machine gun came into action. Before von Mücke could get to the rear to assess the situation Matrose Joseph Rademacher was shot and killed, and Schmidt badly wounded.

The enemy fire, which had grown in intensity and accuracy, then suddenly stopped. Von Mücke looked up and saw two of the Coonfidah gendarmes waving white cloths and running towards the enemy; another approached him and said that his comrades wished to parley with their assailants. Von Mücke seized the opportunity to close up and fortify his position. Knowing they were outnumbered and surrounded, he began setting up for all-round defence while waiting for his opponent to make the next move. It came in the form of an envoy with escort. The envoy demanded that all camels, provisions, water, arms and ammunition be surrendered, as well as £11,000 in gold – then they would be free to go. Von Mücke replied that they had no money, and that Germans do not surrender their arms. The Turkish government official, who had been acting as interpreter, and his wife then accompanied the envoy back to the enemy camp to 'negotiate'; the camel drivers also took the opportunity to slip away.

Firing recommenced a short time later and continued until nightfall. There were no further casualties amongst the Germans, though a number of camels were killed. Von Mücke expected the enemy to make a night attack, but when none eventuated he used the cover of darkness to improve the defences and to bury Schmidt, who died at 9pm. He also instructed his most reliable Arab guide to take a message to the military authorities in Djidda, some eight hours' march away, explaining the situation and requesting assistance.

Hostilities resumed just after dawn on 2 April. Von Mücke told his men to reply vigorously with heavy bursts of machine gun fire, and this quickly dampened the enthusiasm of the Bedouins. Sniping continued throughout the day, however, forcing the Germans to keep movement to a minimum. Daytime temperatures in this part of the country in April peaked well above 30° Celsius, but for those forced to lie on the hot sand with no shade and no water it felt like double that. Two men suffered greater discomfort when they were hit by bullets. One of them, Heizer Friedrich Lanig, later died from his wounds. Mercifully, firing again ceased at sunset, allowing food, water and ammunition to be distributed. Von Mucke calculated that there was only enough water for another day, so as soon as it became dark he tried to get another message through to Djidda. This time he sent two of the remaining gendarmes, disguised as Bedouins. Just before sunrise he informed his men that if help did not come during the course of the day they would try to fight their way out after sunset.

Saturday, 3 April started like the previous day. The brisk exchange of machine-gun and rifle fire at dawn was followed by sniping and a steady rise in temperature. Later in the morning, however, distant rifle fire could be heard. Then, towards midday, all local shooting ceased and an Arab carrying a white flag was seen approaching. The envoy announced that all previous demands were withdrawn on the proviso that they now pay £22,000 in gold for safe passage. Von Mücke believed that a relief column from Djidda was responsible for the distant firing, so stalled for time before eventually declining the offer. The envoy withdrew, only to return thirty minutes later with the same demand. When a third attempt to extract money failed, the Bedouins fired several volleys into the German camp and withdrew. About an hour later two men on camels appeared in the distance.

The men proved to be emissaries of the Emir of Mecca, Hussein bin Ali. Salvation was at hand, and arrived shortly thereafter in the form of the Emir's second son, Abdullah, with seventy men. Abdullah brought greetings from his father, and an assurance that von Mücke and his men would be able to continue their journey in peace. The surviving camels were then loaded, and early in the afternoon the caravan began moving again, escorted by Abdullah and his bodyguard. They stopped and rested that night and reached Djidda the next morning.

Despite the risks associated with a sea passage, von Mücke decided to undertake the next phase of the journey by boat. He obtained a large sambuk and an experienced pilot, and after waiting several days for the sick and wounded to recover their strength, secretly set sail on the night of 8/9 April.[69] Once again they slipped through the British blockade, and after changing boats at Sherm Rabigh, managed to reach Sherm Munnaiburra, ten miles short of their intended destination of El Wegh (Al Wajh), on 28 April. That night a gendarme organised camels for the land leg of the journey, and the following evening the detachment rode into El Wegh. Upon arrival von Mücke was informed that it would take two days to assemble camels for the overland trek to El Ula. This was not unwelcome news, as it allowed everyone to enjoy a good bath and a good sleep.

The detachment rode out of El Wegh on the morning of 2 May, accompanied by the local sheikh. It would take five days to reach El Ula, where von Mücke hoped to order a special train for the last part of their journey. The first four days passed without incident, but each night von Mücke ordered his men to dig defensive positions just in case. The greatest risk of attack would come on the last day, when they had to cross territory controlled by another sheikh. Von Mücke was mindful of the fact that this man was not on friendly terms with his current host, and was 'ill disposed toward us because we had not hired camels off him for the last four hours of our march, while passing through his territory'.[70] Luck again favoured von Mücke:

When we were but a few hours' march distant from El Ula, letters were brought to us. They had been sent to inform us that the angry sheikh who, we had supposed, would attack us, was at the time embroiled in a fight farther to the north, and that we could therefore continue on our way without fear of being molested.[71]

Upon receipt of this information von Mücke rode ahead to El Ula to arrange food, accommodation and rail transport for his men. To his surprise he found that the local Turkish military authorities had organised everything, including a special train. There was even a German newspaper reporter waiting to interview him. Emil Ludwig wrote of von Mücke's arrival:

From the rugged mountains a small caravan descended. I ran up to it. The tall, blond man had already dismounted and smiled at my welcome. He stood there in a completely ruined tropical uniform with his involuntary beard and the bluest seaman's eyes, next to his white camel. 'A bath or Rhine wine?' was my first question, 'Rhine wine!' the decisive answer. Then we sat in the stationmaster's room, and without any fuss Mücke began to tell his story.[72]

From newspapers Ludwig was carrying von Mücke discovered that he had been awarded the Iron Cross 1st Class, as well as Bavarian and Saxon decorations, and that all his officers and men were to receive the Iron Cross 2nd Class.

When his men appeared a few hours later von Mücke rode out to meet them, and with 'flag flying, and cameras pointed at us from every side, we marched together into the little town'. After an abundant meal, a greater abundance of drink, and a quick bath, *Emden*'s landing party boarded their train. Von Mucke was delighted: 'Then the train moved northward at the wonderful speed of thirty kilometres an hour, and we could yield our weary limbs to the comfort of red-cushioned seats, a luxury long denied us.'[73] At two points in their journey they had to travel by wagon or on foot, otherwise they went by train to Damascus and Aleppo, and then through Asia Minor to Constantinople. Along the way they were feted, showered with gifts and flowers, and given new clothing. At Aleppo the detachment received mail from home, their medals, and brand new parade uniforms.

The surviving landing party officers, with selected ratings paraded behind them, at Constantinople in May 1915. Standing, left to right: Kapitänleutnant von Mücke (facing the boy), Leutnant Gyssling, and reserve Leutnants Gerdts and Wellmann. (*Sea Power Centre-Australia*)

Their remarkable six-and-a-half-month journey came to a fitting end on the afternoon of 23 May 1915 when the train pulled into Haidar Pasha (Haydarpaşa) Station in Constantinople. Waiting to meet von Mücke and his men was Konteradmiral Wilhelm Souchon, commander of the *Kaiserliche Marine*'s Mediterranean Squadron and Commander-in-Chief of the Ottoman Navy. Kapitänleutnant Helmuth von Mücke paraded his officers and men before Souchon, saluted, and reported, 'By your leave, landing party from SMS *Emden*, five officers, seven petty officers, and thirty-seven seamen, at your service, reporting for duty.'[74]

9

The Wreck

The "Emden" is lying on a sloping coral bottom, her bow
being about 200 yards from the beach, with heavy surf
breaking, and as in ordinary weather she has motion on
her, I think it highly probably [sic] that in the first very
heavy weather, she will probably slide off into deep water.
Commander Hugh Marryat

After *Sydney* steamed away from the Cocos Islands on 11 November
1914, *Emden* was left in the care of her dead. The task of relieving
them of their eternal duty, clearing away the detritus of battle, and
searching the wreck for anything of value would fall to a lesser ship of
the Royal Navy. This was the sloop *Cadmus*, under the command of
Commander Hugh Marryat.

On 13 November HMS *Cadmus* sailed from Singapore, reaching
Cocos on Wednesday, 18 November. A work party went onboard
Emden the following day and, assisted by the EEACTC cable ship
Patrol, spent all of Friday on the wreck. Seaman Gunner Bertram Kiel
was told that they were to bury the dead as reverently as possible:

> We got inboard and the Officers told us it would be impossible to get the
> bodies ashore ... we got hold of a bloke's legs and two arms and tried
> to carry him to the gangway. His legs came out; he had been there nine
> days and you can imagine the fumes that came out from that body.[1]

Some bodies were torn, badly decomposed and crawling with maggots.
Others, like the one Kiel tried to move, were bloated and full of gas:

> It was twice the size of an ordinary man – blown out. The gullet was
> seized and all the gases were [trapped] inside the body and we released
> all this lot so you can imagine what it was like ... We didn't do any more
> that day.[2]

201

Heavy surf on Saturday prevented anyone boarding *Emden*, but conditions eased on Sunday, allowing the men to resume their gruesome work. Surgeon George Fergusson was mindful of the conditions on the wreck, and this time supplied everyone with heavily scented nose and mouth pads. According to Kiel, 'All plastered up we decided the neatest thing was to go down to the stokehold, try to get hold of some shovels and get the bodies along to the gangway.' Cable hooks were used to drag the corpses to the gangway, where they were shovelled over the side – to the dismay and disgust of the men in the nearby workboat. Kiel recalled:

> When we started putting these bodies over, through the sea gangway, the sharks came up . . . Some of them must have weighed ten ton. They were the biggest fish I ever have seen. They used to grab the body and turn right over. You can imagine what these two Boat Keepers were like down there. They called us everything because they were so near to the sharks and the water was coming into the boat right over the top of them and they could smell the bodies.[3]

Surgeon Fergusson's corpse disposal team on *Emden*'s upper deck amidships; the 'thousand-yard stare' of the sailor on the right betrays the horrors he has seen. (*AWM P11611.055.001*)

The men were ordered not to interfere with private property, but were permitted to take a souvenir or two. Kiel obtained a telescope which he believed was taken from a merchant vessel, but then caught one of his shipmates trying to remove rings from a dead German's hand: 'I walked round and there was a fellow ... cutting the finger off and taking the rings. I said, "I wouldn't do anything like that ... It won't bring you no good."'[4] Commander Marryat was not informed of the incident; he had enough to worry about just trying to complete his work on *Emden*:

> Owing to the heavy surf I was only able to board her on two days and on these two days, examination was made very difficult owing to the appalling stench from decomposed bodies. A party of four men under Surgeon G.D.G. Fergusson, RN, working under most objectionable circumstances did most excellent work in removing these bodies.[5]

He added that the after part of *Emden* as far as the mainmast was completely burnt out, and it was in this section of the ship that his men found the confidential chest and a safe. The latter, evidently damaged, was very difficult to get at owing to torn and twisted steel blocking access; it appeared to contain 'a certain number of dollars, all of which were melted'. *Emden*'s signal logs could not be found, but the burnt remains of the confidential books were secured for inspection by Vice Admiral Jerram.

Marryat noted that *Emden*'s 10.5cm guns were missing their breech blocks and recoil pistons. He made inquiries with the cable station staff, and was told that they had been removed by the raider's crew and thrown overboard:

> All accessible storerooms were searched and no spare parts except for one Maxim [machine gun] were found; these were removed. All other compartments were under water and it was unsafe to send divers down owing to the motion of the ship; and also for the foul air which would have been pumped down to them.[6]

Marryat was obviously hoping to secure a complete gun for Admiralty inspection and evaluation. The Australian authorities, on the other hand, wanted trophies. The Commonwealth Minister for Defence,

Emden, photographed on or about 19 November 1914. (*Western Australian Museum*)

Senator George Pearce, had requested that items such as guns or other fittings be recovered which could be kept 'at the Federal capital as mementoes of Australia's first naval victory'.[7] Marryat wrote in his report, 'The conning tower binnacle and compass, and electric telegraphs, were obtained for the Australian Government, but, owing to time and weather, it was impossible to obtain anything else.'[8]

Marryat also landed a party on North Keeling Island to search for 'treasure', or anything else of value that the Germans might have hidden. They found nothing, so set about collecting the dead from the beach and burying them. Once this work was finished the men were given a few days to rest and recover before preparing *Cadmus* for sea. They sailed for Singapore on 27 November.

Empress of Japan subsequently visited the Cocos Islands and inspected *Emden*'s wreck. Commander Morshead Baillie-Hamilton's men found and recovered *Emden*'s signal log, as well as unspecified mementoes.[9] Other small items and a large quantity of coins were taken when HMAS *Pioneer* examined the wreck on 18 January 1915. Ship's Writer Harold Grice was one of those who went onboard *Emden*, and was shocked by what he saw. In a letter to his sister, he wrote:

> I never realised the effect of a modern sea fight until I saw this mangled mass of steel twisted into every imaginable shape ... It is almost

204

impossible for you to realise the awful effects of a modern 6 in. naval gun firing lyddite shell. Everything it came into contact with was blown to atoms and great gaping holes appeared where it pierced.[10]

Grice had little trouble imagining what it must have been like on *Emden* during the battle. 'I could not but admire those brave Germans who managed to live and fight to the last in that living hell.' He added:

There were still a few dead bodies scattered amongst the wreckage and these were flattened like a piece of wood, apparently caused by the effects of shell explosion. On the aft part of the ship was discovered three money safes. We broke one open and it was found to contain thousands of Mexican dollars. Of course we brought these on board and the Paymaster took charge of them. I collected a few curios, viz Von Müller's (the German Commander) boot brush, a couple of dollars and a few other articles, but we were not allowed to take away any articles of war.[11]

Pioneer's commanding officer, Commander Thomas Biddlecombe, RAN, duly informed Jerram that two intact safes remained on the wreck.

Emden was now showing the effects of constant pounding by the sea; the poop deck aft of the No. 5 guns had collapsed, pulling the

Emden, prior to *Cadmus'* second visit; the lower portion of the toppled foremast with searchlight platform attached remains in place, and the No. 2 port gun can still be seen in its sponson. The No. 5 port gun is now trained on an aft bearing. (*Western Australian Museum*)

upper hull plates inwards and seriously weakening an already structurally compromised stern. In addition, decks, bulkheads and ship's fittings damaged by shell hits or fire were rapidly corroding. Despite the rust, the gaping holes in the hull, and the mangled funnels and superstructure, someone tried to restore a little dignity to *Emden* by training her upper deck guns on fore and aft bearings.[12]

When Jerram informed the Admiralty that he intended to send *Cadmus* back to recover the safes, as 'they may contain important papers or money', he received the instruction, 'If it can be done without risk, salve one or more of *Emden*'s guns.'[13] The Admiralty also desired a torpedo. Knowledge of the capabilities of German guns and torpedoes was vital, so Marryat was instructed to recover one of *Emden*'s torpedoes, as well as one or more 10.5cm guns.

Cadmus, carrying explosives and two NCOs from the Royal Engineers, departed Singapore on 23 January and reached North Keeling six days later. As conditions were favourable, a working party was immediately sent across to *Emden*. Marryat's men located the paymaster's safe, and when blown open was found to contain forty gold coins and 6,350 Mexican silver dollars. On 30 January a 10.5cm gun and mounting was recovered, and the following day a gun barrel and a torpedo were secured. An unnamed *Cadmus* sailor wrote that the ship's divers were tasked with recovering the torpedo, and they 'got one all complete':

> We had a hard job getting it out of the submerged torpedo flat. There were a lot of dead German sailors down there, and when the divers stirred things up it was very disagreeable. We also got two of her guns. One is going to England with the torpedo, and the other to Australia as a curio. Another thing we got was a searchlight, and 6,000 Chinese [Mexican] dollars and some good sets of doctors' instruments.[14]

Bert Kiel recalled that the recovery of the 5.15m, 630kg torpedo was not without its problems, or its humour:

> We sent one of our Divers down. He was an Able Seaman and a bit of a comic and the Gunner told him to unscrew the pistol from the head of the torpedo. Before he could do that we had to get boats' tackles to pull it back [out of the torpedo tube] to get at the pistol. Then, when we

got the thing back he said, 'I can't unscrew this. Send me down a hammer.'[15]

Everyone knew that a smart tap on the pistol would detonate the torpedo warhead, so there was a mild panic when the diver requested a hammer. Kiel continued: 'We had a young Armourer there and he said, "I've nearly got the bolt out of that gun, can I go and finish it off, Sir?", and the Gunner replied, "You remain here. If we go you will go with us."'[16] The torpedo was safely disarmed and transferred to *Cadmus*. On 1 February a gun mounting and a searchlight were removed. The work party spent one more day on the wreck removing items of interest, and on 3 February *Cadmus* departed for Singapore. The items recovered from *Emden* were then cleaned, cased, and shipped to Australia in the steamship *Montoro*.[17]

Emden's notoriety, and Australian newspaper accounts of her battle with *Sydney*, resulted in a great deal of public interest in the story and the wreck. Ships passing near the Cocos Islands deviated from their routes so that passengers and crew might see the infamous German raider. The steamship *Mataram* allegedly stopped and permitted passengers to board the wreck. One, Mr T M Lamb, claimed that he took as souvenirs a revolver and a Luger pistol (both badly damaged by fire), as well as a cat-o'-nine-tails (used for beating dust off uniforms after coaling).[18]

Meanwhile, members of a Sydney-based organisation known as the Millions Club were seeking to make the wreck accessible to the Australian public through the medium of film.[19] They formed the Cocos Islands Film Syndicate, and engaged Charles Cusden to make a documentary film of the battle. Cusden sailed for Cocos on 20 March in the steamship *Hanley*, and reached North Keeling on 19 April. A heavy swell forced *Hanley* to anchor three miles from the wreck, and it also made boarding *Emden* from a lifeboat extremely hazardous. One sailor eventually managed to clamber aboard, passed a rope to Cusden, and hauled him and his equipment onto the upper deck. Cusden filmed the cruiser's stern, collapsed funnels and torn superstructure before moving forward, towards the bridge. In the process he dislodged a loose deck plate and fell into the compartment below. It was later reported, 'It was a great shock, and was intensified when he landed into several feet of water, so stale that the smell was unbearable.'[20] Cusden was lucky not to be killed or injured. After being rescued he explored the lower decks and made a gruesome discovery; away in a remote corner he found the lower half of a former *Emden* sailor. The trousers had gone, but the boots remained on the feet, and the flesh on the legs was so dry and shrivelled it resembled brown leather.[21]

When Cusden returned to Sydney on 27 May he learned that the Commonwealth government had called for tenders for the salving of the German cruiser. He warned against this, stating that *Emden* lies 'battered, twisted and broken on a reef'. In his opinion, salvage operations would be arduous and dangerous. 'Heavy seas have surged over her, and so close inshore does she lie that it is a matter of extreme difficulty for even a small boat to get alongside.'[22]

The Australian Minister for Defence had invited tenders for the salvage of *Emden*'s wreck on 9 May. A Defence Department advertisement stated that all tenderers must undertake to forward to the Navy Office in Melbourne, and hand over free of charge, all guns and gun mountings, torpedoes and torpedo tubes, fire-control instruments and apparatus, money in whatever form it might be found, and all confidential books and documents that may be salved. Furthermore, should the ship be salved and brought into port, the Commonwealth government was to have the option of purchasing her 'at a price to be determined by arbitration in the event of any dispute arising'.[23] Seven tenders were received by the end of June. On 1 July *The Daily Telegraph* reported:

> Offers have been made to raise the *Emden* and bring her to Australia as the property of the Commonwealth Navy for a cash consideration; to buy the wreck, float it, and bring it here for sale, with the first offer of purchase to the Federal Government; and the alternative of salving the guns and stripping the wreck of all valuable material for a stated price. The Navy Board has considered the tenders and referred them with its recommendation to the Minister.[24]

On 5 July Sydney resident Edward Darnley was informed that his tender had been accepted. He and three others planned to form a public company, to be known as the Emden Salvage Company. Darnley, a diver and salvage contractor, stated:

> As soon as that is done we will despatch an expedition to Cocos Island, and I am confident that the *Sydney*'s victim will soon be recovered. We have all the necessary machinery in readiness, and have engaged the captain and engineer for the vessel we will send out. As soon as the *Emden* is recovered, she will be patched up and brought direct to Sydney. She will then be exhibited in the various ports of the Commonwealth, and may finally be sold to the Commonwealth Government under the terms of the tender.[25]

Darnley hoped to have *Emden* in Australia by Christmas, but a problem arose when he sought permission to retain possession of the wreck for eighteen months after recovery, as he wished to exhibit the cruiser around the world. The Minister for the Navy, Jens Jensen, refused the request, and on 9 October announced that 'all negotiations with private firms for the salvage and floating of the cruiser had been broken off. Instead, the Navy department would undertake the work.'[26]

A letter published in *The Sydney Morning Herald* on 29 October cast doubt on even the navy being able to refloat *Emden*. The unnamed correspondent wrote (on 12 September):

> On passing the wreck at the end of last month [August] on the voyage to Singapore, I noticed that the ship had apparently broken her back. All the gutted after-part ... is now under water and her remaining mast has gone. She has evidently only started breaking up quite recently, as a ship passed a fortnight before we did, and then the *Emden* appeared quite normal.[27]

This prompted the navy to send HMAS *Protector* and a skilled diver to the Cocos Islands to report on the practicality of salving *Emden*, or removing anything still onboard which might be of interest or value. When she reached North Keeling on 14 November it was discovered that *Emden*'s stern had completely disappeared, and heavy surf was breaking over the remainder of the ship. Commander Patrick Weir,

209

RAN, reported that the wreckage cast up on the beach 'gave evidence of terrific seas, such as would account for the damage done to the wreck'. Weir and his men remained on site for several days in the hope of boarding *Emden*, but bad weather prevented it.[28] On 20 November *The Age* newspaper informed its readers that *Emden*'s salvage was 'an engineering impossibility':

> The Minister for the Navy stated yesterday that the gunboat *Protector* was despatched from Fremantle a fortnight ago to view the wreck, and determine the advisability of proceeding with the much delayed salvage. A wireless message received from the *Protector* by the Navy department stated that the *Emden* was a total wreck, only the forepart of the vessel remaining on the beach [reef].[29]

On 11 January 1916 the Minister for the Navy announced that 'nothing more can be done towards either salving the remains of the *Emden* or any trophies from her, except such as may be cast ashore'.[30]

Members of *Protector*'s ship's company pose in front of *Emden*'s wreck in November 1915; the mainmast has collapsed and the stern section has broken up and slipped beneath the waves. (*State Library of Victoria, H91.108/154*)

Waste not, want not

John Clunies-Ross did not agree, believing that much could still be salvaged from *Emden*'s wreck. On 25 January 1916 he and his cousin (Edmund Clunies-Ross) established a camp on North Keeling which was occupied by Edmund and a team of salvage workers for ten months from mid-February.[31] John purchased a quantity of steel wire to make a flying fox to transfer heavy items from ship to shore, and joined Edmund in early May to begin salvage operations.

On 9 May John recorded the removal of 'some clothing and loose pieces of metal'. Over the next four weeks they salvaged 274 tins of boiled beef, 230 tins of corned beef, 144 tins of salmon, cases of soap, medical stores, mess tables and seats, and a large amount of ferrous and non-ferrous metal. His workers also dismantled the shield on the port forecastle gun, moved the barrels of the two amidships guns (No. 3 port and starboard) to the forecastle deck, and erected the flying fox. After considerable effort, the first barrel was landed on the beach on 6 June. A second gun barrel went ashore the next day, and on 8 June the salvage crew recovered deck planks, water tanks, more scrap metal,

Cocos Islanders work on *Emden*'s No. 1 starboard gun mount in June 1916. The barrel has been removed and the dismantling of the gun cradle and shield is under way. (*AWM H16074*)

211

and commenced dismantling the starboard forecastle gun. By 1 July two complete guns and two barrels had been shipped to Home Island.[32]

On 4 July John sent a cable to the Prime Minister of Australia, advising that he had salved two guns with pedestals and shields from *Emden*, as well as two barrels. The wording of the cable indicated that he was trying to sell the guns to the Commonwealth. On 14 October he wrote a letter to the Mayor of the City of Sydney, informing him that he had 'salved two 4in guns off the *Emden* complete with pedestals and shields, also two barrells [sic] only, as the mountings have gone overboard in the breakers'. Clunies-Ross continued:

> Some months ago I telegraphed to the Australian Government but I have had no reply whatever. I was under the impression the guns were wanted in Australia, so went to some expense and trouble to get the guns ashore through the surf.
>
> Will you please to let me know if your City wants the guns. If not I will otherwise dispose of them to recover some of the expense in procuring and rigging the gears for the salving of such weights in a difficult place.
>
> I am communicating with Mayor of Melbourne.[33]

The mayors of Sydney and Melbourne, like the prime minister's office, did not take up his offer. On 21 December *The Daily News* published extracts from another letter written by Captain Partridge, master of the motor-schooner *Rainbow* owned by Clunies-Ross:

> We have been to North Keeling Island, where Mr Cluny Ross [sic] and forty people have been working at the *Emden*. We have brought back [to Home Island] two upper deck guns complete, and about 15 tons of metal – brass and copper. The Australians have been wanting the guns, but whether they will care to pay the price the Governor (Mr Cluny Ross) asks for them I do not know. The *Emden* is very small now – just half ... from the stem to the second funnel.[34]

Salvage operations were suspended in December 1916 when Edmund and his workers returned to Home Island; the centre section of the ship appears to have broken up in heavy seas a few months later.[35]

On 3 July 1917 two Royal Navy torpedo boat destroyer flotillas conducted target practice off the Cocos Islands while 'proceeding on Admiralty Service'. One vessel examined the remains of *Emden* by steering close to the island. The commanding officer of the flotillas wrote in his Letter of Proceedings:

> I find that only the fore part of the ship is still remaining to just about the after part of the bridge. The cables to the shore are still standing, but Mr [Clunies] Ross has suspended salvage operations. I saw four guns that he had already salved, on the home island – two guns with mountings complete and two gun barrels; breech blocks of course are missing, and breeches of guns damaged. The Governor informed me that the cost of salvage, after obtaining necessary wire hawsers etc from Batavia was £600; £200 for each gun and mounting, and £100 for each gun barrel. I understand that he is willing to sell the guns. I believe the weight of each gun, with shield, pedestal and mounting, is about 4½ tons.[36]

The Naval Board had known about the guns for some time, and even sought legal advice on their ownership. A similar case of an individual proposing to exhibit, then sell, items recovered from *Emden* resulted in the navy stating that he could not do so, because the wreck was the property of the Admiralty.[37]

On 31 October 1917 the Naval Secretary wrote to Clunies-Ross, informing him that the Commonwealth government wished to 'secure' the guns and any other items salvaged from *Emden*, 'which are of special interest to the people of Australia in view of the destruction of this ship by the Australian Cruiser *Sydney*'. The letter asked for details of the items recovered, 'and the expense likely to be incurred in arranging for their transfer to the Commonwealth Government'. Clunies-Ross replied on 2 February 1918, informing the Naval Secretary that he had two guns complete with mountings, two barrels, a 'steering telltale standard', a pair of telegraph meters, two shells, one shell case, a shell carrier, and a steam siren. He wanted £660 for the lot.[38]

The Commonwealth government, tactfully avoiding the ownership issue, accepted the offer. The guns and items were shipped via Singapore, and arrived in Australia on 19 September 1918 in *Montoro*.

A fortnight later the *Emden* relics were delivered to the Captain-in-Charge, HMA Naval Establishments, Sydney; ironically, this was Captain John Glossop, the very man responsible for the destruction of the German cruiser.

It was Glossop's second reunion with the weapons that killed four of his men. On 21 December 1917 he attended the unveiling of the 10.5cm gun recovered by *Cadmus* nearly three years earlier. The gun now surmounted a stone monument in Hyde Park, Sydney, which had been erected to commemorate the destruction of SMS *Emden* by HMAS *Sydney* on 9 November 1914.[39] Panels on the monument listed the dignitaries present at the unveiling, *Sydney*'s officers at the time of the action, award recipients, and the names of those killed and wounded. Glossop was invited to speak, and concluded his speech by quoting lines from Rudyard Kipling's poem 'Recessional':

> Lord God of Hosts, be with us yet,
> Lest we forget – lest we forget![40]

Glossop was clearly thinking of his own men, but perhaps also spared a thought for *Emden*'s dead.

The 10.5cm gun on the Hyde Park memorial in Sydney, *c*1920. (*Rocky Media Archive*)

Many other items recovered from *Emden* were on display in various Royal Australian Navy establishments, two were placed in Queen's Hall, Federal Parliament House, Melbourne, and some were earmarked for a future national war museum.[41] In September 1919 a list of relics was compiled (exclusive of coins), showing what had been distributed, and what remained in storage.

Relic	To whom distributed
10.5cm gun & mounting	City of Sydney (on display at Hyde Park)
10.5cm gun & mounting	With Admiralty, for expert examination
Torpedo	With Admiralty, for expert examination
Searchlight	With Admiralty, for expert examination
Stern scroll	Federal Parliament House, Melbourne
Nameplate	Federal Parliament House, Melbourne
Ship's bell	Garden Island, Sydney
Ship's compass & pedestal	Garden Island, Sydney
Sub-calibre gun	Naval Depot, Williamstown
Range clock	Naval Depot, Williamstown
Wooden shield (City of Emden coat of arms)	HMAS Tingira
Wooden shield (City of Emden coat of arms)	Navy Office
Binnacle	RAN College
Ship's compass on pedestal	RAN College
Steering wheel	RAN College
Flags, plans & charts	RAN College
Engine room telegraphs (from conning tower)	Port Melbourne Drill Hall
Line-throwing rifle	Birkenhead Drill Hall
Steaming lights (2)	Brisbane Drill Hall
Boat's compass	Sydney Drill Hall
Diver's helmet	Sydney Drill Hall
Electric gongs (2)	Fremantle Drill Hall
Rocket apparatus	Hobart Drill Hall

Relics not yet distributed	Number
10.5cm gun barrels	4
10.5cm gun cradle, pivot, pedestal, shield & component parts	2
10.5cm brass cartridge cases	4
Ammunition transporting case (empty)	1
Box containing two projectiles	1
Telegraph	1
Helm telegraph	1
Brass steam whistle	1
Hose connections	2
Hose strainers	2
Revolution indicators	2
10.5cm projectile	1
Shell	1
Electric fire gong	1
Torpedo director	1
Box containing tools for rifles, etc	1
Fire control instrument	1
Box containing electrical fittings	1

An earlier stocktake of the coins listed two US twenty-dollar gold pieces and 6,429 Mexican silver dollars. One of the gold coins was presented to Glossop and the other was retained by the Naval Board. One thousand of the silver dollars were set aside as souvenirs in the form of medallions. These were to be mounted with a crowned, curved silver suspender reading, 'NOV 9 1914 HMAS • SYDNEY • SMS • EMDEN'. Of the thousand, 702 were reserved for members of *Sydney*'s ship's company, 268 were distributed to 'persons as per Navy Board List', and thirty were allocated to 'others'. In July 1918 the remaining 5,429 unmounted silver dollars were offered to the public for £1 each. Proceeds from the sale, less expenses for the making of the medallions, would go to the Royal Australian Navy's Families' Relief Fund. Members of *Sydney*'s ship's company purchased 614 of the unmounted coins, 343 were sold to the public, twenty-five were gifted to charities or visiting 'Allied Officers', and fourteen went to libraries or museums. The unsold coins (4,433) were smelted down and the four silver bars produced sold by tender. In April 1920 the sum of £1,074 11s 1d was paid into the relief fund.[42]

Some of the items recovered by HMS *Cadmus* in 1915; the nameplate and stern scroll (centre) are flanked by the City of Emden coat of arms panels which once adorned *Emden*'s bows. The badly damaged ship's bell sits on the deck. (*AWM P10929.002*)

By this stage these relics and coins, and the various souvenirs in private hands, represented all that was likely to be recovered from *Emden*. In October 1922 the steamship *Narkunda* called at the Cocos Islands and noted that the wreck was almost completely broken up, with 'big seas breaking over the remains'.[43]

Emden's wreck, lying in shallow but treacherous water, remained undisturbed until 1937, when the promise of easy pickings lured several fishing boats to North Keeling. There was a market for scrap metal in Singapore, and one local vessel, the 75-ton *Ankyo Maru*, returned to harbour with 400 unexploded shells reputedly taken from *Emden*.[44] Singapore marine police seized the cargo and had it dumped at sea. Two months later, on 28 December, they discovered 30 tons of copper, bronze and other metal taken from *Emden*'s wreck in *Ankyo Maru*'s holds. The police believed that *Emden* was the property of the Commonwealth of Australia, so the scrap metal, valued at £400, was confiscated and *Ankyo Maru*'s master warned that any further interference with the wreck would result in the seizure of his boat.[45]

The master did not own *Ankyo Maru*, so had nothing to lose. He was caught again in February 1938 with 20 tons of brass and machinery scrap from *Emden*. Told that his £500 cargo was to be confiscated, he slipped out of harbour in the early hours of 12 February and disposed of the evidence.[46] *Ankyo Maru* was seized upon return to Singapore, forcing the owner to hire lawyers to get his boat back. When they raised the question of ownership of *Emden*'s wreck, the Australian Minister for External Affairs wrote that the Commonwealth government 'makes no claim to the wreck of SMS *Emden*'. As the Cocos Islands were administered by the government of the Straits Settlements, he believed that the wreck, being Crown property, was their problem.[47]

The next unauthorised commercial salvage effort came to light in March 1953, when the pilot of a Singapore-bound Qantas Skymaster spotted a vessel near the wreck. Upon investigation it was found that Japanese skin divers working from the 110ft motorised sampan *Kaiyo* were stripping *Emden* of non-ferrous metal. As the Japanese had not sought permission to operate in British territorial waters, they were reported to the Malaysian government, which now administered control of the Cocos Islands.[48]

The Commonwealth government finally became responsible for *Emden*'s wreck on 23 November 1955, when the Cocos (Keeling) Islands became an Australian Territory. Another twenty-six years would pass before the wreck received protection. On 12 March 1982 what remained of *Emden*, and all articles associated with the ship, were declared historic under the Australian Historic Shipwrecks Act of 1976, thus making it illegal to damage, remove, or dispose of any items from the wreck.[49] The Act also imposed a protected zone around the wreck, prohibiting trawling, diving, spearfishing or any other underwater activity within the zone without a valid permit. This decision effectively saved the not insignificant remains of the ship from further interference and depredation, allowing *Emden* to finally rest in peace.

A report from an authorised dive on *Emden* on 4 February 1990 identified a number of items within the protected zone which should remain recognisable as components of the cruiser for decades to come. Richard Mathews, a member of the four-man dive team and author of the report, noted that the only visible remains of *Emden* above water were two badly rusted boilers on the beach near the wreck site, and 'several condensers lying on the edge of the inner lagoon'. Below water, at a depth of no more than 9m, the layout of the ship was still clearly defined by several large artefacts.[50]

Approximately 65m from the beach lay two large bow anchors and the forward capstan.[51] Astern of the capstan were piles of corroding steel plates and a quantity of live 10.5cm ammunition, the latter, no doubt, having once been stored in the forward magazines. Aft of this was a small engine, followed by an extended area of plating which once formed the bottom of the boiler rooms. Mathews reported:

> Very little of the hull plating remains and what does exist consists of scattered bottom plating lying flat on the ocean floor and several pieces of side plating still standing vertically. These latter pieces are no more than 2 metres high and 8 metres long. Also visible are several thicker plates about 4 metres long and triangular in shape. These plates are lying on the bottom and appear to be about 25 mm thick.[52]

An unidentified object was seen in this area (port side), and the main engines, port and starboard, sat on the seabed aft of it.[53] 'Two guns remain, one on the port side aft of the engines and the other on the starboard side forward of the engines.' Mathews noted that neither gun had 'any armour or turret', which suggests they were sponson guns (No. 4 port and starboard).

Well aft lay the port and starboard propellers (still attached to their shafts) and the rudder machinery with a section of the stern. Two spare propeller blades (originally stowed on the upper deck) were also seen, and the stern anchor was found encrusted on the starboard propeller shaft. Thousands of smaller items lay scattered about.

> The bottom of the ocean where the wreck lies is mainly coral rock which is barren of marine growth because of the surge action of the ocean swells. Filling up all the crevices and cracks in the bottom is a huge assortment of non-corrodible fittings (ie brass, copper and bronze) such as pipe joints, piping, wheels, cogs, portholes etc. Most of these items show signs of having once been connected to iron or steel which has since rusted away.[54]

A quantity of live 10.5cm ammunition was also found adjacent to the wreck, starboard of the main engines.[55]

Imagery from another authorised dive in 2004, which was permitted to leave a plaque on the wreck commemorating the ninetieth anniversary of the action between *Emden* and *Sydney*, suggests that components seen in 1990 remained undisturbed.

An honourable act

On 9 November 2014 descendants of *Emden* and *Sydney* crew members visited the Cocos Islands to commemorate the hundredth anniversary of the battle. Most had attended the opening of *The Last Gentlemen of War* exhibition at the Western Australian Maritime Museum three nights previously, which told the story of the battle, and displayed relics recovered from *Emden* in 1915, as well as *Sydney*-related items. Some of the artefacts had never been publicly exhibited before, but all lent gravitas to the 'Two ships, two nations, two extraordinary stories' theme. Unfortunately, the one item which encapsulated the essence of gentlemanly conduct could not be displayed. This was *Emden*'s nameplate.

In 1931 members of the Commonwealth government and the War Memorials Board discussed the possibility of offering Germany an *Emden* relic in recognition of the bravery exhibited by her captain and crew. They had in mind the nameplate, so inquiries were made through the British government to ascertain if the gesture would be interpreted as friendly.[56] The response from Germany was positive, and on 2 March 1932 *The Sydney Morning Herald* reported that the German Chancellor, Heinrich Brüning, had expressed 'grateful thanks to Australia for the impending return of the cruiser *Emden*'s nameplate'.[57]

The nameplate was taken to Berlin and formally presented to German President Paul von Hindenburg by Australian Minister Stanley Bruce on 27 February 1933. A reporter wrote of the exchange of words:

> Mr Bruce paid a tribute to the courage and chivalry of the *Emden*'s captain and crew. Their deeds, he said, must have stirred the hearts of Germany, as they had wrung respect from their enemies.
>
> Replying to Mr Bruce, President von Hindenburg said the whole of Germany was grateful to Australia. Germany wished to strengthen the

ties of friendship with Australia, and that the day's event would doubtless contribute towards that end. 'Mr Bruce's praise of Captain von Müller and his crew has deeply moved me,' added the President.[58]

Von Hindenburg went on to say, 'I regret that a brave officer has not survived to see this day. The nameplate will find an honourable place in the new *Emden*.' Karl von Müller had died from pneumonia on 11 March 1923, aged forty-nine.

The new *Emden* entered service in 1925, and was the third light cruiser to carry the name. Like *Emden* II (1916–19), *Emden* III wore a large Iron Cross on her bow, authorised by the Kaiser in 1914 'as a remembrance of the glory of the old *Emden*'.[59] The nameplate was subsequently mounted on *Emden* III's after superstructure deck, above the aft gun, and unveiled during a ceremony on 19 March 1933.[60]

The British press reported favourably on Australia's decision to present the nameplate to Germany. According to *The Times*:

Emden's nameplate is unveiled by Vizeadmiral Richard Foerster onboard *Emden* III at Wilhelmshaven on 19 March 1933. Seven former *Emden* crew members attended the ceremony. (*Western Australian Museum*)

This unique sequel of the *Sydney*'s encounter with *Emden* ... marks Australia's remembrance of an adversary's gallantry in a combat which will always hold a special place in her history. Australians were often matched conspicuously against brave opponents on land, and now mutual respect held in wartime has been confirmed by a friendly exchange in time of peace.[61]

The *Daily Express* wrote that it was 'a fitting end to one of the last stories of personal chivalry in modern war. Captain von Müller, of the *Emden*, fought like a knight of the seas.'[62]

The Admiralty had honoured von Müller by permitting him to retain his sword after capture. Australia had honoured the entire ship's company by returning *Emden*'s nameplate.

Appendix 1: SMS *Emden* ship's company on 9 November 1914

Onboard for the action with HMAS *Sydney*
Fate:
K – denotes killed in action, drowned or died of wounds
W – denotes wounded in action
M – denotes prisoner of war (Malta)
A – denotes prisoner of war (Australia)

Name	Rank or Rate	Fate
Aden, Heyo Hermann	Obermaschinistenmaat	W A
Adlung, Adolf	Heizer	M
Andresen, Fritz	Marine-Ingenieur	M
Astor, Gustav	Oberheizer	K
Bakmeyer, Albert Johann	Obermatrose	W A
Bartocha, August	Obermatrose	K
Bauer, Johann Peter	Heizer	M
Bauer, Joseph	Heizer	K
Bauke, Manfried	Obersignalgast	K
Baum, Richard	Oberheizer	K
Bednors, Alfred Max	Matrose	M
Behrendt, Paul	Oberheizer	M
Benthien, August	Heizer	W A
Bergien, Walter Karl	Obermaschinist	W A
Bergmann, Friedrich	Matrose	K
Bergmann, Wilhelm	Bootsmannsmaat	K
Bieber, Arnold	Funkentelegraphiemaat	K
Blauenburg, Peter	Obermaschinistenmaat	M
Blecher, Otto	Heizer	M
Blecker, Franz	Heizer	M
Blümel, Karl	Heizer	M
Bolt, Wilhelm	Diensttuender Maschinistenoberanwärter	M
Book, Albert	Obermatrose	K
Borski, Anton	Matrose	K
Böttjer I, Karl	Matrose	K
Böttjer II, Karl	Matrose	K
Brackmann, Heinrich	Heizer	K
Bredehorn, Hans	Diensttuender Maschinistenoberanwärter	K
Bredenkötter, Heinrich	Matrose	K
Brockmann, Hans	Obermaschinistenmaat	K

Brunning, Adolf	Heizer	M
Buck, Johann	Matrose	W A
Bülow, Ernst Karl	Matrose	W A
Bunke, Robert	Maschinistenmaat	W M
Bürger, Georg	Oberheizer	M
Burmann, Emil	Schreibersmaat	K
Büsing, Hermann	Obermatrose	K
Cziba, Bernhard	Oberwachtmeistersmaat	K
Daams, Josef	Oberheizer	W A
Dammann, Julius	Heizer	M
Danschke, Franz	Heizer	M
Debelius, Wilhelm	Maschinistenmaat	M
Dehorn, Theodor	Heizer	M
Diekmann, Karl	Oberheizer	M
Diesel, Fritz	Maschinistenmaat	M
Dietze, Ernst	Heizer	K
Dopheide, Rudolf	Matrose	K
Dressler, Arthur	Obermaschinist	K
Dreyer, Friedrich	Heizer	K
Ehlers, Walter	Funkentelegraphiegast	K
Ellerbroek, Friedrich	Marine-Stabsingenieur	M
Engel, Paul	Matrose	W A
Engels, Heinrich	Bootsmannsmaat	K
Erfurt, Richard	Maschinistenmaat	M
Ewegen, Hermann von	Maschinistenmaat	K
Fenske, Wilhelm	Oberbootsmannsmaat	K
Ferber, Johann	Oberbottelier	W M
Feukert, Kurt	Diensttuender Obersignalgast	W A
Fiedler, Emil	Matrose	K
Fischer, Josef	Heizer	K
Flint, Martin	Heizer	M
Formberg, Heinrich	Heizer	K
Fornacon, Ernst	Obermaschinistenanwärter	W M
Forst, Hans	Heizer	M
Franz, Joseph, Prinz von Hohenzollern	Leutnant zur See	M
Franz, Wilhelm	Bäckersgast	K
Freye, Heinrich	Zimmermannsmaat	M
Friedrich, Arthur	Heizer	M
Friese, Hermann	Maschinistenmaat	K
Gaede, Ernst	Kapitänleutnant	K
Garbe, Friedrich	Obermaschinistenmaat	W M
Geerdes, August	Oberleutnant zur See	W A

Geibel, Jacob	Heizer	W M
Gierloff, Richard	Maschinist	M
Goldbaum, Hermann	Heizer	M
Gollatz, Paul	Maschinistenmaat	M
Gonscherowski, Ewald	Heizer	M
Gottschalk, Hermann	Heizer	M
Gräwe, Walter	Signalgast	K
Grenz, Friedrich	Obermatrose	K
Gropius, Hans	Kapitänleutnant	K
Grumbach, René	Funkentelegraphiegast	W A
Grün, Karl	Obermaterialienverwaltersmaat	M
Grzybowski, Bruno	Obermatrose	W A
Guérard, Albert von	Leutnant zur See	K
Gurak, Otto	Heizer	W A
Gutman, Adam	Obermatrose	K
Haas, August	Heizer	K
Haaß, Hugo	Marine-Ingenieur	M
Haase, Paul	Segelmachersmaat	K
Habben, Martin	Malersgast	W A
Hackemesser, Paul	Sanitätsmaat	K
Handel, August	Obermaschinistenmaat	M
Handtke, Anton	Heizer	K
Harms, Hans Heinz	Maschinistenmaat	M
Hartung, Fritz	Artillerieobermechanikersmaat	W A
Heering, Heinrich	Obermaschinistenmaat	M
Heinzelmann, Friedrich	Bootsmannsmaat	M
Hellwege, Harry	Maschinistenmaat	W M
Hellwig, Willi	Matrose	K
Henkes, Nikolaus	Bäckersgast	K
Henninger, Ludwig	Matrose	K
Henseler, Peter	Diensttuender Maschinistenoberanwärter	M
Herwartz, Leonard	Heizer	M
Hilbig, Karl	Matrose	K
Hilgenstock, Fritz	Torpedooberheizer	W A
Hilbold, Jacob	Heizer	K
Hoef, Peter	Maschinistenmaat	M
Hoffmann, Josef	Schumachersgast	W A
Holthausen, Paul	Heizer	K
Holze, Otto Wilhelm	Heizer	W A
Huch, Otto	Heizer	W A
Huhn, Heinrich	Schumachersgast	K

Hülsbusch, Heinrich August	Heizer	W M
Hülsmann, Bernhard	Obermaschinistenanwärter	M
Huster, Hermann	Funkentelegraphiegast	K
Hutsch, Peter	Torpedoheizer	M
Issleib, Richard	Heizer	K
Jaguttis, Michael	Obermaschinistenmaat	M
Jung, Heinrich	Heizer	K
Junk, Johann	Heizer	M
Junker, Friedrich	Heizer	K
Jürgens, Karl	Maschinistenmaat	M
Kaiser, Johann	Kriegsfreiwilliger Heizer	W A
Kalbe, Albert	Matrose	K
Kammer, Wilhelm	Oberheizer	W A
Kampf, Willy	Maschinist	M
Kapuszinsky, Apollinarius	Matrose	K
Kaufner, Heinrich	Zimmermannsgast	K
Keil, Hermann	Obermaschinistenmaat	M
Keller, Georg	Obermaschinist	W M
Kienapfel, Wilhelm	Heizer	M
Kirchhoff, Ernst	Heizer	K
Klages, Alfred	Maschinistenmaat	M
Klawitter, Paul	Bootsmannsmaat	W A
Klee, Karl	Matrose	K
Klein, Ludwig	Oberheizer	W A
Kleinecke, Otto	Matrose	K
Klöppel, Johann	Heizer	M
Kluge, Gustav	Maschinistenmaat	M
Kluth, Heinrich	Heizer	M
Knabe, Paul	Heizer	M
Knasiak, Josef	Matrose	M
Knittel, August	Heizer	M
Koczwara, Johann	Kriegsfreiwilliger Heizer	M
Koplin, Friedrich	Matrose	W M
Köppen, Walter	Obermaschinistenmaat	K
Körber, Georg	Maschinist	M
Körver, Theodor	Heizer	M
Köster, Paul	Torpedomaschinistenmaat der Reserve	W M
Köster, Georg Wilhelm	Heizer	W A
Kröhling, Wilhelm	Matrose	K
Kruggel, Adolf	Feuerwerksmaat	M
Kugelmeyer, Georg	Matrose	K
Kühl, Wilhelm	Matrose	K

Kuhlmann, Richard	Torpedoheizer	M
Kühnel, Herbert	Matrose	K
Kunkel, Adolf	Matrose	W A
Kutzmutz, Paul	Heizer	M
Laabs, Heinrich Wilhelm	Heizer	W A
Ladewig, Richard	Matrose	K
Lange, Karl	Heizer	M
Leicht, Georg	Obermaschinist	M
Leuk, Matthias	Oberheizer	M
Léveque, Fritz	Heizer	M
Leven, Heinrich	Obermatrose	K
Levetzow, Ernst von	Oberleutnant zur See	K
Levy, Gustav	Matrose	K
Liebe, Albert	Artilleriemechanikeroberanwärter	M
Lindner, Hans	Signalgast	M
Linnemann, Wilhelm	Heizer	W A
Linnig, Paul	Signalmaat	K
Lochau, Friederich	Matrose	M
Löffler, Ludwig	Schneidersgast	K
Löhrer, Peter	Heizer	M
Luther, Dr Johannes	Marine-Stabsarzt	M
Maaß, Robert	Torpedooberheizer	W A
Machelett, Karl	Heizer	M
Martini, Alois	Heizer	M
Martz, Eugen	Heizer	K
Marx, Hans	Obermatrose	K
Mayer, Nicolaus	Matrose	W A
Metzing, Theodor	Signalgast	K
Meybohm, Friedrich	Heizer	W A
Meyer, Heinrich	Bootsmannsmaat	K
Meyer, August	Obermatrose	K
Meyer, Karl	Zimmermannsgast	W A
Mischel, Fritz	Torpedooberheizer	W A
Möller, Ludwig	Signalgast	K
Möller, Walter	Heizer	K
Mönkediek, Otto	Steuermann	W A
Müller, Ernst Friedrich	Heizer	M
Müller, Friedrich	Heizer	W M
Müller, Karl von	Fregattenkapitän	M
Müller, Leo	Matrose	K
Müller, Paul	Torpedomatrose	M
Müller, Walter	Oberheizer	M
Nagels, Cornelius	Heizer	M

Niebuhr, Wilhelm	Matrose	W A
Nohke, Max	Signalgast	K
Odenthal, Wilhelm	Heizer	K
Offermann, Otto	Matrose	W A
Olm, Wilhelm	Maschinistenmaat	M
Pallida, Paul	Heizer	W M
Park, Wilhelm	Matrose	K
Peters, Gerhard	Bootsmannsmaat	K
Peyronnie, Eugen	Oberheizer	M
Pfeiffer, Karl	Feuerwerker	K
Pfeil, Heinrich	Heizer	K
Pieper, Wilhelm	Maschinistenmaat	M
Pieritz, Erich	Heizer	W M
Plotha, Johann	Oberheizer	W A
Plötz, Hugo	Steuermannsmaat	M
Pohlmann, Wilhelm	Heizer	K
Pörrer, Georg	Torpedoheizer	M
Possehl, Friedrich	Torpedomatrose	W A
Pries, Paul	Offiziersbarbier (civilian)	K
Puls, Karl	Heizer	M
Püschel, Ernst	Torpedomaschinistenmaat	M
Pyttlik, Georg	Torpedoobermaschinist	K
Quadflieg, Joseph	Heizer	M
Reche, Karl	Oberheizer	M
Reich, Heinrich	Matrose	K
Reichelt, Alfred	Oberzimmermannsgast	M
Riegelmeyer, Otto	Maschinistenmaat	M
Rieger, Paul	Signalmaat	K
Riehl, Johannes-August	Heizer	K
Rohr, Joseph	Heizer	K
Rombach, Nicolaus	Matrose	M
Ross, Wilhelm	Heizer	K
Röttgen, Jakob	Matrose	W A
Ruhmer, Robert	Heizer	M
Ruscinski, Joseph	Bootsmannsmaat	W A
Rütz, Carl	Maschinistenmaat	M
Rysse, Nicolaus van	Feuerwerksmaat	K
Sablowski. Kurt	Bootsmannsmaat	K
Sanders, Dietrich	Heizer	K
Schaller, Paul	Heizer	W A
Schau, Kurt	Matrose	K
Scheller, Emil	Heizer	K
Schember, Heinrich	Heizer	W M

Schepputat, Gustav	Diensttuender Maschinistenoberanwärter	M
Scherer, Nicolaus	Matrose	K
Schlauß, Felix	Heizer	M
Schlechtweg, Wilhelm	Matrose	K
Schmidt, Adam	Heizer	M
Schmidt, Josef	Heizer	W M
Schmiedtke, Rudolf	Diensttuender Maschinistenoberanwärter	K
Schneider, Max	Maschinistenmaat	K
Schnelle, Rudolf	Matrose	K
Schoolmann, Johann	Diensttuender Maschinistenoberanwärter	K
Schuhmacher, Max	Heizer	M
Schulz, Gustav	Offizierskoch (civilian)	K
Schulze, Ludwig	Maschinist	K
Schütz, Michael Isidor	Heizer	W A
Schwabe, Dr Ludwig	Assistenzarzt	K
Schwarz, Hermann	Obersignalgast	M
Schwarz, Wilhelm	Maschinistenmaat	M
Sellmeyer, Heinrich	Matrose	K
Siemens, Klaus	Oberheizer	K
Spielmann, Albert Hans	Bootsmannsmaat	W A
Stauch, Max	Bootsmannsmaat	K
Stechmeyer, Konrad	Oberheizer	M
Steidle, Theodor	Heizer	W A
Steinfurth, Heinrich	Feuerwerksmaat	K
Stoffers, August	Marine-Ingenieur	K
Straka, August	Heizer	M
Tannert, Gerhard	Matrose	K
Teschner, Bernhard	Matrose	W A
Thomas, Theodor	Oberheizer	K
Tietz, Paul	Matrose	K
Treppens, Willi	Matrose	K
Tull, Josef	Maschinist	M
Uebe, Hermann	Diensttuender Maschinistenoberanwärter	M
Uhde, Karl	Heizer	M
Unger, Bernhard	Heizer	M
Unidentified Chinese National	Waschmänner (civilian)	K
Unidentified Chinese National	Waschmänner (civilian)	K
Unidentified Chinese National	Waschmänner (civilian)	K
Uster, Theodor	Heizer	K

Veith, Gustav	Heizer	K
Velten, Wilhelm	Oberfeuerwerksmaat	W A
Vieregg, Fritz	Maschinistenmaat	M
Vogt, Wilhelm	Diensttuender Maschinistenoberanwärter	M
Vorwerk, Karl	Heizer	K
Wachtel, Ferdinand Karl	Heizer	M
Wagner, Gustav	Matrose	W A
Wecke, Otto	Oberhoboistenmaat	M
Weise, Alfred	Matrose	W M
Welher, Peter	Heizer	M
Welhing, Johann Clemens	Heizer	M
Werkmeister, Adam	Maschinistenmaat	M
Werner, Arthur	Matrose	M
Wesemann, Diedrich	Maschinistenmaat	M
Wetzel, Hermann	Heizer	K
Wex, Ernst	Heizer	K
Wieland, Wilhelm	Heizer	K
Wilking, Hermann	Schreibersmaat	K
Wille, Paul	Funkentelegraphiegast	K
Willms, Johannes	Matrose	M
Wilzepolsky, Goldap	Heizer	K
Winter, Jacob	Heizer	W A
Wirth, Johann	Heizer	W M
Witt, Walter	Matrose	K
Wittenberg, Arnold	Maschinistenmaat	K
Wittenbrock, Theodor	Matrose	K
Witthoeft, Robert	Oberleutnant zur See	W M
Wittig, Walter	Heizer	M
Wolff, Friedrich	Heizer	M
Wollburg, Wilhelm	Matrose	M
Woytakowsky, Franz	Zimmermannsmaat	W M
Woytschekowsky, Arthur	Marine-Oberzahlmeister	K
Zeidler, Paul	Matrose	K
Ziehr, Willi	Matrose	K
Zimmer, Georg	Wachtmeistersmaat	M
Zimmer, Peter	Heizer	K
Zimmermann, Fritz Karl	Leutnant zur See	K

Detached for duty on Direction Island

Fate:
K – denotes died of wounds or disease
W – denotes wounded

Name	Rank or Rate	Fate
Bartholomäus, Georg	Torpedomatrose	
Becker, Bernhard	Heizer	
Berg, Arnold	Matrose	
Booch, Alfred	Torpedomaschinistenmaat	
Burgwedel, Heinrich	Bootsmannsmaat	
Dorl, Albert	Matrose	
Goldmann, Bruno	Signalgast	
Grube, Hermann	Obermatrose	
Gyssling, Eugen	Leutnant zur See	
Härttrich, Adam	Maschinistenmaat	
Hegel, Otto	Obermatrose	
Heimann, Paul	Oberheizer	
Hilbers, Georg	Funkentelegraphieobermatrose	
Holen, Adolf	Maschinistenmaat	
Hoff, Walter	Obersignalgast	
Keil, Wilhelm	Matrose	K
Kirbach, Erich	Matrose	
Knopp, Heinrich	Obermatrose	
Koschinsky, Heinrich	Obermatrose	W
Krause, Fritz	Obermatrose	
Kreutz, Jakob	Heizer	
Lanig, Friedrich	Heizer	K
Löhmann, Walter	Obermatrose	
Luther, Gustav	Oberheizer	
Mauritz, Julius	Matrose	W
Michaelis, Erich	Bootsmannsmaat	
Mücke, Hellmuth von	Kapitänleutnant	
Münch, Walter	Heizer	
Ostermann, Carl	Heizer	
Petersen, Wilhelm	Torpedomatrose	
Pinkert, Fritz	Matrose	
Rademacher, Joseph	Matrose	K
Reich, Erich Oskar	Obermatrose	
Rossbach, Paul	Maschinistenmaat	
Sangen, Alarich	Matrose	
Schmidt, Roderich	Leutnant zur See	K

Schmidtberger, Philipp	Matrose	
Schwalbe, Gustav	Heizer	
Schwenteidt, Carl	Matrose	
Siebert, Alfred	Matrose	
Steege, Willi	Matrose	
Stephan, Johann	Heizer	
Stoves, Walter	Heizer	
Süss, Wilhelm	Obermatrose	
Tiedemann, Hendrik	Obermatrose	
Wadephul, Alfred	Matrose	
Wichert, Rudolf	Funkentelegraphiegast	
Winterling, Fritz	Oberheizer	
Witt, Hermann	Matrose	W
Wolff, Rudolf	Matrose	

Appendix 2: HMAS *Sydney* ship's company on 9 November 1914

Fate:
K – denotes killed in action or died of wounds
W – denotes wounded in action

Name	*Rank or Rate*	*Fate*
Adams, James	Stoker, RAN	
Adams, Robert John	Able Seaman, RAN	
Alexander, Edward James	Able Seaman, RN	
Anderson, Ralph Augustus	Ordinary Seaman 2nd Class, RAN	
Anderson, Walter Ernest	Ordinary Seaman, RAN	
Andrews, Charles James	Shipwright 2nd Class, RAN	
Atkins, Bertie John	Petty Officer, RN	
Atkinson, George Thomas	Stoker, RAN	
Attwater, Albert	Engine Room Artificer 3rd Class, RAN	
Ayres, Charles Stephens William	Able Seaman, RAN	
Badger, Cecil Williams	Stoker, RAN	
Bainbrigge, Phillip	Stoker, RAN	
Baird, Stanley Edward	Able Seaman, RAN	
Baker, Frederick Ernest	Able Seaman, RAN	
Baker, Walter	Chief Stoker, RAN	
Ball, Herbert David	Stoker, RAN	
Banks, Harold Wall	Stoker, RAN	
Bannier, Frank John	Leading Stoker, RAN	
Barber, Herbert Henry	Leading Stoker, RN	
Barker, Albert Mortyn	Officers' Steward 3rd Class, RAN	
Barker, Joseph William	Officers' Steward 2nd Class, RN	
Barnett, Charles Henry	Ordinary Seaman, RAN	
Barratt, Stanley Gordon	Stoker, 2nd Class, RAN	
Barry, Thomas John	Stoker, RN	
Bates, George	Able Seaman, RAN	
Batty, Frank	Stoker, RN	
Behenna, Edward Charles	Carpenter, RN	
Belcham, Walter Ryly	Stoker, RN	
Bell, Robert William	Ordinary Seaman, RAN	K
Bell-Salter, Basil Owen	Lieutenant, RN	
Bellamy, William Leonard	Officers' Steward 2nd Class, RAN	
Bennett, Alfred	Acting Chief Stoker, RN	
Benney, William John	Able Seaman, RAN	
Bent, Thomas Hurbert	Ordinary Seaman, RAN	
Bird, Henry Thomas	Able Seaman, RAN	
Boston, Ernest Cyril	Boy 1st Class, RAN	

233

Bourke, Walter Bernard	Ordinary Seaman 2nd Class, RAN
Brady, Charles	Ordinary Signalman, RAN
Brady, Thomas Edward	Boy 1st Class, RAN
Brazendale, Herman	Able Seaman, RAN
Brien, Jerry	Leading Stoker, RN
Brien, Thomas Linsley (George Alfred)	Acting Stoker, RAN
Broc, John Francis	Able Seaman, RN
Broome, Richard Henry	Able Seaman, RN
Brougham, Frederick Henry	Engine Room Artificer 4th Class, RAN
Brown, Albert Edward	Painter, RAN
Brown, James	Leading Seaman, RAN
Brown, John	Chief Stoker, RAN
Brownlow, Alfred James	Officers Steward 1st Class, RAN
Brydie, William Corstorphine	Cooper, RAN
Budgen, Arthur James	Stoker Petty Officer, RAN
Bunkin, Edward	Shipwright 2nd Class, RN
Butcher, John Arthur	Able Seaman, RAN W
Cahill, Denis	Leading Stoker, RN
Carsley, Charles	Leading Stoker, RN
Carter, Henry William	Ships' Corporal, RAN
Cavaye, Frederick Langton	Lieutenant, RN
Cave, Sidney Edward	Ordinary Seaman, RAN
Chapman, Allan Thomas	Stoker, RAN
Chitts, Thomas James	Ordinary Seaman, RAN
Clague, Frank	Ordinary Seaman, RAN
Clark, Ernie	Ordinary Seaman, RAN
Clarke, John	Leading Stoker, RAN
Clifford, James Reynolds	Telegraphist, RAN
Clifford, John William	Able Seaman, RAN
Coleman, Arthur Wheatley	Engineer Lieutenant Commander, RN
Coleman, John Albert	Chief Yeoman of Signals, RAN
Colless, Alan	Ordinary Seaman 2nd Class, RAN
Collins, Harold Mark	Acting Able Seaman, RAN
Colton, Joseph	Stoker, RN
Colwill, Richard	Chief Stoker, RN
Connell, Peter	Yeoman of Signals, RN
Connelly, John Davis	Able Seaman, RAN
Conroy, Henry	Able Seaman, RN
Cook, Arthur Benjamin	Ordinary Seaman, RAN
Cook, Wilfred Thomas	Electrical Artificer 2nd Class, RN
Cooksey, William	Sailmaker, RAN
Corder, Reuben John	Ordinary Seaman, RAN

Corigliano, Charles David	Stoker, RAN	
Cornish, Frederick James	Stoker 2nd Class, RAN	
Coughlan, Rupert	Stoker, RAN	
Coulson, Tettrell	Stoker, RN	
Coulter, Charles	Chief Stoker, RN	
Crosby, Albert Edward	Able Seaman, RAN	W
Crowther, William	Officers' Steward 2nd Class, RN	
Culph, Henry John	Stoker, RAN	
Currie, John McCallum	Leading Stoker, RAN	
Darby, Leonard	Surgeon, RAN	
Dardel, James Henry	Engine Room Artificer 4th Class, RAN	
Darragh, James	Engine Room Artificer 4th Class, RAN	
Davey, Joseph Henry	Blacksmith's Mate, RAN	
Davis, Frederick Bernard	Ship's Musician, RAN	
Davis, George	Petty Officer, RN	
Davis, William	Stoker, RAN	
Dawes, Alfred	Butcher 3rd Class, RAN	
Day, Edward George	Cook's Mate, RAN	
Day, John	Leading Seaman, RAN	
Deer, Hubert Victor	Stoker, RAN	
Dell, Bertie Glyn	Leading Seaman, RN	
Denham, George Dunlop	Mechanician, RAN	
Denholm, Colin	Stoker, RAN	
Dennis, Cleon	Engineer Lieutenant, RAN	
Denyer, Alfred Samuel	Stoker, RAN	
Dobson, Charles William	Stoker Petty Officer, RAN	
Dogger, Leslie	Stoker, RAN	
Doll, Godfrey Edward	Ordinary Seaman, RAN	
Donnelly, John Henry	Petty Officer, RN	
D'Ornay, John Walter	Boy 1st Class, RAN	
Dott, Frederick	Stoker, RN	
Dowers, John Frederick	Able Seaman, RN	
Dowley, Reginald Thomas	Officers Steward 3rd Class, RN	
Drew, Henry Edward	Stoker Petty Officer, RN	
Eastlake, Arthur Charles Edward	Able Seaman, RN	
Edson, Harry Harold	Able Seaman, RAN	
Edwards, George William	Officers Steward 1st Class, RN	
Edwards, Harry	Able Seaman, RN	
Ehlert, Carl Bergenhagen	Boy 1st Class, RAN	
Elliott, Aubrey John	Stoker, RAN	
Emslie, Alexander	Engine Room Artificer 4th Class, RAN	
Etheridge, Frank Richard	Petty Officer, RN	
Evans, George Edwin	Ordinary Seaman 2nd Class, RAN	

Every, Frederick	Stoker, RAN	
Fahey, James Joseph	Acting Leading Stoker, RN	
Feeley, Frank Howard	Stoker, RAN	
Fehr, Thomas Edward	Stoker, RAN	
Finlay, Frederick	Chief Ship's Cook, RN	
Finlayson, John Francis	Lieutenant Commander, RN	
Fisher, Frank	Leading Seaman, RAN	
Fleming, William	Stoker, RAN	
Fletcher, Samuel Horace	Engine Room Artificer 1st Class, RN	
Flewellen, Eric Clarence	Boy 1st Class, RAN	
Fowler, Lawrence Parsons	Engineer Lieutenant, RAN	
Frampton, George	Leading Stoker, RN	
Freathy, Archibald Ernest	Leading Seaman, RN	
Freeman, Harold Arthur	Ordinary Seaman 2nd Class, RAN	
Frost, Herbert	Able Seaman, RN	
Fulton, John William	Second Cook's Mate, RAN	
Gable, Albert	Stoker, RAN	
Garland, John	Stoker, RAN	
Garsia, Rupert Clare	Lieutenant, RAN	
Gascoigne, Thomas	Able Seaman, RAN	W
George, Stanley Bertram	Officers' Steward 3rd Class, RN	
Gilliot, Walter Willoughby	Leading Stoker, RAN	
Glossop, John Collings Taswell	Captain, RN	
Glue, Benjamin James	Stoker, RAN	
Goad, William Samuel Watts	Leading Carpenter's Crew, RN	
Gorlich, Frederick	Able Seaman, RAN	
Grace, Cecil Gordon	Stoker 2nd Class, RAN	
Green, Bertie Fredrick	Able Seaman, RAN	W
Green, Mervyn Henry Newton	Stoker, RAN	
Griffin, Thomas	Plumber, RAN	
Griffith, Norman Eric	Stoker, RAN	
Grigor, Bruce	Boy 1st Class, RAN	
Grigor, Wallace	Boy 1st Class, RAN	
Grimley, Reginald Francis	Ordinary Seaman 2nd Class, RAN	
Gullick, Alfred William	Able Seaman, RN	
Hales, Thomas	Engine Room Artificer 3rd Class, RAN	
Halford, John	Leading Stoker, RN	
Hall, William	Stoker 2nd Class, RAN	
Hammond, James	Stoker, RN	
Hampden, Geoffrey Cromwell Edward	Lieutenant, RN	W
Hansen, Ernest Robert	Ordinary Seaman, RAN	
Harris, John	Acting Stoker, RAN	

236

Harry, Herbert (Beaton, Blaise Hanley)	Ordinary Seaman, RAN	
Hart, Arthur Asaph	Petty Officer, RN	
Harte, John Albert	Able Seaman, RAN	
Harvey, Mark Beer	Petty Officer, RN	W
Hawkes, Thomas	Stoker, RN	
Haworth, Claude Frederick	Stoker 2nd Class, RAN	
Hayden, Thomas	Leading Stoker, RN	
Hayler, Albert Waldegrave	Able Seaman, RN	
Hearfield, Frank Hermann	Ship's Steward's Boy, RAN	
Heath, George William	Able Seaman, RAN	
Herlihy, Denis Frank	Leading Telegraphist, RN	
Hickson, Thomas William	Stoker Petty Officer, RAN	
Hill, James Alexander	Able Seaman, RAN	
Hoar, George Auldren	Able Seaman, RN	
Hoffman, George	Cook's Mate, RAN	
Holley, Francis William	Master at Arms, RAN	
Holloway, Frederick James	Leading Stoker, RN	
Holmes, Herbert	Able Seaman, RN	
Hood, Charles	Able Seaman, RAN	
Hooper, Arthur James	Able Seaman, RAN	W
Horne, Richard	Able Seaman, RAN	W
Houlton, John Francis	Ship's Corporal, RN	
Houston, Robert Thomas	Stoker, RAN	
Howells, Robert Harold Henry	Boy 1st Class, RAN	
Hoy, Albert	Able Seaman, RN	K
Hubbard, Henry	Canteen Assistant (civilian)	
Hughes, John	Stoker Petty Officer, RAN	
Hughes, Thomas	Leading Signalman, RN	
Humphreys, Leslie George	Boy 1st Class, RAN	
Humphry, Reginald	Signalman, RN	
Hunt, Leonard	Stoker, RN	
Hunter, Norman Charles	Ordinary Telegraphist, RAN	
Hutchison, George Arnold	Artificer Engineer, RN	
Hutton, William	Stoker, RAN	
Huxford, Alfred Ernest	Able Seaman, RAN	
Hyde, Stephen Charles	Ordinary Seaman, RAN	
Jacob, Edward Frederick	Stoker Petty Officer, RN	
James, Charles	Stoker, RAN	
Jamieson, Edward	Able Seaman, RAN	
Jeffery, Douglas Robert	Petty Officer, RAN	
Jeffery, Oswald Richard	Ordinary Seaman, RAN	
Jessop, Morris	Officers' Steward 2nd Class, RN	

Johnstone, Arthur Kenrick	Stoker, RAN	
Johnstone, James Montagu Cholmeley	Acting Lieutenant, RN	
Jones, Arthur Edwin	Able Seaman, RAN	
Jones, Frank Trevor	Able Seaman, RN	
Joyce, William George	Armourer's Crew, RN	
Joyner, Arthur	Leading Stoker, RN	
Kelly, Daniel	Stoker, RAN	
Kemp, Arthur Frederick	Stoker, RAN	
Kent, Edwin Hamilton	Able Seaman, RAN	
Kimber, Harry	Stoker, RAN	
King, John Thomas	Chief Stoker, RN	
Kingsford-Smith, Eric	Assistant Paymaster, RAN	
Kinniburgh, Joseph Leslie	Able Seaman, RAN	W
Kirby, James Edward	Stoker, RAN	
Knowles, Arthur Frederick	Able Seaman, RAN	
Laird, Joseph Ernest	Acting Leading Stoker, RAN	
Lake, Thomas	Ordinary Seaman, RAN	
Lambert, Arthur William	Chief Petty Officer, RAN	
Lander, Thomas	Leading Cook's Mate, RN	
Leahy, Gerald	Able Seaman, RAN	
Leaning, Frederick	Stoker, RAN	
Lee, Leonard Charles	Able Seaman, RAN	
Lee-Gray, Charles John	Chief Writer, RN	
Lemon, Arthur Thomas Handford	Stoker, RAN	
Levy, Jack	Sick Berth Attendant, RAN	
Little, Vivian Agincourt Spence	Chaplain, RAN	
Longley, Edward Elkins	Stoker, RN	
Lucas, Claude Merlin	Stoker 2nd Class, RAN	
Lynch, Thomas	Petty Officer, RN	K
Macrow, Albert Charles	Able Seaman, RAN	
Maher, William	Stoker, RAN	
Malone, Arthur James	Ordinary Seaman, RAN	
Mansell, Jesse	Officers' Cook, RN	
Marland, John Stanley	Ordinary Seaman 2nd Class, RAN	
Marshall, William Nankivel	Stoker, RAN	
Martin, Alfred Moule	Boatswain, RN	
Mason, Alfred Edward	Ship's Steward, RN	
Matthew, Wallace	Ordinary Seaman 2nd Class, RAN	
Matthews, Robert	Acting Engine Room Artificer 4th Class, RAN	
Matthews, William Henry	Able Seaman, RN	
Mauger, Herbert James	Shipwright 2nd Class, RAN	

May, Francis James	Officers' Steward 3rd Class, RN
McCabrey, David	Acting Leading Stoker, RN
McCarthy, Thomas	Leading Seaman, RAN
McCarthy, William George Henry	Stoker, RN
McCleery, Thomas	Chief Stoker, RAN
McClure, John	Mechanician, RAN
McComas, Robert Croydon	Able Seaman, RAN
McFarlane, John Clement	Gunner (Torpedo), RAN
McGowan, Henry	Stoker, RAN
McGregor, Benjamin	Stoker, RAN
McIntyre, Henry	Stoker 2nd Class, RAN
McKay, Duncan	Able Seaman, RAN
McKay, Leslie Vickers	Stoker, RAN
McLarty, Donald	Engine Room Artificer, RN
McLennan, Cecil	Stoker, RAN
Meldrum, William Ernest	Ordinary Seaman, RAN W
Mellor, Arnold	Ordinary Signalman, 2nd Class, RAN
Merrilees, Alexander James	Boy 1st Class, RAN
Millar, Roy Maxwell	Boy 1st Class, RAN
Mitchell, Sydney Reuben	Electrical Artificer 2nd Class, RN
Moriarty, Edward Henry	Stoker, RAN
Morris, George Otto	Ordinary Seaman, RAN
Moss, Horace William	Able Seaman, RAN
Mullins, Thomas Edward	Sick Berth Steward, RAN
Napper, Percy	Acting Chief Stoker, RN
Neale, Charles Alfred	Stoker, RAN
Neher, Howarth Rolf	Stoker, RAN
Neill, William Boswell	Able Seaman, RAN
Newham, James Edward	Petty Officer, RN
Newman, Ernest	Leading Seaman, RAN
Newton, Thomas	Petty Officer, RAN
Nielsen, Neils Peter Henry	Stoker, RAN
Norman, Eric Henry	Officers Steward 3rd Class, RAN
Norris, Frederick	Yeoman of Signals, RAN
Norton, Ernest Claude	Staff Paymaster, RAN
Nugent, James Laurence	Stoker, RAN
Oliver, Walter Albert	Able Seaman, RAN
O'Neill, Thomas	Stoker, RN
Organ, Alfred	Stoker, RN
Overell, Joseph James	Stoker, RAN
Palmer, James	Stoker, RAN
Parkes, James William	Leading Seaman, RAN

Parsell, James	Blacksmith's Mate, RAN
Parsons, Thomas Walter	Stoker, RN
Payling, John Peter	Boy 1st Class, RAN
Pearce, George Wilson	Engine Room Artificer 3rd Class, RAN
Pearce, Henry	Engine Room Artificer 3rd Class, RAN
Pedelty, John Francis	Boy 1st Class, RAN
Perry, Samuel	Chief Armourer, RAN
Perry, Thomas Lewis	Petty Officer Telegraphist, RN
Pert, James Watt	Engine Room Artificer 4th Class, RAN
Peterson, Albert Victor	Ordinary Seaman 2nd Class, RAN
Peterson, Theodore	Stoker, RAN
Phillips, James Thomas Henry	Chief Ship's Cook, RN
Pope, Cuthbert John	Lieutenant, RN
Powell, Ivo	Stoker, RAN
Poyner, Herbert Leonard	Stoker Petty Officer, RN
Prebble, Edward Brennan	Stoker, RAN
Pullar, John	Stoker, RAN
Purcell, Arthur Joseph	Stoker, RAN
Rahilly, Denis Edward	Lieutenant, RN
Randell, Isaac	Able Seaman, RAN
Rayner, Ernest Moss	Ordinary Seaman, RAN
Real, Alfred Ernest	Stoker, RAN
Reeves, Reginald John	Stoker, RAN
Rhoades, William Smith	Chief Petty Officer, RN
Rich, Edgar Lindsay	Leading Ship's Stewards Assistant, RN
Rickards, Henry (Bridger, Henry)	Stoker, RAN
Riddle, Henry	Leading Seaman, RN
Rigney, William	Stoker 2nd Class, RAN
Robb, John	Stoker, RAN
Roberts, Bernard Neil Goldsmith	Boy 1st Class, RAN
Robertson, John Love	Leading Stoker, RAN
Robinson, James Harold	Stoker, RAN
Robinson, Samuel	Acting Chief Stoker, RN
Robson, Joseph Henry	Leading Signalman, RAN
Rogan, Thomas John	Stoker 2nd Class, RAN
Rollo, Allan James	Engine Room Artificer 3rd Class, RAN
Rumley, Arthur	Stoker, RAN
Ruskin, Alfred	Stoker, RAN
Russell, Sydney Frank	Leading Seaman, RAN
Russell, William	Able Seaman, RAN
Ryan, John William	Boy 1st Class, RAN
Sadler, William Charles	Able Seaman, RN

Salter, Frank	Able Seaman, RN	
Salter, George Body	Gunner, RN	
Saunders, Lionel	Stoker, RN	
Sayer, Louis Alfred	Chief Engine Room Artificer, RN	
Scammell, George Henry Joseph Payne	Leading Cook's Mate, RN	
Scoble, Frederick William	Stoker, RAN	
Seabrook, Arthur	Stoker, RN	
Seabrook, John William	Signalman, RN	
Shallcross, Alfred	Able Seaman, RAN	
Sharp, John	Stoker, RN	
Sharp, Leonard Nairn	Officers' Steward 3rd Class, RAN	
Sharpe, Reginald Albert	Able Seaman, RN	K
Sheedy, Frederick Allen	Ordinary Seaman 2nd Class, RAN	
Slark, William Starbuck	Leading Stoker, RN	
Smale, Henry Alex	Stoker 2nd Class, RAN	
Smale, Samuel Gilbert	Able Seaman, RN	
Smart, Ernest John	Able Seaman, RAN	
Smith, Albert Edward	Chief Stoker, RN	
Smith, Alfred James	Stoker, RN	
Smith, George	Stoker, RN	
Smith, William	Able Seaman, RAN	
Smith, William Patrick	Stoker, RAN	
Sneezum, Rickmer Jasper	2nd Cook's Mate, RAN	
Spence, David Robert	Stoker, RAN	
Spencer, Charles Herbert	Officers' Steward 2nd Class, RN	
Staunton, James Leslie	Able Seaman, RAN	
Stephens, Thomas	Armourer's Crew, RAN	
Stevenson, Thomas Victor	Ordinary Signalman 2nd Class, RAN	W
Stewart, James Officer	Able Seaman, RN	
Stewart, James Pitts	Stoker Petty Officer, RAN	
Stewart, Sydney	Stoker, RAN	
Stewart, Wilfred Horace	Able Seaman, RAN	
Stonz, Cecil Hermann Jacob	Able Seaman, RAN	
Sullivan, Thomas	Able Seaman, RAN	
Sweeney, Joseph	Petty Officer, RN	
Sweetland, William Pearce	Ship's Steward 2nd Class, RAN	
Tamblin, William James Reid	Able Seaman, RN	
Taylor, Adolphus	Ordinary Seaman, RAN	
Taylor, Benjamin James	Stoker Petty Officer, RN	
Taylor, Ernest	Leading Stoker, RN	
Taylor, John Henry Havelock	Ordinary Seaman 2nd Class, RAN	
Taylor, Leonard	Stoker, RAN	

Taylor, William Alfred	Able Seaman, RAN
Telfer, Stanley James	Ordinary Seaman, RAN
Terry, Charles	Chief Shipwright, RN
Terry, Ernest	Able Seaman, RAN
Thomas, Valentine Gordon Geoffrey	Stoker, RAN
Thomson, Samuel	Leading Stoker, RAN
Thorndike, Leonard Jack	Ordinary Telegraphist, RAN
Tilbrook, Fred Archibald	Officers' Steward 2nd Class, RAN
Timmins, Thomas John	Chief Stoker, RAN
Todd, Arthur Charles Robert	Surgeon, RAN
Toner, Peter	Stoker, RN
Topp, Archibald Henry	Ordinary Seaman, RAN
Townsend, Walter Charles	Stoker, RAN
Trodd, John Charles	Stoker Petty Officer, RN
Truscott, William Charles Curnow	Able Seaman, RN
Turnbull, Thomas	Engine Room Artificer 4th Class, RAN
Turner, Charles Percival	Able Seaman, RN
Turner, Frederick	Chief Electrician, RN
Turner, George Edward	Stoker, RAN
Turner, John Joseph	Stoker, RAN
Vaughan, John	Stoker Petty Officer, RN
Veitch, Robert	Officers' Cook, RAN
Waldron, Arthur	Stoker, RAN
Walke, Harold Philip	Signalman, RAN
Warburton, William	Able Seaman, RAN
Ward, Jack	Telegraphist, RAN
Ward, William	Able Seaman, RN
Warner, George Graham Gordon	Stoker, RAN
Watson, Haylock Frederick	Officers' Cook 3rd Class, RN
Webb, George James	Leading Stoker, RAN
Webb, Henry	Petty Officer, RAN
Welford, Arthur John	Yeoman of Signals, RN
Westerman, Albert	Stoker 2nd Class, RAN
Wheeler, Alfred	Stoker, RAN
Whelan, Francis William	Able Seaman, RN
Whiddett, Alfred	Leading Stoker, RAN
Whitby, Arthur Raymond	Ordinary Seaman 2nd Class, RAN
White, Andrew	Engine Room Artificer 3rd Class, RAN
White, William John Thomas	Shipwright, 2nd Class, RAN
Wilkinson, James Leonard	Stoker, RAN
Willett, Alfred Elliott	Able Seaman, RAN

Williams, Charles Edward	Stoker Petty Officer, RAN	
Williams, Ernest	Stoker Petty Officer, RAN	
Williams, George Henry	Able Seaman, RAN	
Williams, John Robert	Ordinary Seaman 2nd Class, RN	
Williams, Joseph Gould	Stoker Petty Officer, RN	
Williamson, Tom	Ordinary Seaman 2nd Class, RAN	W
Wilson, Henry	Ordinary Seaman 2nd Class, RAN	
Wilson, John William	Acting Leading Stoker, RN	
Winder, John	Able Seaman, RN	
Wilson, George Henry	Able Seaman, RAN	
Withers, John	Stoker Petty Officer, RAN	
Wood, Ernest Claudius	Leading Stoker, RAN	
Wood, William	Leading Stoker, RAN	
Woodhead, Thomas	Carpenter's Crew, RAN	
Woodhouse, Edward	Canteen Manager (civilian)	
Woods, Alfred Charles	Ordinary Seaman 2nd Class, RAN	
Wootton, Robert	Able Seaman, RN	
Wyatt, Roderick Joseph	Stoker, RAN	
Yeomans, Percy Victor	Stoker 2nd Class, RAN	
Yetton, Charles	Chief Stoker, RN	
Young, Thomas	Petty Officer, RN	

Appendix 3: Honours and Awards

HMAS *Sydney*

On 1 January 1915 Captain John Collings Taswell Glossop was made a Companion of the Order of the Bath (CB) for distinguished services whilst commanding HMAS *Sydney* on 9 November 1914. Glossop was subsequently awarded the Japanese Order of the Rising Sun, 3rd Class, and the French Legion of Honour (Officer), for distinguished services rendered during the war.

Six members of the ship's company were awarded the Distinguished Service Medal for their conduct on 9 November 1914, these being Chief Petty Officer Arthur Lambert, Able Seamen Harold Collins, Bertie Green, Joseph Kinniburgh and William Taylor, and Sick Berth Steward Thomas Mullins.

In recognition of his work, Engineer Lieutenant Commander Arthur Coleman was promoted to Engineer Commander, effective from 9 November 1914.

Glossop also recommended the following members of the ship's company for promotion:

Name	From	To
Atkins, Bertie John	Petty Officer	Chief Petty Officer
Harvey, Mark Beer	Petty Officer	Chief Petty Officer
Webb, Henry	Petty Officer	Chief Petty Officer
McClure, John	Mechanician	Warrant Mechanician
Rollo, Allan James	Engine Room Artificer 3rd Class	Chief ERA 2nd Class
Currie, John McCallum	Leading Stoker	Stoker Petty Officer
O'Neill, Thomas	Stoker	Leading Stoker
Davis, William	Stoker	Leading Stoker

SMS *Emden*

On 4 November 1914, in recognition of *Emden*'s raid on Penang, Fregattenkapitän Karl von Müller was awarded the Iron Cross (*Eisernen Kreuz*), 1st and 2nd Class. All other commissioned officers, all warrant officers, and fifty petty officers were awarded the Iron Cross 2nd Class.

In February 1915 Kapitänleutnant Helmuth von Mücke and the members of *Emden*'s landing party were recognised for their achievements and devotion to duty. Von Mücke was awarded the Iron Cross 1st Class, the Saxon Military Order of St Henry (*Militär-St Heinrichs Orden*) Knight's Cross, and the Bavarian Military Merit

Order (*Militär-Verdienstorden*) 4th Class with Swords; all officers and men under his command at that time were awarded the Iron Cross 2nd Class. Leutnant zur See Eugen Gyssling was also awarded the *Militär-Verdienstorden*.

On 1 December 1914 von Müller was granted honorary citizenship of the City of Emden. German Admiralty recognition of his actions on 9 November 1914 came much later. On 21 March 1918 von Müller was awarded the *Pour le Mérite* (commonly known as the 'Blue Max'). On 1 October 1918 he was promoted to Kapitän zur See.

In 1921 surviving *Emden* crew members were granted a unique privilege; they were permitted to add '-Emden' to their family name to honour and perpetuate their association with the ship.

Appendix 4: Ships intercepted by SMS *Emden* 4 August – 9 November 1914

Ship	Date	Fate
Ryazan	4 August	Captured and converted to an auxiliary cruiser. Became SMS *Cormoran* (II). Later interned at Guam and scuttled by her crew on 7/4/17
Pontoporos	10 September	Captured and employed as a collier. Recaptured on 12/10/14 by HMS *Yarmouth*
Indus	10 September	Sunk
Lovat	11 September	Sunk
Kabinga	12 September	Captured and later released
Killin	13 September	Sunk
Diplomat	13 September	Sunk
Loredano	13 September	Stopped and released
Dandolo	13 September	Stopped and released
Trabboch	14 September	Sunk
Clan Matheson	14 September	Sunk
Dovre	18 September	Stopped and released with prisoners
King Lud	25 September	Sunk
Oceanus	25 September	Stopped and released
Tymeric	25/26 September	Sunk
Gryfevale	26 September	Captured and later released with prisoners
Buresk	27 September	Captured and used as collier. Scuttled on 9/11/14 to prevent recapture by HMAS *Sydney*
Ribera	27 September	Sunk
Foyle	27 September	Sunk
Djoca	27 September	Stopped and released
Clan Grant	16 October	Sunk
Ponrabbel	16 October	Sunk
Benmohr	16 October	Sunk
Fernando Po	18 October	Stopped and released
Troilus	18 October	Sunk
St Egbert	18 October	Captured and later released with prisoners
Exford	18 October	Captured and used as collier. Recaptured on 11/12/14 by HMS *Himalaya*
Chilkana	19 October	Sunk
Zhemchug	28 October	Sunk
Glenturret	28 October	Stopped and released
Mousquet	28 October	Sunk
Newburn	30 October	Stopped and released with prisoners

Appendix 5: SMS *Emden* ship's company detachments prior to 9 November 1914

Detached for duty on *Buresk*

Name	Rank or Rate
Ellermann, Heinrich	Obermaschinistenmaat
Fikentscher, Erich	Leutnant zur See
Giersch, Richard	Oberheizer der Reserve
Goltz, Hermann	Bootsmannsmaat der Reserve
Granzow, Julius	Obermatrose
Gronau, Wilhelm	Obermatrose
Kelle, Fritz	Obersignalgast
Klöpper, Oskar	Kapitänleutnant der Reserve
Lakay, Wilhelm	Kriegsfreiwilliger Heizer
Lapp, Heinrich	Obermaschinistenmaat
Leucht, Martin	Obermaschinistenmaat
Meyer, Karl	Matrose der Reserve
Rölle, Fritz	Funkentelegraphiegast
Schall, Robin Vidal	Leutnant zur See
Warnecke, Henry	Oberheizer der Reserve
Wittkopf, Friedrich	Torpedomaschinist

Detached for duty on *Exford*

Name	Rank or Rate
Eckstein, Joseph	Heizer
Fischer, Otto	Maschinist
Heinrich, Otto	Kriegsfreiwilliger Heizer
Huber, Wilhelm	Torpedomatrose
Jahnke, Franz	Maschinistenmaat
Kern, Eugen	Kriegsfreiwilliger Heizer
Klein, Paul	Funkentelegraphiemaat
Kliemt, Karl	Kriegsfreiwilliger Heizer
Köhler, Gustav	Matrose
Lauterbach, Julius	Oberleutnant zur See der Reserve
Müller, Karl	Bootsmann
Oettiger, Hermann	Bootsmannsmaat
Olschewsky, Emil	Maschinistenmaat
Piduch, Joseph	Matrose
Redlich, Willy	Steuermannsmaat
Siat, Ludwig	Maschinistenmaat
Wahlmann, Marcel	Matrose

Detached for duty on _Markomannia_

Name	Rank or Rate
Bordeaux, Franz	Marine-Zahlmeisterapplikant

Detached for duty on _Pontoporos_

Name	Rank or Rate
Becker, Hans	Heizer
Doleszyck, Friedrich	Matrose
Engel, Wilhelm	Matrose
Freund, Gerhard	Maschinist
Fürchtenicht, Richard	Matrose
Lehnigk, Richard	Maschinistenmaat
Look, Hermann	Heizer
Meyer, Martin Paul	Vizesteuermann der Reserve
Michuletz, Kurt	Torpedomaschinistenmaat
Paschkewitz, Ewald	Matrose
Patzig, Friedrich	Matrose
Rohde, Georg Johann	Matrose
Saake, Ernst	Heizer
Wöhner, Erich	Maschinistenmaat

Notes

1 Swan of the East

1 P Huff, *SMS Emden*, Hamecher, Kassel, 1994, pp11–12.
2 H Herwig, *'Luxury' Fleet*, Allen & Unwin, London, 1980, p125.
3 NAA, MP1049/1, 1918/047.
4 Huff, op cit, pp16–17.
5 *Dresden* was fitted with steam turbines, as were all cruisers ordered after *Emden*.
6 NAA, MP1049/1, 1918/047.
7 *Emden*'s 10.5cm guns were given the designation I/40, which was the overall length of the gun in bore calibres (ie 40 x 10.5cm = 420cm).
8 Huff, op cit, p19.
9 R Lochner, *The Last Gentleman-of-War*, Stanley Paul, London, 1988, pp305–6.
10 N Friedman, *Naval Weapons of World War One*, Seaforth, Barnsley, 2011, p336.
11 As completed, *Emden* carried one steam pinnace, one pulling pinnace, one motor boat, one gig, two cutters and two jolly boats.
12 Huff, op cit, pp38–41.
13 C Stephenson, *Germany's Asia–Pacific Empire*, Boydell Press, Suffolk, 2009, pp4–6, 54–7.
14 Ibid, p31.
15 T Gottschall, *By Order of the Kaiser*, Naval Institute Press, Annapolis, 2002, pp134–5.
16 D van der Vat, *The Last Corsair*, Panther Books, London, 1984, p36.
17 Huff, op cit, p140.
18 F Lochau, *On The Raging Seas*, Reach Publishers, Wandsbeck, 2012, p17.
19 F Joseph, Prince of Hohenzollern, *Emden*, Herbert Jenkins, London, 1928, p1.
20 B Tuchman, *The Guns of August*, Four Square, London, 1965 (reprint), p91.
21 Joseph, op cit, p6.
22 Franz Bordeaux, MLMSS 685/Item 1, Mitchell Library, State Library of New South Wales.
23 Joseph, op cit, pp8–9.
24 The additional 10.5cm ammunition (double what *Emden* normally carried) was stowed in lockers near the guns and in the 5.2cm magazines. The 5.2cm guns and ammunition are believed to have been removed from the ship prior to her departure from Tsingtao, probably to provide storage space for 10.5cm ammunition.
25 Bordeaux, op cit.
26 Ibid.
27 Ibid.
28 Lochner, op cit, p28.
29 Bordeaux, op cit.
30 The warships sighted were almost certainly the Russian cruisers *Askold* and *Zhemchug* with accompanying torpedo boats, on their way from Vladivostock to Hong Kong.
31 Von Mücke, *The Emden*, Ritter & Company, Boston, 1917, p17.
32 A Jose, *The Royal Australian Navy*, Angus & Robertson, Sydney, 1935 (reprint), pp1–8.
33 J Corbett, *Naval Operations*, vol 1, Naval & Military Press, East Sussex, reprint of the 1938 (revised) edition, pp44, 152.
34 Stephenson, op cit, pp67–70.
35 *Naval Staff Monographs (Historical)*, vol 5: *The Eastern Squadrons, 1914*, Naval Staff, Training and Staff Duties Division, April 1922, p33.
36 Corbett, op cit, p129.
37 W Churchill, *The World Crisis*

1911–1914, Australasian Publishing Company, Sydney, 1923, p295.
38 Bordeaux, op cit.
39 Joseph, op cit, p15.
40 *Newcastle* was at Nagasaki, and *Triumph* was at Hong Kong.
41 Churchill, op cit, p206.
42 It was later established that the vessel at Singapore was *Geier* (like *Cormoran*, now classified as a gunboat). She departed Singapore on 29 July and was last seen heading east.
43 *Naval Staff Monographs (Historical)*, vol 5, op cit, pp38–40.
44 Churchill, op cit, p207.
45 D Stevens, *In All Respects Ready*, Oxford University Press, South Melbourne, 2014, p21.
46 Jose, op cit, p10.
47 *Naval Staff Monographs (Historical)*, vol 5, op cit, p42.
48 The transmissions suggested that von Spee was moving deeper into the South Pacific, when in fact he was heading northeast, towards the Marianne Islands.
49 *Ryazan* was fitted with eight 10.5cm guns taken from *Cormoran*, and commissioned on 10 August as SMS *Cormoran* (II).
50 Huff, op cit, p147.
51 NAA, MP367/1, 580/2/1664. *Emden*'s war song was 'Watch on the Rhine'. Bordeaux knew it by its first line, '*Es braust ein Ruf wie Donnerhall*' which, loosely translated, means 'There resounds a call like thunder'.
52 Jose, op cit, pp11–14.
53 *Naval Staff Monographs (Historical)*, vol 5, op cit, p46.
54 Bordeaux, op cit.
55 Ibid. There were actually only seven merchantmen in the bay: *Gouverneur Jaeschke, Holsatia, Loongmoon, Mark, Prinz Waldemar, Staatssekretär Kraetke,* and *Yorck*.
56 Gyssling and Schmidt had been exchanged for Kapitänleutnant der Reserve Metzenthin, who had joined *Emden* on 6 August at Tsingtau.
57 Lochner, op cit, p50.
58 *Emden* was chosen because

Nürnberg's boilers were in poor condition.
59 Bordeaux, op cit.
60 Lochner, op cit, p55.
61 Joseph, op cit, p34.
62 Von Mücke, op cit, p41.
63 Joseph, op cit, pp35–6.
64 Stephenson, op cit, p106.
65 *Naval Staff Monographs (Historical)*, vol 5, op cit, p48.
66 Bordeaux, op cit.
67 Warships were permitted to use disguise and fly the flag of another nation, provided they displayed their true national flag before opening fire.
68 Corbett, op cit, pp280–2.
69 Ibid, pp146–9.

2 Cry Havoc
1 Lochner, op cit, pp77–9.
2 NAA, MP472/1, 16/15/8367.
3 Bordeaux, op cit.
4 Ibid.
5 Joseph, op cit, p67.
6 Bordeaux, op cit.
7 Ibid.
8 Ibid.
9 Joseph, op cit, p70.
10 A naval officer was now required on *Markomannia*, so Klöpper was sent to the collier. *Markomannia*'s first officer was assigned to *Pontoporos*, and Lauterbach returned to *Emden*.
11 Lochau, op cit, pp51–2.
12 Bordeaux, op cit.
13 Lochner, op cit, p94.
14 E Fayle, *Seaborne Trade*, vol 1, The Battery Press, Nashville, 1997 (reprint), p205.
15 Lochner, op cit, p97.
16 Joseph, op cit, p87.
17 *Naval Staff Monographs (Historical)*, vol 5, op cit, pp63–4.
18 Stevens, op cit, p50.
19 Jose, op cit, pp150–1.
20 Ibid, p158.
21 *Swiftsure, Dartmouth* and *Fox* were assigned to the convoys to protect them against possible attack by *Königsberg*.
22 *Naval Staff Monographs (Historical)*, vol 5, op cit, p64.
23 *Emden*'s forward sponson guns were at the greatest risk of damage during

coaling operations at sea. Each 10.5cm gun was fitted with two telescopic sights; the more important layer's sight was on the left, and the auxiliary sight was on the right side of the gun. As the sponson guns were normally pointed forward when not in use, *Emden* always coaled from the starboard side to avoid damaging the layer's sight on the No. 2 port gun.

24 Bordeaux, op cit.

25 The collier, with a prize crew from *Emden* onboard, was instructed to head south and wait for *Markomannia* off Simeulue Island during the second week of October.

26 NAA, MP367/1, 580/2/1664.

27 Ibid.

28 The French warships *Dovre*'s captain had seen in Penang were actually *Dupleix* and the gunboat *D'Iberville*.

29 Bordeaux, op cit.

30 Joseph, op cit, p102.

31 Bordeaux, op cit.

32 Ibid.

33 Trade routes in the Bay of Bengal had been reopened at 8.00am on 22 September, only to be closed again at 2.00am on 23 September after *Emden*'s reappearance rendered them unsafe.

34 Fayle, op cit, pp210–11.

35 Corbett, op cit, p298.

36 Ellerbroek was promoted to Marine-Stabsingenieur on 19 September.

37 Lochau, op cit, p62.

38 Joseph, op cit, p113.

39 Bordeaux, op cit.

40 Ibid.

41 Ibid.

42 *Naval Staff Monographs (Historical)*, vol 5, op cit, p75.

43 Joseph, op cit, p123.

44 Bordeaux, op cit. *Markomannia* steamed east and rendezvoused with *Pontoporos* off Simeulue Island on 6 October. They were caught by HMS *Yarmouth* six days later, whereupon *Markomannia* was seized and sunk, and *Ponotoporos* captured. Franz Bordeaux and his companions became prisoners of war.

45 Joseph, op cit, p129.

46 Jose, op cit, pp171–2.

47 *Naval Staff Monographs (Historical)*, vol 5, op cit, p81.

48 AWM, 1DRL/0658.

49 J Walter, *The Kaiser's Pirates*, Arms & Armour, London, 1994, p80.

50 AWM, 1DRL/0658.

51 Joseph, op cit, p154.

52 AWM, 1DRL/0658.

53 Lauterbach now took up the duties of navigating officer, as he had intimate knowledge of Penang harbour, which *Emden* was soon to visit.

54 *Naval Staff Monographs (Historical)*, vol 5, op cit, pp85–6.

55 *Buresk* was ordered to rendezvous with *Emden* west of Sumatra on 31 October.

56 Joseph, op cit, p170.

57 Lochau, op cit, pp95–6.

58 Von Mücke, op cit, p148.

59 Lochau, op cit, p97.

60 Von Mücke, op cit, p152.

61 *Zhemchug* had a complement of 340. One officer and ninety men were killed, whilst two officers and 106 men were wounded.

62 Before leaving *Glenturret*, Lauterbach handed Captain Jones a note from von Müller for delivery to the authorities in Penang. It was an apology for having fired on the unarmed launch.

63 Von Mücke, op cit, p161.

64 Joseph, op cit, pp181–2.

65 *Naval Staff Monographs (Historical)*, vol 5, op cit, p93.

66 Joseph, op cit, pp196–7.

67 Jose, op cit, p193.

3   The Cocos Raid

1 P Plowman, *Voyage to Gallipoli*, Rosenberg, Kenthurst, 2013, p96. The New Zealand transports were *Arawa, Athenic, Hawkes Bay, Limerick, Maunganui, Orari, Ruapehu, Star of India, Tahiti* and *Waimana*.

2 The Australian transports were *Afric, Anglo-Egyptian, Argyllshire, Armadale, Ascanius, Benalla, Clan MacCorquodale, Euripides, Geelong, Hororata, Hymettus, Karroo, Katuna, Marere, Medic,*

Miltiades, Omrah, Orvieto, Pera,
Port Lincoln, Rangatira, Saldanha,
Shropshire, Southern, Star of
England, Star of Victoria, Suffolk
and Wiltshire.
3 Jose, op cit, p158.
4 The Admiralty had received word
that Scharnhorst and Gneisenau had
bombarded Papeete, the capital of
French Tahiti, on 22 September.
Subsequent intelligence, based on a
German wireless message
intercepted on 4 October, placed
them halfway between Tahiti and
South America.
5 Naval Staff Monographs
(Historical), vol 5, op cit, p82.
6 Jose, op cit, p158. Yahagi did not
join the convoy escort, instead being
employed in the hunt for Emden
after the Penang raid.
7 The Chathams were the third sub-
class of the Royal Navy's Town-class
light cruisers which were built in
response to the small German
cruisers then in service or under
construction. The Bristols (Bristol,
Glasgow, Gloucester, Liverpool,
Newcastle), built under the 1908/9
programme, were capable of 25
knots and armed with two 6in and
ten 4in guns. They were followed by
the Weymouths (Weymouth,
Yarmouth, Falmouth, Dartmouth)
of the 1909/10 programme, which
carried eight 6in guns. The
Chathams (Chatham, Dublin,
Southampton, Melbourne, Sydney,
Brisbane) were an improved version
of the Weymouths.
8 AWM35, 24/1.
9 Sydney carried seven 21in
torpedoes, as well as a 12pdr field
gun and two .303in Maxim machine
guns. As completed, Sydney also
carried eleven ship's boats, these
being one 35ft steam cutter, one 34ft
barge, two 30ft sailing cutters, two
30ft gigs, three 27ft whalers and
two 16ft skiffs.
10 F Ethridge, HMAS Sydney Log,
courtesy of Sea Power Centre-
Australia.
11 Arthur Todd, MLMSS 274, Mitchell
Library, State Library of New South

Wales.
12 There were 434 officers and ratings
onboard Sydney on 9 November
1914; of these, 229 were ex-RN or
RN personnel on loan. Sydney's
peacetime complement was 392
officers and men.
13 Todd, op cit.
14 R Martin, A Sound Defence, Town
of Albany, Albany, 1988, p15.
15 Philomel and Pyramus sailed for
Singapore via Fremantle. Ibuki and
Pioneer were to provide escort for
Ascanius and Medic after their
departure from Fremantle.
16 AWM35, 17/1.
17 AWM, PR02076.
18 C Bean, The Story of ANZAC, vol
1, Angus & Robertson, Sydney,
1921, p98.
19 AWM, 2DRL/0885.
20 Todd, op cit.
21 AMWA, PD 1044.
22 AWM35, 24/47. The W/T buzzer
used by the escorts had a range of
about fifteen miles. The transports
could receive W/T messages, but
were forbidden to transmit.
23 Todd, op cit.
24 Cradock and his men were avenged
on 8 December 1914, when von
Spee's squadron was destroyed off
the Falkland Islands. Scharnhorst,
Gneisenau, Leipzig and Nürnberg
were sunk with heavy loss of
life.Only Dresden managed to
escape.
25 Jose, op cit, p194.
26 Ibid.
27 Joseph, op cit, p204.
28 NAA, MP1185/6, 1915/9907.
29 Jose, op cit, p194.
30 H von Mücke, The Ayesha, Ritter &
Company, Boston, 1917, p3.
31 Jose, op cit, p568. Vice Admiral
Jerram had foreseen such a raid by
Emden or Königsberg, and had
instructed Farrant as to the
precautions to adopt, and the
necessity of giving immediate
warning in case of attack. Farrant
duly ordered his staff to bury or
hide tools, spare telegraph
equipment and several battery cells.
These were not found by von

Mücke's men.
32 Bean, op cit, p103.
33 Jose, op cit, p194.
34 Ibid, p180.
35 Diary of Edward 'Ted' Gwyther, courtesy of Mr Bruce Minchin.
36 Jose, op cit, p568.
37 AWM, PR01724. Seven men remained with the pinnace, tasked with locating, lifting and cutting the underwater telegraph cables.
38 AWM45, 1/94.
39 Jose, op cit, p568.
40 AWM, PR01724.
41 Jose, op cit, p569.
42 *Naval Staff Monographs (Historical)*, vol 5, op cit, p101.
43 Jose, op cit, p195.
44 NAA, MP1049/1, 1918/047.
45 NAA, MP1049/14, 1955/999.
46 Ibid.
47 AWM35, 24/50.
48 AWM35, 24/2. *Sydney*'s boilers, although coal-fired, were fitted with oil sprayers to enable steam to be raised more quickly in an emergency.
49 Diary of Ernest William Newman, courtesy of Sea Power Centre-Australia. Helm orders in 1914 were given in accordance with the old convention of steering a vessel by oar or tiller, which was opposite to the direction in which the wheel was turned.
50 *The Mail*, Wednesday, 16 December 1914.
51 Newman, op cit.
52 NAA, MP472/1, 5/15/8561.
53 Todd, op cit.
54 Von Mücke, *The Ayesha*, p7.
55 History of the Atlantic Cable & Undersea Communications: 1915 – How submarine cables are made (see Atlantic-cable.com).
56 Lochau, op cit, p116.
57 Ibid, p116.
58 Ibid, p117.
59 Jose, op cit, p195.
60 Joseph, op cit, p207.
61 NAA, MP1185/6, 1915/9907. The aiming gear in question was probably the auxiliary sight bracket on the No. 2 starboard gun, which had been damaged during coaling

operations.
62 AWM, 1DRL/0658.
63 Lochau, op cit, pp117–18.
64 NAA, MP1049/1, 1918/047.
65 Jose, op cit, p195.
66 NAA, MP1185/6, 1915/9907.
67 AWM45, 1/94.
68 AWM, PR01724.
69 Von Mücke, *The Ayesha*, p9.
70 Joseph, op cit, p215.
71 Ibid, pp215–16.
72 Jose, op cit, p195.
73 NAA, MP1049/1, 1918/047.
74 Ibid.
75 Ibid.
76 C Daw & L Lind, *HMAS Sydney 1913–1929*, The Naval Historical Society of Australia, Garden Island, 1973, p33.
77 R Strong, *Chaplains in the Royal Australian Navy*, UNSW Press, Sydney, 2012, p73.
78 *The Book of Common Prayer, The Church of England*, HM Printers, London, pp344–5.
79 AWM, PR00196.
80 AWM, 2DRL/0900.
81 AWM, 1DRL/0668.
82 AWM35, 24/50. The report, 'Enemy in Sight', was recorded in the log at 9.20am.
83 Jose, op cit, p195.
84 NAA, MP1185/6, 1915/9907.
85 Huff, op cit, p202.

4 Action

1 AWM, 2DRL/0900.
2 *Naval Review* (1915:1), 'Narrative of the Proceedings of HMAS *Sydney*, Part I'.
3 AWM, 2DRL/0900.
4 AWM35, 24/47. This coded message was transmitted at 9.40am, just after fire was opened.
5 Jose, op cit, p564.
6 Garsia later discovered that the order to load had been given by Rahilly, but he failed to hear it. The gun was quickly loaded, and immediately afterwards the order 'Control' was received. The gun was then brought to the ready and fired in the first salvo.
7 AWM, 2DRL/0900.
8 The muzzle velocity of the 10.5cm

shell was 710m per second, but this would have been much reduced by the time the shell reached *Sydney*, some 9,500m away.

9 AWM, 2DRL/0900.

10 Glossop and Rahilly had planned to open fire on the enemy ship when the range had reduced to 9,500yds (8,687m).

11 AWM, 2DRL/0900.

12 Ibid.

13 *Naval Review* (1915:1), op cit.

14 AWM, 2DRL/0900.

15 Ibid.

16 *Naval Review* (1915:1), op cit.

17 Glossop was unaware that the 10.5cm guns fitted to *Emden* were capable of being elevated to 30°, giving them a maximum effective range of 12,200m (13,342yds). Comparable British guns (4in QF MkI–III) could only be elevated to 20°, and had a maximum effective range of 8,230m (9,000yds).

18 Eric Kingsford-Smith, letter 13/11/14, courtesy of Creswell Historical Collection. Eric's younger brother, Charles Kingsford-Smith, served in the Australian Imperial Force and the Royal Flying Corps during the First World War. He was later knighted for his services to civil aviation.

19 *Reader's Digest* (27:162), The Reader's Digest Association, New York, October 1935, pp49–50.

20 Ibid, p50.

21 Joseph, op cit, pp217–18.

22 AWM, 2DRL/0900.

23 Ibid.

24 *The Sydney Morning Herald*, Friday, 4 December 1914.

25 Diary of John William Seabrook, courtesy of Sea Power Centre-Australia.

26 AWM, 2DRL/0900.

27 This shell also cut away a pair of signal halyards, sliced through a bridge rail, and chopped a pair of binoculars in half.

28 Jose, op cit, pp187–8.

29 C Pope, 'Description of Action between HMAS *Sydney* and SMS *Emden*', *Royal Australian Naval College Magazine* (1915), p8.

30 AWM, 2DRL/0900.

31 Ibid.

32 A 'Statement of hits by the enemy' contained in AWM, 2DRL/0900 records three hits on the upper deck in the vicinity of No. 2 starboard gun, but does not indicate where the third shell struck.

33 Report by James Stewart, courtesy of Sea Power Centre-Australia.

34 *The Scone Advocate*, Friday, 18 December 1914.

35 The other two members of the gun crew, Able Seamen Harold Collins and William Taylor, were assisting the wounded from the after control when the shells struck. Upon their return they took Ordinary Seaman Bell below for treatment.

36 M Carlton, *First Victory, 1914*, William Heinemann, North Sydney, 2013, p269.

37 Kingsford-Smith, op cit.

38 AWM, 2DRL/0900.

39 Ibid.

40 Carlton, op cit, p270.

41 Newman, op cit.

42 The observed mix of high-explosive and shrapnel shell indicates that *Emden*'s gun crews were firing whatever came to hand in order to maintain a high rate of fire. The reason why so many shells failed to explode (on *Sydney* and in the sea) was perhaps due to faulty fuzes or poor loading drill; some shells might have been fired with their safety pins still in place, preventing detonation.

43 Newman, op cit.

44 Stewart, op cit.

45 AWM, PR00196.

46 NAA, MP472/1, 5/15/8561.

47 Todd, op cit.

48 NAA, MP472/1, 5/15/8561.

49 AWM, 2DRL/0900.

50 The maximum rate of fire for *Sydney*'s 6in guns was 7 rounds per minute (under ideal conditions). It is believed that *Sydney*'s guns were firing at a rate of 3–4 rounds per minute in controlled battery fire on 9 November. When each gun was permitted to fire independently the rate would likely have been in the order of 5–6 rounds per minute.

51 AWM, 2DRL/0900.
52 Ibid.
53 Ibid.
54 'Common' denotes a shell which has a hole in the nose for a fuze, and a very large cavity which is completely filled with explosive. 'Lyddite' is the picric acid explosive filling. Lyddite was dark yellow in colour and gave off yellow smoke and choking fumes when detonated.
55 NAA, MP1185/6, 1915/9907.
56 L Writer & D Sellick, *First Blood*, Media Publishing, Sydney, 2009, p167.
57 Lochau, op cit, p124.
58 NAA, MP1049/1, 1918/047.
59 Ibid.
60 Ibid.
61 Lochau, op cit, p124.
62 *The Reader's Digest* (27:162), op cit, p50.
63 Joseph, op cit, p218.
64 NAA, MP1049/1, 1918/047.
65 Jose, op cit, pp196–7.
66 Lochau, op cit, p124.
67 NAA, MP1049/1, 1918/047.
68 Ibid.
69 Ibid.
70 Jose, op cit, p197.
71 NAA, MP1049/1, 1918/047.
72 Huff, op cit, p234.
73 Jose, op cit, p197.
74 F McClement, *Guns in Paradise*, McClelland & Stewart, Toronto, 1968, p185.
75 NAA, MP1049/1, 1918/047. Heinzelmann stated that fifteen rounds were fired by his No. 3 gun before the No. 5 gun 'was disabled', indicating that the No. 5 starboard gun was hit early in the action.
76 Ibid.
77 Fire control had also become more difficult because the electric transmitters to the guns were no longer working, forcing Gaede to pass his orders via damaged speaking tubes.
78 AWM35, 24/47.
79 AWM, PR02076.
80 P Schuler, *Australia in Arms*, Fisher Unwin, London, 1917 (reprint), pp43–4.
81 NAA, MP1049/1, 1918/047.

82 Lochau, op cit, p124.
83 NAA, MP1049/1, 1918/047.
84 Lochau, op cit, p126.
85 NAA, MP1049/1, 1918/047.
86 Ibid.
87 Oakum was a caulking or packing material made from old rope and tar.
88 NAA, MP1049/1, 1918/047.
89 Jose, op cit, p197.
90 Writer & Sellick, op cit, p180.
91 NAA, MP1049/1, 1918/047.
92 Joseph, op cit, p223. The two wounded men, Wilhelm Hartmann (who had been transmitting orders to the guns) and Paul Tietz (who had been attending the engine room telegraphs), then left the conning tower and were subsequently killed.
93 NAA, MP1049/1, 1918/047.

5 **The Reckoning**
1 *Naval Review* (1915:1), op cit.
2 AWM, 2DRL/0900.
3 H Bywater, *Cruisers in Battle*, Constable & Company, London, 1939, p97.
4 Pope, op cit, p8.
5 Lochau, op cit, p131.
6 NAA, MP1049/1, 1918/047.
7 Ibid.
8 *Naval Review* (1915:3), 'Narrative of the Proceedings of HMAS *Sydney*, Part II'. Gropius was one of those blown overboard. A short time earlier, Heizer Bauer had observed Gropius and Heizer Pieritz 'busy with a capstan bar at the hand steering gear' on the poop deck. Erich Pieritz survived, but suffered serious burns (NAA, MP1049/1, 1918/047).
9 NAA, MP1049/1, 1918/047.
10 Ibid.
11 Ibid.
12 Ibid.
13 Ibid.
14 Ibid.
15 Ibid.
16 Ibid.
17 Ibid.
18 Ibid.
19 Lochau, op cit, p129.
20 Ibid, p130.
21 NAA, MP1049/1, 1918/047.

22 Ibid.
23 Ibid.
24 AWM, 2DRL/0900.
25 Joseph, op cit, p209.
26 NAA, MP1049/1, 1918/047.
27 Von Hohenzollern was correct. Maschinist Richard Gierloff stated that the port auxiliary engine room was temporarily abandoned due a dangerous accumulation of smoke and gas in the compartment following a shell hit. The explosion burst open the 'door leading from the port auxiliary engine-room to the main engine-room … bending it out of shape to such an extent that it was impossible to close it again properly' (NAA, MP1049/1, 1918/047).
28 AWM, 2DRL/0900. The torpedo bars were extendable guide rails, designed to prevent the torpedo becoming jammed in the tube by water pressure when the ship was steaming at high speed.
29 *Sydney*'s torpedoes could be set to run at 28 knots over 10,000yds, or 44 knots over 4,000yds. McFarlane appears to have calculated that the range would reduce to less than 4,000yds by the time he fired his torpedo, so ordered the faster setting.
30 AWM, 2DRL/0900.
31 McFarlane reported that the torpedo was fired at '10 hours 38 min 18 sec by stop-watch', but all other accounts indicate that the time of launch was around 10.25am. It is possible that McFarlane's watch was not synchronised with ship's time. A similar discrepancy can be found in Engineer Lieutenant Commander Coleman's report, which noted a six-minute variance between engine-room time and *Sydney*'s deck time.
32 This was due to the range being underestimated. *Emden* survivors stated that the torpedo was seen running straight for them, but stopped a short distance away (AWM, 2DRL/0900).
33 Jose, op cit, 198.
34 AWM, 2DRL/0900.
35 *Naval Review* (1915:3), op cit.
36 Joseph, op cit, p221.
37 NAA, MP1049/1, 1918/047.
38 AWM, 2DRL/0900. The barrel of the S-2 gun (Serial No. 2289) is preserved at the Australian War Memorial.
39 Lieutenant Garsia reported that during this phase of the action spray was driving over the forecastle gun, drenching the gun crew and himself. He added that from this point onwards, the gun was not 'running out properly' after recoil. Later this got worse, and all efforts to push the barrel back into position failed, rendering it unserviceable.
40 NAA, MP1185/6, 1915/9907.
41 Ibid.
42 The concussion also caused tools and spare parts to fall from their hooks and brackets on the centreline bulkhead. Heizer Josef Fischer, working in the port engine room, was struck on the head by a falling object and killed.
43 NAA, MP1049/1, 1918/047.
44 Ibid.
45 Ibid.
46 Ibid.
47 AWM, 2DRL/0900.
48 Ibid.
49 Lochner, op cit, p180.
50 AWM, 2DRL/0900.
51 Stewart, op cit; 17-year-old Ordinary Seaman 2nd Class Alan Colless was also praised for his work on the forecastle gun.
52 AWM, 2DRL/0900.
53 Stewart, op cit.
54 AWM, 2DRL/0900.
55 AWM35, 24/47.
56 NAA, MP1049/1, 1918/047.
57 Jose, op cit, p198.
58 NAA, MP1049/1, 1918/047.
59 Ibid.
60 Ibid.
61 Jose, op cit, p198.
62 Kingsford-Smith, op cit.
63 NAA, MP472/1, 5/15/8561.
64 AWM, 2DRL/0900.
65 Ibid.
66 Stewart, op cit.
67 AWM, 2DRL/0900.
68 Ibid.

69 NAA, MP1049/1, 1918/047.
70 Ibid.
71 Ibid.
72 Lochner, op cit, p180.
73 NAA, MP1049/1, 1918/047.
74 Ibid.
75 Ibid.
76 Ibid.
77 Ibid.
78 Ibid.
79 Lochner, op cit, p181.
80 Joseph, op cit, p213.
81 Ibid.
82 NAA, MP1049/1, 1918/047.
83 Ibid.
84 Joseph, op cit, p226.
85 AWM, 2DRL/0900.
86 Ibid.
87 Stewart, op cit.
88 AWM, 2DRL/0900.
89 NAA, MP1049/1, 1918/047. The shell killed Henkes and badly wounded Otto Gurak in the left leg. Nagels was uninjured.
90 Ibid.
91 Ibid.
92 Ibid.

6 Beached and Done For
1 Kingston valves (seacocks) allow sea water to be admitted into a ship's hull or hold for flooding purposes. 'Draw fires' involved raking the burning coal out of the boiler furnaces to quickly stop steam production.
2 NAA, MP1049/1, 1918/047.
3 Ibid.
4 Ibid.
5 Ibid.
6 Ibid.
7 Ibid.
8 AWM35, 24/47.
9 AWM, 2DRL/0900.
10 Ibid.
11 Hoef swam forward to the fallen mast, from which he was pulled back onto *Emden*.
12 Lochau, op cit, pp135–6.
13 Ibid, p138.
14 NAA, MP1049/14, 1915/999.
15 AWM35, 24/47.
16 NAA, MP472/1, 5/15/8561.
17 Ibid.
18 Ibid.

19 AWM, 2DRL/0900.
20 Ibid.
21 NAA, MP1049/14, 1915/999.
22 AWM, PR03295.
23 *The McIvor Times*, Thursday, 28 January 1915.
24 AWM, PR00196.
25 AWM, 3DRL/3479.
26 McClement, op cit, p195.
27 AWM35, 24/1.
28 AWM, 2DRL/0900.
29 Von Hohenzollern thought that von Müller had simply forgotten to lower the ensign. A more likely scenario is that the flag could not be lowered. Access to the ensign halyards on the upper section of the mainmast was via a steel ladder on the starboard side of the mast. Photographs of *Emden*'s wreck reveal that the poop deck around the base of the mainmast was subjected to an intense fire. Eyewitness reports indicate that this fire started during the action and burned for several hours. Such a fire would have prevented access to the ladder, and the ladder itself would have remained too hot to touch for a considerable period of time.
30 Joseph, op cit, pp214–15.
31 NAA, MP1049/1, 1918/047.
32 Ibid.
33 Ibid.
34 Ibid.
35 Ibid.
36 Ibid.
37 Joseph, op cit, p229.
38 Ibid, p232.
39 *Emden*'s two main drinking water tanks had a capacity of 21,540 litres. In all likelihood both were ruptured and the contents contaminated with sea water when the ship grounded. The only other drinkable water, that which was contained in the condensers and the feed water tanks for the boilers, was drained into the bilge after *Emden* ran aground.
40 The birds were actually a local species of Booby.
41 NAA, MP1185/6, 1915/9907. Mayer was obviously referring to 10.5cm cartridges 'cooking off' in

the fires.
42 Jose, op cit, p200. *Sydney*'s deck log recorded that the *Buresk* boats were slipped at 3.45pm.
43 AWM, 2DRL/0900.
44 Huff, op cit, p214.
45 AWM35, 24/50.
46 Glossop clearly interpreted von Müller's failure to respond to *Sydney*'s Morse flag signals as an act of belligerence. In reality, it was probably a case of *Sydney* being too far away for her signals to be read. Under normal circumstances two signalmen were required to read and make Morse flag signals. One, equipped with a telescope, would read the signal, and the other, equipped with the hand flag, would acknowledge the signal and make the response. It is not known if Schwarz and Lindner were supplied with a telescope or binoculars, but they clearly had trouble seeing *Sydney*'s flag hoist. Correctly reading hand flag signals at two miles without such optical instruments would have been extremely difficult, if not impossible.
47 Newman, op cit.
48 Jose, op cit, p200.
49 NAA, MP1185/6, 1915/9907.
50 NAA, MP1049/1, 1918/047.
51 Ibid.
52 Ibid.
53 Ibid.
54 Lochau, op cit, p140.
55 NAA, MP1049/1, 1918/047.
56 AWM, 2DRL/0900.
57 Ibid.
58 Arthur Werner, MLDOC 3232, Mitchell Library, State Library of New South Wales.
59 AWM, PR00196.
60 *Naval Review* (1915:3), op cit.
61 AWM, PR00196.
62 NAA, MP472/1, 5/15/8561.
63 AWM, PR00196.
64 *Naval Review* (1915:1), op cit. Darby wrote that they 'hung about till morning, on the lookout for *Königsberg* or any other German ships which might have been about' (NAA, MP472/1, 5/15/8561). The transmission received by *Sydney*'s

wireless operators was possibly Batavia trying to contact Direction Island.
65 AWM, 3DRL/4183.
66 Von Mücke, *The Ayesha*, op cit, pp16–17.
67 AWM45, 1/94.
68 Von Mücke, *The Ayesha*, op cit, p19.
69 AWM, PR01724.
70 Von Mücke, *The Ayesha*, op cit, p23.
71 AWM, PR01724.

7   Rescue
1 Joseph, op cit, p235.
2 NAA, MP1049/1, 1918/047.
3 Joseph, op cit, p237.
4 Writer & Sellick, op cit, p202.
5 NAA, MP1049/1, 1918/047.
6 Joseph, op cit, p236.
7 *Sydney* had patrolled to the southeast after recovering the German sailor at 6.55pm, and did not set course for Direction Island until midnight.
8 AWM, 3DRL/4183.
9 *Barrier Miner*, Sunday, 3 January 1915.
10 AWM35, 24/2.
11 AWM, 3DRL/4183.
12 AWM, PR00196.
13 NAA, MP472/1, 5/15/8561.
14 Ibid.
15 Ibid.
16 AWM, 2DRL/0885.
17 AWM, 2DRL/0900.
18 Ibid.
19 Leading Seaman Newman heard von Müller promise that he, his officers and men, 'would consider themselves under Naval Discipline & would not interfere with the ship's fittings'.
20 AWM35, 24/50.
21 NAA, MP1185/6, 1915/9907.
22 Jose, op cit, p567.
23 AWM35, 24/50. This message later led to confusion ashore because the entrance to the lagoon was actually on the northeastern side of the island.
24 AWM, 2DRL/0900.
25 Joseph, op cit, p238.
26 NAA, MP472/1, 5/15/8561.

27　*The McIvor Times*, Thursday, 28 January 1915.
28　AWM, 2DRL/0900.
29　NAA, MP472/1, 5/15/8561.
30　Newman, op cit.
31　*The Don Dorrigo Gazette and Guy Fawkes Advocate*, Saturday, 15 May 1915.
32　Petty Officer Raphael Hargraves, *The Sinking of the Emden*, courtesy of Creswell Historical Collection (Hargraves served as Arthur Kendrick Johnstone in *Sydney*).
33　Kingsford-Smith, op cit.
34　AWM, 2DRL/0900.
35　Todd, op cit.
36　Darby commended Cook's Mate John Fulton for performing 'some exceedingly disagreeable work' cleaning up the patients.
37　NAA, MP472/1, 5/15/8561.
38　Schuler, op cit, p57.
39　NAA, MP472/1, 5/15/8561.
40　Darby also thought Plotha's chances of survival slim, but he struggled on and was later admitted to hospital in Colombo. 'Later news tells us that the patient is doing well and they hope to fit him out with an artificial right half to his face.'
41　Darby, letter, 23/11/14, courtesy of Sea Power Centre-Australia.
42　NAA, MP1185/6, 1915/9907.
43　AWM, 3DRL/2190.
44　Able Seaman Reg Sharpe was buried at sea with full naval honours that evening at 8.30pm.
45　Specialists, including Petty Officers George Davis and John Donnelly, and Carpenter Behenna, were also sent to *Emden* to examine the ship, assess damage, and remove anything of value. A book of range tables was recovered from the conning tower, Davis and Donnelly each came off with a torpedo director sight, and Behenna's notes formed the basis of a damage report.
46　AWM35, 24/50.
47　Joseph, op cit, p238.
48　Jose, op cit, p201.
49　Daw & Lind, op cit, p40.
50　Todd, op cit.
51　Plowman, op cit, p178.
52　Joseph, op cit, p251.
53　Daw & Lind, op cit, p41.
54　AWM, 2DRL/0900.
55　Lochau, op cit, p155.
56　AWM, 2DRL/0900.
57　NAA, MP472/1, 5/15/8561.
58　A half-crown coin had a diameter of 32mm.
59　NAA, MP472/1, 5/15/8561.
60　Ibid.
61　Ibid.
62　Glossop wrote in his diary that he had to wait thirty minutes for a boat to come out to *Sydney* to collect Ollerhead and his assistants. The delay made him worry that von Mücke's party had returned and taken control of the island.
63　NAA, MP472/1, 5/15/8561.
64　AWM35, 24/2.
65　Jose, op cit, p201.
66　AWM, 2DRL/0900.
67　Ibid.
68　AWM38, 3DRL/606/264/1.
69　AWM35, 24/2. The log entry stated that the list of 199 survivors was exclusive of officers and men taken from *Buresk*. This is incorrect. On the morning of 11 November there were 184 survivors from *Emden* onboard *Sydney*. The sixteen officers and men taken from *Buresk* brought the total number of captives to 200.
70　Todd, op cit.
71　Jose, op cit, p567.
72　Joseph, op cit, p257.
73　NAA, MP472/1, 5/15/8561.
74　Ibid.
75　Ibid.
76　*The McIvor Times*, Thursday, 28 January 1915.
77　NAA, MP472/1, 5/15/8561.
78　Ibid.
79　AWM, PR00196.
80　NAA, MP472/1, 5/15/8561.

8　Prisoners
1　AWM, 2DRL/0885.
2　NAA, MP1049/14, 1915/999. *Empress of Asia* was ordered to remain at Cocos until the arrival of the sloop *Cadmus*, which was to make a thorough search of *Emden*'s wreck and guard Direction Island in case *Ayesha* should return.
3　With *Emden* accounted for, and

Königsberg blockaded, the Admiralty ordered *Melbourne* to proceed to Colombo and thence to Malta in preparation for her next assignment.

4 Todd, op cit.
5 The deaths of Stoffers (11/11) and Scheller (12/11) reduced the number of survivors to 182.
6 NAA, MP472/1, 5/15/8561.
7 AWM, PR03295.
8 NAA, MP472/1, 5/15/8561.
9 AWM, 2DRL/0885.
10 NAA, MP472/1, 5/15/8561.
11 AWM, 2DRL/0885.
12 AWM35, 24/50.
13 AWM35, 24/2.
14 NAA, MP472/1, 5/15/8561.
15 NAA, MP1185/6, 1915/9907.
16 Glossop's Letter of Proceedings was completed on 15 November. It was essentially a six-page report on the action between *Sydney* and *Emden*, the pursuit of *Buresk*, the recovery of survivors, and *Sydney*'s status after the action (casualties, damage sustained, ammunition expended, etc). A copy of the Letter of Proceedings is contained in MP1049/14, 1915/999.
17 NAA, MP472/1, 5/15/8561.
18 AWM, 2DRL/0885. Once the track chart was complete Rahilly used it to produce several hectograph copies. A number of hand-drawn copies were also produced and circulated.
19 *Hampshire* had been ordered to return to Colombo, leaving *Ibuki* as the sole escort for the convoy. *Hampshire* took the ten New Zealand and three Australian transports (*Anglo-Egyptian*, *Rangatira* and *Karroo*) with her as they needed coal and water.
20 AWM35, 24/50.
21 Ibid.
22 Ibid.
23 Ibid.
24 Plowman, op cit, p188.
25 Newman, op cit.
26 NAA, MP1185/6, 1915/9907.
27 Todd, op cit.
28 NAA, MP472/1, 5/15/8561.
29 Coleman was suffering from

appendicitis and was put ashore for surgery.
30 Jose, op cit, p567.
31 Joseph, op cit, p258.
32 Churchill, op cit, p434.
33 Ibid.
34 NAA, MP1185/6, 1915/9907.
35 AWM, 2DRL/0885.
36 The coaling was performed by local labour, and took two days to complete. In total, 850 tons of coal and 150 tons of furnace oil were embarked.
37 Todd, op cit.
38 The forty-seven admitted to hospital were later sent to Australia for internment. Five of them, August Benthien, Paul Klawitter, Adolf Kunkel, Johann Plotha and Joseph Ruscinski, were later deemed unfit for further military service and repatriated back to Germany.
39 E Proud, *Triple Odyssey*, Idea Generation, London, 2003, p133.
40 *Daily News*, Thursday, 25 April 1974.
41 A Paterson, *Happy Dispatches*, Lansdowne Press, Sydney, 1981 (reprint), p95.
42 Ibid, p97.
43 NAA, MP472/1, 5/15/8561.
44 *The Corowa Free Press*, Tuesday, 2 February 1915.
45 Thomas Bent failed to recover, and died on 13 February 1915.
46 NAA, MP472/1, 5/15/8561.
47 Numbers confirmed by *Oberhaupt Emdenfamilie*, Flottillenadmiral aD Henning Bess.
48 Lochau, op cit, p159.
49 Joseph, op cit, p266.
50 Jose, op cit, p205.
51 Lochner, op cit, p226.
52 *Naval Staff Monographs (Historical)*, vol 5, op cit, p110.
53 Von Mücke, *The Ayesha*, op cit, p66.
54 Vice Admiral Jerram had requested the British Consul General at Batavia to press the Dutch authorities to have *Ayesha* interned should she arrive in their waters.
55 Von Mücke, *The Ayesha*, op cit, p69.
56 Lochner, op cit, pp230–1.

57 Ibid, p232.
58 Von Mücke, *The Ayesha*, op cit,
    p73.
59 Ibid, p82.
60 The vessel was indeed British, and
    upon arrival at Colombo on 16
    December her master reported
    having sighted a three-masted
    schooner resembling *Ayesha* at
    6.00am on 9 December, in position
    3° 24' S 99° 38' E, steering east.
61 The landing party now numbered
    five officers (including von Mücke),
    one doctor and forty-seven men.
    One man, Heizer Jakob Kreutz, had
    been ordered to remain on *Choising*
    for disciplinary reasons.
62 AWM45, 1/94.
63 Van der Vat, op cit, p209.
64 *Choising* had been instructed to
    return that night to re-embark the
    landing party, should this prove
    necessary. Minkwitz did not see von
    Mücke's signal, assumed that his
    services were no longer required,
    and set course for Massawa in
    Italian Eritrea (the agreed Plan B).
    Ship and crew were later interned.
65 Two sick sailors were left at
    Menakha. They resumed their
    journey several days later with
    Turkish guides and rejoined the
    main body at Sanaa.
66 Von Mücke, *The Ayesha*, op cit,
    p142.
67 Ibid, p164.
68 Ibid, p169.
69 Three men had bullet wounds.
    Obermatrose Heinrich Koschinsky
    and Matrose Julius Mauritz were
    severely wounded, whilst Matrose
    Hermann Witt was slightly
    wounded.
70 Von Mücke, *The Ayesha*, op cit,
    p213.
71 Ibid, p215.
72 Van der Vat, op cit, pp238–9.
73 Von Mücke, *The Ayesha*, op cit,
    p219.
74 Lochner, op cit, p247.

9 The Wreck
1 H Baynham, *Men from the
   Dreadnoughts*, Hutchinson,
   London, 1976, p226.

2 Ibid, p227.
3 Ibid.
4 The man in question died later in
   the war when his ship was sunk in
   the English Channel.
5 AWM45, 1/95.
6 Ibid.
7 *The West Australian*, Friday, 5
   February 1915.
8 AWM45, 1/95.
9 Jose, op cit, pp164 (footnote), 207.
10 *The Southern Record and
    Advertiser*, Saturday, 3 April 1915.
11 Another *Pioneer* crew member, Able
    Seaman Frederick Blake, took as a
    souvenir one of the Mexican 8 reales
    coins (silver dollar), and engraved it
    with his personal details. The coin
    was subsequently acquired by a
    shipmate, Chief Stoker George
    Blake, who over-stamped it with his
    own personal details. The
    coin/identity disc is now held by the
    Australian War Memorial (AWM,
    REL36514).
12 The No. 1 starboard and both No. 4
    guns were left on their original
    bearings, no doubt because of battle
    damage to their training gear.
13 Van der Vat, op cit, p271.
14 *The Don Dorrigo Gazette and Guy
    Fawkes Advocate*, Saturday, 15 May
    1915.
15 Baynham, op cit, p227.
16 Ibid.
17 The two 10.5cm guns recovered
    were sponson guns (without
    shields). Photos taken of the wreck
    after the *Cadmus* visit indicate that
    these were the No. 2 port and
    starboard guns. These were the
    closest to *Emden*'s torpedo flat,
    where lifting gear would have been
    rigged. The recovered items arrived
    in Australia in April. One gun, the
    torpedo and the searchlight were
    subsequently sent to the Admiralty
    for 'expert examination', and public
    display in London. The second gun
    was placed in storage; in December
    1917 it was put on permanent
    display in Hyde Park, Sydney.
18 *The Register*, Friday, 5 March 1915.
    Lamb's story is doubtful. He
    probably bought the souvenirs off a

Cadmus crew member in Singapore, as each item had a note of authenticity signed by Surgeon Fergusson.

19 The Millions Club was founded in 1912 with the aim of making Sydney the first city in Australia to reach a population of one million.

20 *The Sun*, Thursday, 27 May 1915.

21 Cusden took 1,000ft of film of *Emden* and around Direction Island for the documentary *How We Fought the Emden* (aka *The Fate of the Emden*), which was released in Australia in June 1915. Footage from the documentary was then used in the Australasian Films silent movie, *How We Beat the Emden*, released in December 1915. Footage from this movie and another (*For Australia*) was used in the film *For the Honour of Australia*, which screened in Britain in November 1916. The preserved film, and what remains of Cusden's original footage, can be seen online at: https://aso.gov.au/titles/features/for-the-honour-of-australia.

22 *The Sun*, Thursday, 27 May 1915.

23 *The Sunday Times*, Sunday, 9 May 1915.

24 *The Daily Telegraph*, Thursday, 1 July 1915.

25 *The Sun*, Monday, 5 July 1915.

26 *The Age*, Monday, 11 October 1915.

27 *The Sydney Morning Herald*, Friday, 29 October 1915.

28 *The Age*, Wednesday, 12 January 1916.

29 Ibid, Saturday, 20 November 1915.

30 Ibid, Wednesday, 12 January 1916.

31 NAA, A9752, 59.

32 NAA, A9752, 111.

33 Copy of letter dated 14 October 1916, courtesy of Geoff Vickridge.

34 *The Daily News*, Thursday, 21 December 1916.

35 There appears to be no record of what was recovered from the wreck between February and May, or between July and Christmas Eve 1916. Salvage operations resumed on 1 November 1917 and concluded at the end of the December 1917.

36 NAA, MP472/1, 1/17/6743.

37 Ibid.

38 Ibid.

39 Although not the original intention, the Hyde Park gun also serves as a memorial to *Emden*'s fallen. Battle damage to the training wheel, next to where the gun-layer stood, suggests that this was the gun Bootsmannsmaat Joseph Ruscinski was serving (No. 2 port) when he was wounded.

40 *The Sydney Morning Herald*, Saturday, 22 December 1917.

41 The national war museum opened on 11 November 1941 as the Australian War Memorial. Amongst the *Emden* items currently on display at the AWM is the ship's bell, and one of the 10.5cm guns (believed to be No. 1 port) recovered by John Clunies-Ross. The other complete gun recovered by Clunies-Ross can be seen at the RAN's Heritage Centre, Garden Island, Sydney.

42 NAA, MP472/1, 1/17/6743.

43 *The Advocate*, Monday, 30 October 1922.

44 Reports stated that markings on the cartridge cases indicated that they came from *Emden*, but the projectiles were claimed to be of 6in calibre. This caused naval experts to believe that they could not have come from the German cruiser, as her shells were smaller (4.1in).

45 *The Argus*, Wednesday, 29 December 1937. The seized cargo was sold to a Singapore scrap metal dealer in 1939.

46 *The Western Mail*, Thursday, 17 February 1938.

47 Sea Power Centre-Australia, 1938 correspondence relating to the ownership of *Emden*'s wreck. The Straits Settlements (Singapore, Penang, Malacca, Dinding, Labuan, Christmas Island, Cocos Islands) were administered by a governor based in Singapore.

48 *The West Australian*, Saturday, 4 April 1953.

49 *Commonwealth of Australia Gazette*, No. S42, Friday, 12 March

1982.

50 R Mathews, *Report: Diving on the SMS Emden*, courtesy of the Western Australian Maritime Museum.

51 The location of these large, heavy objects suggests that the front portion of the ship slipped back into deeper water when the bow section was relatively intact.

52 Mathews, op cit.

53 A small drawing of this unidentified object suggests that it is a support column and pedestal for a 10.5cm gun (possibly No. 3 port).

54 Mathews, op cit.

55 The location of this ammunition (outside the wreck) suggests that it was removed from the after magazines and dumped, possibly by a salvage crew using explosives to remove more valuable items like auxiliary machinery and the aft guns. There is also evidence of

10.5cm cartridges having been recovered for the brass cases, as there are several detached, unfired projectiles on the wreck.

56 *Emden* had originally carried two nameplates, one on each side of her stern, but only one was recovered by *Cadmus*.

57 *The Sydney Morning Herald*, Wednesday, 2 March 1932.

58 Ibid, Tuesday, 28 February 1933.

59 Lochner, op cit, p285.

60 The nameplate is believed to have been removed from *Emden* III in April 1945. It was later placed in the officers' mess of the Karl von Müller Barracks in the the city of Emden. It now resides in the chief petty officers' mess at the Wilhelmshaven naval base.

61 *The West Australian*, Wednesday, 1 March, 1933.

62 Ibid.

Bibliography

Archives

National Archives of Australia

A2, 1917/3501 Part 3 Enemy Subjects –
German Prisoners of War ex SS [sic]
Emden

A2911, 1834/1914 European War 1914
Emden, destruction of by HMAS
Sydney

A9752, 59 Expenses in connection with
Emden

A9752, 111 Pages from notebook 1916
and 1917 – John S Clunies Ross
about *Emden* salvage

MP367/1, 580/2/1664 Bordeaux, F, Diary
of Deputy Paymaster of *Emden*

MP472/1, 1/16/1743 HMAS *Sydney–
Emden* engagement, recommenda-
tions for awards of medals and
advancements

MP472/1, 5/15/391 Forwarding Lists of
Prisoners of War ex *Emden*

MP472/1, 1/17/6743 *Sydney Emden*
Engagement – Distribution of
Mementoes

MP472/1, 5/15/8561 Report of Surgeon
Darby

MP472/1, 16/15/8367 Diary of
Steuermannsmaat Hugo Plötz

MP1049/14, 1915/999 *Sydney–Emden*
Engagement

MP1049/1, 1918/047 *Sydney–Emden*,
Action notes of crew of *Emden*

MP1185/6, 1915/9907 *Emden*, Forwards
copy of a translation from the diary
of a sailor

Australian War Memorial

AWM25, 519/39 [Operations]
Engagement with German ship
Emden

AWM35, 17/1 HMAS *Melbourne* Ship's
Book, 30/12/13 – 9/12/14

AWM35, 24/1 HMAS *Sydney* Ship's Book,
26/6/13 – 27/1/25

AWM35, 24/2 HMAS *Sydney* Ship's Log,
18/6/14 – 9/6/15

AWM35, 24/47 HMAS *Sydney* Wireless
Telegraphy Signal Log, 28/8/14 –
9/11/14

AWM35, 24/50 HMAS *Sydney* Signal Log,
31/10/14 – 4/3/15

AWM35, 24/51 HMAS *Sydney* Wireless
Telegraphy Signal Log, 9/11/14 –
19/3/15

AWM36, Bundle 14/1 HMAS *Sydney* –
Letters of Proceedings

AWM36, Bundle 14/7 HMAS *Sydney* –
Naval superstitions

AWM38, 3DRL/606/264/1 Records of C
E W Bean

AWM45, 1/75 Statement of hits by
enemy, HMAS *Sydney*

AWM45, 1/94 Translation of letter to
Engine Room Petty Officer 1st Class
Jaguttis from Härttrich of the *Emden*

1DRL/0658 Signal log of SMS *Emden*,
1914

1DRL/0663 SMS *Emden*

1DRL/0668 Glossop, John Collings
Taswell

1DRL/0669 Seabrook, John William

2DRL/0885 Glossop, John Collings
Taswell

2DRL/0900 Glossop, John Collings
Taswell (contains reports of officers)

3DRL/1760 Garsia, Rupert Clare

3DRL/2190 Dardel, J H

3DRL/3479 Glossop, John Collings
Taswell

3DRL/4183 Kirby, James

3DRL/6560 Mayer

PR86/218 Newman, Ernest William

PR00196 White, W J

PR01724 Saunders, R J

PR02076 Gedling, Stanley Alfred

PR03158 Clifford, James Reynolds

PR03174 Todd, Arthur Charles Robert
PR03295 Little, Vivian Agincourt Spence

Army Museum of Western Australia
PD 1044 Arthur Croly

HMAS *Creswell – Creswell Historical Collection*
Paymaster Lieutenant Eric Kingsford-Smith, letter, 13/11/14
Petty Officer Raphael Hargraves, *The Sinking of the Emden*

Sea Power Centre-Australia
Diary of Ernest William Newman
Diary of John William Seabrook
Ethridge, F, *HMAS Sydney Log*
Report by Mr James Stewart

State Library of New South Wales, Mitchell Library
Arthur Todd, MLMSS 2741
Arthur Werner, MLDOC 3232
Franz Bordeaux, MLMSS 685/Item 1

Western Australian Museum
Mathews, R, *Report: Diving on the SMS Emden*, MA-11/83/1

Published sources

Official publications
Admiralty, Naval Staff Intelligence Division, *A Dictionary of Naval Equivalents*, vol I, Oxford University Press, 1922
Admiralty, Naval Staff Intelligence Division, *A Dictionary of Naval Equivalents*, vol II, HMSO, London, 1924
BR634G, *A Dictionary of German-English, English-German Naval Equivalents*, Naval Intelligence Division, London, 1943
Naval Staff Monographs (Historical), vol 5: *The Eastern Squadrons, 1914*, Naval Staff, Training and Staff Duties Division, April 1922
Treatise on Ammunition, 10th edition, War Office, 1915 (Imperial War Museum/Naval & Military Press reprint)

Books and published works
Atkinson, J, *By Skill & Valour*, Spink & Son, Sydney, 1986
Baynham, H, *Men from the Dreadnoughts*, Hutchinson, London, 1976
Bean, C, *The Story of ANZAC*, vol I, Angus & Robertson, Sydney, 1921
Bennett, G, *Coronel and The Falklands*, Batsford, London, 1962
Bromby, R, *German Raiders of the South Seas*, Doubleday, Sydney, 1985
Bywater, H, *Cruisers in Battle*, Constable & Company, London, 1939
Campbell, J, *Naval Weapons of World War Two*, Conway, London, 1985
Carlton, M, *First Victory, 1914*, William Heinemann, North Sydney, 2013
Churchill, W, *The World Crisis 1911–1914*, Australasian Publishing Company, Sydney, 1923
Corbett, J, *Naval Operations*, vol 1, Naval & Military Press, East Sussex, reprint of the 1938 (revised) edition
Daw, C, & L Lind, *HMAS Sydney 1913–1929*, The Naval Historical Society of Australia, Garden Island, 1973
Drummond, B, *Fine Ships & Gallant Sailors*, self-published, Bristol, 2010
Fayle, E, *Seaborne Trade*, vol 1, The Battery Press, Nashville, 1997 (reprint)
Forstmeier, F, *SMS Emden*, Warship Profile 25, Profile Publications, Windsor, 1972
Freeman, L, *Stories of the Ships*, John Murray, London, 1919
Friedman, N, *British Cruisers of the Victorian Era*, Seaforth, Barnsley, 2017 (reprint)
_____, *British Cruisers: Two World Wars and After*, Naval Institute Press, Annapolis, 2010
_____, *Naval Weapons of World War One*, Seaforth, Barnsley, 2011
Goldsmith, D, *The Devil's Paintbrush*, Collector Grade Publications, Ontario, 2002
Gottschall, T, *By Order of the Kaiser*, Naval Institute Press, Annapolis, 2002
Harper, G, *Letters from Gallipoli*, Auckland University Press, Auckland, 2011
Herwig, H, *'Luxury' Fleet: The Imperial*

German Navy 1888–1918, Allen & Unwin, London, 1980

Hoehling, A, *Lonely Command*, Thomas Yoseloff, New York, 1957

Hohenzollern, Franz Joseph, Prince of, *Emden*, Herbert Jenkins, London, 1928

Hohenzollern-Emden, Franz Joseph, Prinz von, *Emden – The Last Cruise of the Chivalrous Raider 1914*, Lyon Press, East Sussex, 1989

Hoyt, E, *The Last Cruise of the Emden*, Mayflower, London, 1969

Huff, P, *SMS Emden (1909 bis 1914), Baupläne des Kleinen Kreuzers*, Hamecher, Kassel, 1996

_____, *SMS Emden (1909 bis 1914), Schicksal eines Kleinen Kreuzers*, Hamecher, Kassel, 1994

Jose, A, *The Royal Australian Navy*, Angus & Robertson, Sydney, 1935

Juncker, W, *In Kriegsgefagenschaft auf Malta*, self-published, Homburg, 2012

Lochau, F, *On The Raging Seas*, Reach Publishers, Wandsbeck, 2012

Lochner, R, *The Last Gentleman-of-War*, Stanley Paul, London, 1988

McClement, F, *Guns in Paradise*, McClelland & Stewart, Toronto, 1968

Martin, R, *A Sound Defence*, Town of Albany, Albany, 1988

Mücke, H von, *The Emden*, Ritter & Company, Boston, 1917

_____, *The Ayesha*, Ritter & Company, Boston, 1917

Paterson, A, *Happy Dispatches*, Lansdowne Press, Sydney, 1981 (reprint)

Plowman, P, *Voyage to Gallipoli*, Rosenberg, Kenthurst, 2013

Pollen, A, *The Navy in Battle*, Chatto & Windus, London, 1919 (reprint)

Proud, E, *Triple Odyssey*, Idea Generation, London, 2003

Raeder, E, *Der Krieg zur See, 1914–1918, Der Kreuzerkrieg in den ausländischen Gewäassern, Band 2*, Mitler, 1923

Schuler, P, *Australia in Arms*, Fisher Unwin, London, 1917 (reprint)

Stephenson, C, *Germany's Asia–Pacific Empire*, Boydell Press, Suffolk, 2009

_____, *The Siege of Tsingtau*, Pen & Sword, Barnsley, 2017

Stevens, D, *In All Respects Ready*, Oxford University Press, South Melbourne, 2014

Strong, R, *Chaplains in the Royal Australian Navy*, UNSW Press, Sydney, 2012

The Book of Common Prayer, The Church of England, HM Printers, London

Tuchman, B, *The Guns of August*, Four Square, London, 1965 (reprint)

van der Vat, D, *The Last Corsair*, Panther Books, London, 1984

Walter, J, *The Kaiser's Pirates*, Arms & Armour, London, 1994

Witthoef, R, *Unsere Emden*, Ernst Steiniger, Berlin, 1938

Writer, L, & D Sellick, *First Blood*, Media Publishing, Sydney, 2009

Wyllie, W, & M Wren, *Sea Fights of the Great War*, Cassell, London, 1918

Zienert, J, *Unsere Marineuniform*, Helmut Gerhard Schulz, Hamburg, 1970

Journals, periodicals and other publications

Commonwealth of Australia Gazette, No. S42

London Gazette, Supplements of 1 January 1915 and 10 April 1915

Naval Review (1915:1), 'Narrative of the Proceedings of HMAS *Sydney*, Part I'

Naval Review (1915:3), 'Narrative of the Proceedings of HMAS *Sydney*, Part II'

Reader's Digest, vol 27, no. 162, The Reader's Digest Association, New York, October 1935

Royal Australian Naval College Magazine, 1915

Index

Page references in italics refer to illustrations.